BOLLINGEN SERIES LXI · 4

ESSAYS OF ERICH NEUMANN

VOLUME 4

Editorial Committee

Renée Brand†
William McGuire
Julie Neumann†

ERICH NEUMANN

The Fear of the Feminine

AND OTHER ESSAYS ON FEMININE PSYCHOLOGY

Translated from the German by
Boris Matthews, Esther Doughty,
Eugene Rolfe, and Michael Cullingworth

BOLLINGEN SERIES LXI · 4

PRINCETON UNIVERSITY PRESS

THIS IS THE FOURTH VOLUME OF NUMBER SIXTY-ONE
IN A SERIES OF WORKS SPONSORED BY AND PUBLISHED
FOR BOLLINGEN FOUNDATION

Library of Congress Cataloging-in-Publication Data
Neumann, Erich.
The fear of the feminine and other essays on feminine
psychology / Erich Neumann; translated from the German by Boris
Matthews ... [et al.].
p. cm.—(Essays of Erich Neumann; v. 4) (Bollingen series; LXI, 4)
Includes bibliographical references and index.
ISBN 0-691-03474-5—ISBN 0-691-03473-7 (pbk.)
1. Femininity (Psychology) 2. Psychoanalysis. I. Title. II. Series:
Neumann, Erich. Essays. English. Selections; v. 4.
III. Series: Bollingen series; 61.
BF175.4.F45N48 1994
155.3'33—dc20   93-32444

Princeton University Press books are printed on acid-free paper
and meet the guidelines for permanence and durability of the
Committee on Production Guidelines for Book Longevity
of the Council on Library Resources

Printed in the United States of America

1 3 5 7 9 10 8 6 4 2

1 3 5 7 9 10 8 6 4 2
(Pbk.)

CONTENTS

EDITORIAL NOTE

The first three essays in this volume composed Neumann's *Zur Psychologie des Weiblichen,* published by Rascher Verlag in 1953 as the second volume in the author's series *Umkreisung der Mitte: Aufsätze zur Tiefenpsychologie der Kultur* (Circling the Midpoint: Essays on the Depth Psychology of Culture). Neumann's Vorwort to that volume is published here as a preface, as it is equally relevant to the two additional essays. The origins of the original essays were as follows.

"The Psychological Stages of Woman's Development" was expanded and revised from a lecture to the Psychological Clubs of Zurich, Basel, and Tel Aviv. The lecture included an essay, "Die Urbeziehung der Mutter" (The Primordial Relation to the Mother), published in *Der Psychologe* (Bern) III (1951) and later incorporated in Neumann's masterwork *The Great Mother: An Analysis of the Archetype* (B.S. XLVII, 1955).

The second essay, "The Moon and Matriarchal Consciousness" had been published in a special volume of the *Eranos Jahrbuch* (XVIII, 1950) in honor of the seventy-fifth birthday of C. G. Jung. The volume, entitled *Aus der Welt der Urbilder* (From the World of the Archetypes), contained ten other essays by Eranos lecturers.

"On Mozart's 'Magic Flute'" was expanded from a lecture to the Psychological Clubs of Zurich, Basel, and Tel Aviv. Neumann dedicated the published version to his wife, the analytical psychologist Julie Neumann. The translation by Esther Doughty appeared in vol. 11 (1978) of *Quadrant*, the journal of the C. G. Jung Foundation, New York, and has been revised by Boris Matthews, who also translated the first two essays, "The Fear of the Feminine," and Neumann's preface to the volume.

Two other essays on the Feminine have been added to the original three. "The Meaning of the Earth Archetype for Modern Times" was a lecture that Neumann delivered in Tel Aviv and then at the 1953 Eranos conference, thus first published in the *Jahrbuch* for 1953. The present translation appeared in *Harvest*, the journal for Jungian studies of the Analytical Psychology Club of London, in two parts: first, in the 1981 number, in the translation of the late Eugene Rolfe based on a draft by Madeline Lockwood, edited by Ruth Ludgate; second, in the 1983 number, in Michael Cullingworth's translation.

"The Fear of the Feminine" was part of a symposium held at the C. G. Jung Institut, Zürich, and published as *Die Angst* by Rascher Verlag (Studien aus dem C. G. Jung Institut, 1959), containing contributions by eight scholars from various disciplines.

Three essays had been previously translated: "The Psychological Stages of Woman's Development" in Rebecca Jacobson's translation, revised by Hildegard Nagel and Jane D. Pratt, *Spring 1959*; "The Moon and Matriarchal Consciousness" (partially) in Miss Nagel's translation, *Spring 1954*; and "The Fear of the Feminine" in the (partial) translation of Irene Gad and Ruth Horine, edited by Jeanne Walker, *Quadrant* 19 (1986). Those translations have been consulted.

WILLIAM McGUIRE

TRANSLATOR'S NOTE

The translation of certain terms used in these essays merits brief comment. In the original German, Neumann generally uses the term *das Weibliche* when referring both to the individual woman and to the archetypal aspect of the psyche usually called "feminine." One may regularly translate *das Weibliche* as "the feminine," and Neumann's translators have sometimes made this choice. I have found this confusing, however. English usage (or my English usage) does not favor abstract nouns such as "the feminine." Is Neumann speaking of the individual woman or the archetypal energy called feminine or both? In the few instances where Neumann writes *die Frau*, there is no question of his referent, but those passages are infrequent.

Hoping to clarify what the author meant, I have rendered *das Weibliche* in several ways. When context appears to refer to the individual, I have used "woman" or "women." If the reference appears to be archetypal, I have translated *das Weibliche* as "the Feminine" or "the Archetypal Feminine," as in *The Great Mother*. But where the term appears to refer both to the individual woman and to the archetypal energy, I have used "woman," "female," and "the Feminine." I have followed the same principle in translating *das Männliche*—whether as "the Masculine," "male," or "man." Furthermore, I have capitalized "Self" in the Jungian sense.

As Neumann points out in his preface, these distinctions are crucial in considering the therapy not only of individual women and men but also of a culture characterized by a one-sided patriarchal extreme.

Milwaukee, 1989   BORIS MATTHEWS

PREFACE

These essays on the psychology of the Feminine belong in the context of a depth psychology of culture and of a cultural therapy, for the one-sided patriarchally masculine value-canon of occidental consciousness and the fundamental ignorance regarding the essentially different female and feminine psychology have contributed in a major way to the crisis of our time. Hence understanding the Feminine is an urgent necessity not only in order to understand the single individual but also to heal the collective.

The history of the development of consciousness in the West is that of a masculine, actively oriented consciousness whose achievements led to a patriarchal culture. By contrast, other laws govern the development of the Feminine—insofar as it does not participate in any decisive way in "masculine" development such as is the case in modern times. The different nature of the female and feminine psyche must be discovered anew if women are to understand themselves, but also if the patriarchally masculine world that has fallen ill thanks to its extreme one-sidedness is again to return to health.

Analytical psychology has recognized that a female element exists and is active in man's unconscious and a male element in woman's unconscious. A depth psychol-

---

Vorwort to *Zur Psychologie des Weiblichen*. Translated by Boris Matthews. See the editorial note, above. Also see "On Erich Neumann: 1905-1960," by Gerhard Adler, in *Creative Man*, vol. 2 of these *Essays*.

ogy of the Feminine and of women that takes these new insights into account is necessary if we are to comprehend all the problems of relationship and of marriage; but beyond this it also makes it possible for both women and men to understand themselves more fully.

In "The Psychological Stages of Woman's Development" we attempt a comprehensive outline of woman's path of development as it differs from that of men. By contrast, in "The Moon and Matriarchal Consciousness" we attempt to elucidate the essentially different female-matriarchal consciousness that forms the basis of many behaviors and modes of being peculiar to women and to the feminine. "Matriarchal consciousness," a "birth-giving" consciousness in a very specific sense, forms the bridge between the woman and the creative individual—for example, the male artist, in whom the anima, his female side (and with the anima also the matriarchal consciousness), is more strongly accentuated than in the average patriarchal man.

Consequently, the essay on Mozart's *Magic Flute* fits meaningfully in this context, because the *Auseinandersetzung*—the conflict and coming-to-terms with each other—of the matriarchal and the patriarchal worlds (which constitutes the actual object of our contribution to the "psychology of the feminine") stands at the center of the opera and its remarkable libretto. *The Magic Flute* overcomes these antitheses and culminates in a new synthesis. Developing a synthesis of this sort in the psychic reality of the individual and of the collective is one of the fundamental, future-oriented tasks of individual and cultural therapy in our time.

Tel Aviv, 1952   E. NEUMANN

ABBREVIATED REFERENCES

B.S. = Bollingen Series (New York and Princeton).

CW = The Collected Works of C. G. Jung. Edited by Gerhard Adler, Michael Fordham, Herbert Read, and William McGuire. 20 vols. Translated by R.F.C. Hull. New York/Princeton (B.S. XX) and London, 1951-1979.

EJ = *Eranos-Jahrbücher*. Edited by Olga Froebe-Kapteyn (until 1960). Zurich.

Freud, Sigmund, Standard Ed. = The Standard Edition of the Complete Psychological Works of Sigmund Freud. 24 vols. Translated by James Strachey et al. London, 1953-1974.

Jung, C. G., "The Relations." = "The Relations between the Ego and the Unconscious," CW 7, pars. 202-406. Orig.: "Die Beziehungen zwischen dem Ich und dem Unbewussten," Gesammelte Werke (Zurich/Olten), 7. First published Zurich, 1928, as a book, revised from a 1916 lecture.

Neumann, *Amor and Psyche: The Psychic Development of the Feminine, A Commentary on the Tale by Apuleius.* Translated by Ralph Manheim. New York (B.S. LIV) and London, 1956. Orig.: *Amor und Psyche. Mit einem Kommentar von Erich Neumann. Ein Beitrag zur seelischen Entwicklung der Weiblichen.* Zurich, 1952.

Neumann, *Depth Psychology and a New Ethic.* Translated by Eugene Rolfe. New York, 1969. Orig.: *Tiefenpsychologie und neue Ethik.* Zurich, 1948.

Neumann, *The Great Mother: An Analysis of the Archetype*. Translated by Ralph Manheim. New York (B.S. XLVII) and London, 1955. Orig.: *Die Grosse Mutter. Der Archetyp des grossen Weiblichen*. Zurich, 1956.

Neumann, *The Origins and History of Consciousness*. Translated by R.F.C. Hull. New York (B.S. XLII) and London, 1954. Orig.: *Ursprungsgeschichte des Bewusstseins*. Zurich, 1949.

Neumann, U. d. M. = Umkreisung der Mitte. 3 vols. Zurich, 1953.

PEY = Papers from the Eranos Yearbooks. Translated by Ralph Manheim and R.F.C. Hull. 6 vols. New York/Princeton (B.S. XXX) and London, 1955-1968.

THE FEAR OF THE FEMININE

AND OTHER ESSAYS ON
FEMININE PSYCHOLOGY

I

THE PSYCHOLOGICAL STAGES
OF WOMAN'S DEVELOPMENT

In *The Origins and History of Consciousness*[1] we traced the development of the archetypal stages that lead to the formation of consciousness and of an ego that we designate "patriarchal," for the bearers of this predominantly occidental development are men with their characteristic values.

Although development of consciousness in a patriarchal direction is also necessary for the modern woman, her development follows an essentially different course. The normal development of the Western woman, as well as the psychological premises of her neuroses, form the empirical basis for the outline that we will attempt to present here.

The first stage of female as well as of male development is that of a psychic unity characterized by the symbol of the uroboros, the serpent forming a closed circle, the tail-eater. We prefer this symbol over the concept of the unconscious because the vitality and dynamic opposi-

---

"Die psychologischen Stadien der weiblichen Entwicklung," *Zur Psychologie des Weiblichen*. (See the editorial note, above.) Translated by Boris Matthews.

1. Original: *Ursprungsgeschichte des Bewusstseins* (Zurich, 1949).

tion of the processes are visible in it, qualities not conveyed by the notion of the unconscious.

In the original psychic situation a fusion or, better, a non-separation of the ego and the unconscious prevails. Here we are confronted with a pre-ego stage of the psyche that stands phylogenetically and ontogenetically at the beginning of the development of every individual consciousness. In this stage the ego of the female, like the ego of the male, relates to the unconscious as to a mother whose superiority is so great that we cannot yet speak of a separation between mother and child, unconscious and ego. To a certain extent the child is still unborn and contained in the maternal uroboros. Individually this situation is expressed in the child's lack of separation from the mother, just as it is exemplified collectively by the individual's containment in the supra-personal, maternally protective power of the group, the clan, or the family that to a great degree determines what the individual does or does not do.

Initially the unconscious appears as the good mother —that is, the child's primal relationship to her carries a positive accent, for the dependent, infantile ego is protected and nourished by the maternal unconscious. By "primal relation to the mother" we mean the totality of the infant's or small child's relationships with its mother before it has developed a delimited personality with an ego-centered consciousness. More transpersonal than personal factors are operative in the primal relationship since the child is subject to a preponderance of transpersonal, archetypal forces.

Archetypally the primal relationship—i.e., the total dependency of the ego and of the individual on the unconscious and on the group—is experienced in projection on the mother who, despite her individuality, impresses the infant and the small child as the maternal uroboros and Great Mother.[2] The daughter's primal relationship to the mother differs fundamentally from that of the son, and understanding this difference makes an essential contribution to understanding the discrepancy between the psychology of women and of men.

If we say that, following a decisive point in his development, the male child experiences the mother as a "dissimilar thou" different from himself while the girl child experiences mother as a "similar thou" and not different, a question arises: In what sense do we mean this, and how is this sort of "difference" possible, since the infant cannot initially be aware—and indeed, as we know, is *not* aware—of any sexual differences?

The embryonic as well as the infantile relationship of the child to the mother is the prototype of all primary relationships. In this sense the primal relationship actually "originates" from the mother; that is, it is informed by the mother archetype, the psychic prototype of the maternal element living in the human psyche. However, this is not to say that the child's psychic reaction *arises* due to the effects of the primal relationship with the personal mother in the sense that, for example, psychoanalysis assumes the individual's unique personal experiences to be the cause of later developments. The embryonic and infantile relationship to the mother is the prototype of every instance of *participation mystique*, and the ego's

2. That we are dealing with a projection can be seen from the fact that even if another person—or even animal—takes the mother's place, it can assume the role of the projection carrier.

"containment in the uroboros"[3] is merely descriptive of this fact.

In the history of humankind the differentiation of man and woman belongs among the earliest and most impressive projections of opposites, and early humankind took the male and the female as the prototype of opposites in general. For this reason every archetypal opposition easily assumes the symbolism of the Masculine and the Feminine, and hence the opposition of conscious and unconscious is experienced in terms of this symbol, the Masculine identified with consciousness and the Feminine with the unconscious. This symbolic opposition is by no means limited to the secondary phenomena of anima and animus[4] but arises from the original containment in the uroboros, the birthplace of "masculine" consciousness and the "maternal" unconscious. The objectivity of consciousness develops out of the non-differentiation of the unconscious in the course of human history through a symbolic "separation" of the Masculine from the Feminine. The male child experiences this principle of opposition between Masculine and Feminine within the primal relationship to the mother, a relationship that must be surrendered if the male child is to come into his own and find his identity as a male.

The totality of the psyche, the center of which is the Self, exists in a relationship of identity with the body, the vehicle of the psychic processes. The physical changes from infant to boy, youth, man, and graybeard are also accompanied by psychic changes that differ greatly from

3. Neumann, *Origins and History*.
4. See Jung, "The Relations," pars. 296ff. [See above, pp. xiiif. Abbreviated References.]

the corresponding changes in the development of woman. Hence between the sexes we must assume a biospychic difference that is manifested in archetypal and symbolic ways, even if it cannot be expressed in any strict characterological categories. Therefore the Self as the totality of the personality rightly carries secondary sexual characteristics, and both body and psyche are closely connected in their dependence on hormones.[5]

Even when, in pre-patriarchal societies, the male children long remain with the women's groups and are shaped by their *participation mystique*, the experience of dissimilarity is a given from the very beginning, or at any rate from the point at which they perceive differences between the sexes. But how and under which cultural conditions the Masculine-Feminine principle of opposites is manifested is unimportant. Nor does it matter that this difference has been wrongly interpreted and has led to incorrect conclusions owing to culturally conditioned patriarchal prejudices.

Since the male experiences the primal situation— identity with the mother, the Feminine other—as identity with a non-Self, it is only in a later phase of development that Self-discovery as a male[6] is attainable, standing as it does in opposition to the primal relationship. Only the achievement of detachment from the primal relationship and an objective attitude toward it leads to male Self-discovery and stability. When this is not achieved, the

5. That this law is invalid at the beginning of the development of individuation need not concern us here.

6. This Self-discovery must not be confused with the Self-discovery of individuality in the second half of life. Initially it appears to be ego-discovery, but is the first stage of finding one-Self, which, in woman's individuation, we call attaining one-Self.

7

male remains entrapped and castrated in uroboric and matriarchal incest,[7] that is, he is inauthentic and estranged from himself. Elsewhere we have described this fundamental situation and the development arising out of it as depicted in myths where the first stages of the development of consciousness were interpreted as essentially the liberation of the Masculine from the Feminine, of the son from the mother.

It is a fundamental male experience that the primal relationship, the identification with a thou, turns out to be "false." The lasting effects of this experience appear in the male's tendency toward objectivity with the confrontation this necessitates, in his tendency to relate only from the distant, conscious world of logos, and in his unwillingness to identify unconsciously with a thou. This leads to the male's greater degree of isolation but equally to the intensified formation and solidity of ego and consciousness, all in a certain opposition to female psychology. As fear of relationship, this fundamental experience lurks in the background of many neuroses in men.

Since male Self-discovery is bound by its very nature to the development of consciousness and to the separation of conscious and unconscious systems, ego and consciousness always appear symbolized archetypally as masculine. This means that the male identifies his ego with consciousness and with his archetypally masculine role, and identifies himself with the development of consciousness in the course of human history. Individually he lives out the archetypal character of the hero and experiences his

7. *Origins and History.*

Self only in his victorious battle with the dragon, i.e., the natural side of the unconscious that confronts him in the form of the primal relationship.

But for the woman the primary relationship has a completely different significance and effect. When the child—whether female or male—becomes conscious of the principle of Masculine-Feminine opposition in whatever form it appears, the primal relationship to the mother is relatedness itself. But for the girl all the complications that lie in the boy's experience of being different vanish. Even when she "comes into her own" as woman, identity with her mother in the primal relationship can continue to exist to a great extent, and her Self-discovery is primary since Self-discovery and primal relationship, in the case of the girl child, can coincide.

This means that a woman can continue in the primal relationship, expand in it, and come into her own without having to leave the circle of the maternal uroboros and the Great Mother. In so far as she remains in this realm she is, to be sure, childish and immature from the point of view of conscious development, but she is not estranged from herself. While a man in a similar situation is "castrated," i.e., robbed of his authentic being, the woman merely remains fixated, held fast in an immature form of her authentic being. Again and again we find that, even in the midst of an occidental, patriarchal culture, a woman can flourish as a natural whole in this psychologically undeveloped form—that is, without a corresponding development of consciousness—that would have caused a man long since to fail in society and to become neurotic. This basic situation in which Self-discovery and the primal

9

relationship correspond gives women the advantage of a natural wholeness and completeness from the beginning that men lack.

The mother-child relationship is that of mutual identification, and the fact that Self-discovery (in which woman experiences herself as female) coincides with the primal relationship (in which she experiences mother as female) leads to a primary reinforcement of all those relationships that come into being through identification. This also contrasts with the experience of the male, who fundamentally prefers a form of relatedness based on juxtaposition.

While relatedness in opposition or juxtaposition is a culturally shaped, individual form of relatedness, the woman's natural ways of relating through identification derive from the blood bond of pregnancy, that is, from the primal relationship to mother with whom this relationship originates. For this reason the longing for relationships of identity accompanies a woman throughout her life and informs her tendency to create a similar situation again. But only as a grown woman, when she experiences pregnancy and becomes the bearer of the primal relationship for her child, does the matriarchally inclined woman's longing find fulfillment; then her ego, as subject, experiences the containment of the child and identity with it.

The symbolic relationship of Demeter and Kore, whose mythological significance Jung and Kerényi[8] have elucidated, characterizes the phase of Self-conservation

---

8. C. G. Jung and C. Kerényi, *Essays on a Science of Mythology*. (B.S. XXII, 1949.) [Orig. 1941. Jung's essays are republished in CW 9,i.]

in which the female ego remains bound to the maternal unconscious and the Self. The importance of this mythologem for woman's psychology lies in this: here we find a matriarchal psychology that specifically determines the relationship of woman to the Feminine as well as to the Masculine. The effects of this sort of archetypally directed phase are almost always demonstrable in corresponding sociological constellations, while at the same time they rule the unconscious behavior of the individual woman. Consequently in our context it is of no importance to delimit the extent to which the psychological conditions affect the social situation or, vice versa, how far collective social conditions affect the psyche of the individual woman.

It is typical for the phase of Self-conservation that psychologically and often sociologically the woman remains in the women's group—the mother clan—and maintains her continuity "upward" in relationship to the group of mothers and "downward" to the group of daughters. Her solidarity with the proximity to women and the Feminine coincide with her segregation and sense of alienation from men and the Masculine.

The exogamous brother, with whom contact is strictly hindered by taboos from early on, assumes the role of spiritual authority and masculine leadership, even if, as in the exogamous clan, he lives elsewhere. On the other hand, the husband from the alien clan, with whom there is a sexual relationship, remains a foreigner in the women's group and is largely without rights or powers. The alien status of this man is often evidenced by the secrecy of his visits to his wife. The mother-in-law taboo—that is, the husband's anxious avoidance of his wife's mother—points in the same direction. This taboo is characteristic for the alienation, indeed the hostility, prevailing between males and females in this phase. For, psychologically speaking, the essence of the phase of Self-conservation lies in this: the dominance of the maternal element prevents any individual and complete meeting between man and woman, Masculine and Feminine. A part of this is, or is identical with, the woman's experience of the male and of the Masculine as a hostile subjugator and robber.

The phase of Self-conservation of the Feminine can last a long time since it makes healthy human existence possible for woman and for the group. While this phase is to be regarded as positive in terms of preserving life, it has a negative effect when related to the development of consciousness, which is hindered by the arresting power of the unconscious. From this angle, the Great Mother appears as terrifying and devouring, not only as good and protective.

In terms of woman's development, of course, the possibility that the phase of Self-conservation may last a long time does not mean that woman has not already come to terms with the Masculine and with the men with whom she has lived in the most intimate association from the beginning.

The fact that a "modern" married woman who has children and does not necessarily appear neurotic can live in the phase of Self-conservation means that, undisturbed by any conscious *Auseinandersetzung*, she exists in a state of unawareness about life and about living with another person. In this phase everything appears to her "obvious and natural," which often enough indicates that she is filled with her own unconscious notions about the character of the Masculine and of her own husband without her having experienced, as an ego and an individual, the Masculine in general and her husband in particular. For woman, however, the significance of the Masculine far transcends her relationship to her male partner, and a woman whose development is arrested in the phase of Self-conservation is, generally speaking, an incomplete person even if she does not become neurotic. The outer and the inner relationship to the Masculine—that is, to the external man and to the masculine principle at work within her—constitutes part of her wholeness just as a relationship to the outer and inner Feminine does for the man.

Apart from its significance in her own psychological development, a woman's persistence in the phase of Self-conservation also has negative consequences for her family. For the "phases" are not abstract phantoms of an historical past but rather images of unconscious constellations that are operative now as in earlier times, and necessary for the development of personality. Thus, for example, the matriarchal psychology of the maternal clan can still be dominant in an occidental, patriarchal marriage, and the mother-in-law taboo that still betrays its vitality in countless mother-in-law jokes can express the fact that the wife's mother still dominates her and her entire patriarchal-appearing family.

The negative significance of this phase finds expression in a number of marital disturbances or generally in disturbances in the woman's relationship to the Masculine. The alienation from men or hostility toward men prevailing in her often makes an inner relationship to a man impossible and thus becomes a source of frigidity, among other troubles.

Restriction of a woman's interest to her children, who are regarded as the proper meaning of marriage, belongs in the same category. Children's neurotic illnesses arising through this constellation can disappear in the early stages if the mother becomes normal.

But woman's psychology in this phase can also be determined by a relationship to man that is only sexual. This has its prototype in the emphasis on the phallic male found in the matriarchy and in the attendant "Amazon" psychology. While the purely phallic, unrelated, lustful character of sexuality predominates, myth relates that the Amazons used men only for begetting children. In these constellations women preserve the unity of the Amazonian women's group while they relate to the Masculine and to the man as toward something alien, in part hostile, in part "wholly other."

Among the negative effects of this phase we also find a situation in which the woman experiences herself masochistically as sufferer, and consequently she reduces the Masculine and men to the level of mere sadists. Quite often the archetypal constellation of the matriarchy lies behind this sort of "perversion," which, in a more general sense, is characteristic of a great number of women. But precisely this "masochistic" feature becomes understandable only in terms of the next stage of woman's development, which we designate the "invasion of the patriarchal uroboros."

At this level the original, uroboric situation still prevails. But the accentuation of the masculine-patriarchal element in the term "patriarchal" uroboros is intended to point out that here it is a question of a development in the direction of the patriarchy. Now the uroboric situation will be overcome and the archetype of the Great Father emerges. In the matriarchy—that is, under the hegemony of the Great Mother—the Masculine can be experienced only in a diminished form. The matriarchy regards the masculine side of the uroboros, which of course is bisexual, as part of the Great Mother, as her tool, helper, and satellite. The male is loved as child and as youth and used as her tool of fertility, but he continues to be integrated in and subordinated to the Feminine, and his authentic masculine being and uniqueness is never acknowledged.[9]

With the invasion of the paternal uroboros, however, something completely new happens to the woman. She is seized by an unknown, overwhelming power that she experiences as a formless numinosum. In the history of the development of consciousness, the encounter with an anonymous force of this kind is always an experience of the ego's limits, found not only among primitive peoples but also among persons of developed consciousness, for example in their experience of mysticism[10] and of individuation. The ego's experience of its limits therefore does not always signify only that a primitive, easily dissolved ego has encountered the numinous in the likeness of its own formlessness. In transitional phases and in

9. Cf. Neumann, *Origins and History* and *The Great Mother*.
10. Cf. Neumann, *Kulturentwicklung und Religion* (U. d. M., vol. l, 1953). [Including "Mystical Man," *EJ 1948* (tr. in PEY, vol. 6), "The Psychological Meaning of Rituals," *EJ 1950*, and "The Mythical World and the Individual," *EJ 1949* (tr. R. T. Jacobson in *Quadrant* 14 [1981]).]

situations that transform the personality—whenever a new archetypal situation is constellated and for whatever reasons—the archetype, as something numinous and undefined, anonymous and transpersonal, overwhelmingly confronts ego consciousness. Consciousness first reacts, in the individual situation as in collective development, by feeling overwhelmed and defeated. Only gradually does it work out new forms of adaptation to the archetype that, at the subjective level, lead to development, enrichment, and extension of consciousness, and on the objective level manifest in ever more differentiated phenotypes or incarnations of the numinous.

Thus the overwhelming power not only of the anonymous numinosum but also of the numina and of the numen, of the divinity as a male figure, belongs to the paternal uroboric stage. This development commences in the matriarchy with the appearance of pluralistic power groups of a masculine, demonic character, such as the cabiri, satyrs, and dactyls, whose multiplicity still betrays their anonymity and formless numinosity. They are followed by the figures of the phallic-chthonic gods, who indeed are still subordinate to the Great Mother (as, for example, Pan, Poseidon, Hades, and the chthonic Zeus were in Greece), but whom woman can experience as the patriarchal uroboros. Typical deities who appear as the patriarchal uroboros are Dionysus and Wotan, as well as Osiris and, at another cultural level, Shiva, whose transpersonal form is enveloped by a palpable anonymity. Not only are most of these figures venerated orgiastically as fertility gods, but in woman's emotional and ecstatic relationship to them she experiences the unfathomable depths of her own nature.

For woman, invasion by the patriarchal uroboros corresponds to an intoxicating experience of being overwhelmed, of being seized and taken by a "ravishing penetrator" whom she does not experience personally in relation to and projected onto a concrete man, but rather as an anonymous, transpersonal numen. Both impersonality and being overwhelmed are essential constituents in the experience of this stage.

In mythology we find this stage represented in the relationships of the matriarchal "virgin" not to the husband but to a god who overpowers her, now as cloud or wind, as rain, lightning, gold, moon, sun, and so on, or again as a numinous phallus in animal form that penetrates her, be it as serpent or bird, as bull, goat, horse, etc.

Indeed, unconditioned as it is by anything from the outer world, the archetypal character of the experience in this phase is so clear that we must ask what inner experience of the woman we are confronting here. Unconscious inner forces and transpersonal contents whose energetic charge greatly exceeds that of woman's consciousness break into the personality with the emergence of the paternal uroboros. Because the power of the unconscious penetrates and overwhelms, woman experiences it as something Masculine that sweeps her away, seizes and pierces her, and transports her beyond herself. Consequently the movement of the unconscious is always felt to be numinous and creative, since its invasion "fructifies" and changes the personality it seizes.[11]

This pleromatic experience—pleromatic because a nu-

11. We cannot here enter into a discussion of the male's anima experience, which, in the case of a creative and religious man, is completely analogous to woman's experience.

minous divinity is experienced in its formless indeter-
minateness even when it may transitorily assume form—
fills the woman with mortal fear. An obvious symbol of
this is the mythologem of the death-marriage in which
the masculine energy as robber and ravisher can become
Hades, the god of death, who abducts the woman, as
Kore, into his realm.

Associated with this overwhelming and huge masculine presence or force is the woman's transpersonal
feeling of inadequacy—that is, a feeling of inferiority
that has its impersonal and archetypal basis here. Vis-
à-vis the Masculine, the woman feels herself too small.
Understandably it is as fear that she experiences her inability to take into herself the whole phallus of the
godhead.

We find the Masculine as serpent, dragon, and monster
in a large number of women's sexual anxieties and neurotic behaviors that hinder her relationship to men. However, in the feminine Self-surrender of acceptance of this
situation and in her letting herself be overpowered, the
woman is led to victory over fear and her anxiety is
transformed into intoxication and orgasm. In this transformation (whose significance we can only mention here)
the dragon figure of the patriarchal uroboros assumes, for
example, the likeness of a god, and Heraclitus's statement
proves true that Hades and Dionysus are one and the
same figure in the mysteries.[12]

Seized with total and profound emotion by the Masculine, woman overcomes the stage of Self-conservation
and arrives at a new phase of her experience, that of Self-

12. Heraclitus of Ephesus, fr. 15, in K. Freeman, *Ancilla to the Pre-Socratic Philosophers* (1948).

surrender. Although it is also expressed in the body, her profound orgiastic emotion has a spiritual character. This spiritual character, however, has nothing to do with the abstract logic of the masculine, patriarchal spirit but belongs to a specific, feminine form of spiritual experience that is often associated with the symbol of the moon in mythology.[13]

The connection between spiritual emotion and bodily orgasm is still expressed in modern woman; her spiritual excitement can be so intense, for example with music, that she can reach orgasm, and her "understanding" of spiritual contents can be connected with physical sensations. This means that, speaking symbolically, she does not understand with her head but with her entire body; for her, spiritual-emotional and physical processes are bound together in a manner quite foreign to the average man.[14]

But the relation to the patriarchal uroboros also has negative effects if the woman gets caught in it. In contrast to the stage of "Self-conservation," in which woman did not experience the Masculine in its authenticity, the new element in this phase is the overwhelming quality of the Masculine. Where a male consciousness would demand this experience be worked through, for example as "as-

13. See below, essay II, "The Moon and Matriarchial Consciousness."

14. On the other hand, much evidence attests that, for both good and ill, the creative person is more keenly aware of his or her dependency on the body than is the average person. There is no doubt that this is due to a greater degree of sensitivity to and a more acute consciousness of intimately linked processes. But even here, consistent with its development, patriarchal consciousness has the tendency to commence as if free and to deny its dependency on processes of the unconscious and the body.

similation of the contents invading consciousness," for the woman both the overwhelming character of the event and the process of working through her experience of it is made more difficult since for her the Masculine remains numinous, anonymous, and transpersonal.

A human tendency working unconsciously toward formation of the personality, which we have called centroversion,[15] forces the woman—as it does the man—to pass through all the phases necessary for individual development. And tarrying in one phase that progressively must be traversed means a regression in respect to the development of personality.

The positive and the negative figures of the patriarchal uroboros provide one of the essential motifs for problems that, on the personal level, psychoanalysis has described as the woman's experience of the Oedipus complex. But this Oedipus complex is often only "secondarily personalized";[16] that is to say, it is the foreground expression of an archetypal constellation. Frequently the relationship to the patriarchal uroboros stands behind the fantasy of incest with the personal father, but the archetypal image with which the woman experiences the liaison surpasses the features of the personal father and often completely excludes them. However, being held captive by the patriarchal uroboros—as an archetypal constellation—is not restricted to the psyche of the child; rather, it remains a continuing problem also for the adult woman who has not overcome this stage.

One of the characteristic forms in which the patriarchal uroboros operates as a danger—but by no means

15. *Origins and History*, index, s.v. centroversion.
16. Ibid., s.v. Oedipus complex.

the only one—is that of the fascinating spirit-father. The workings of this form constellate the figure of the "daughter of the eternal father," i.e., a woman who as "virgin" remains bound to the spirit-father in visible or invisible form. The woman as prophetess and as nun, as "genius" and as "angel," can be an expression of her fixation in this archetypal phase in which she relates via an intuitive connection to a transpersonal spiritual force whose transpersonal magnitude appears either within a religious framework as the godhead or personalized as the great man, artist, visionary, poet, etc., to whom the woman is bound. In this case she leads her life as the man's "anima," that is, as his inspiratrix, and consequently can forfeit her individual life that also has earthy, maternal, and other qualities that ought to be developed. She "lives beyond her means" and is inflated;[17] she is identified with an archetypal feminine figure that far exceeds her merely human limits and who as Sophia is the female partner of the Spirit-Father. A variant of this constellation is the "Woman without a Shadow"[18] who is unfruitful because she has split herself off from her earthly, shadow side.

This constellation retains the intoxicating component in the relationship of the small female to the great male, and hence a certain infantility and daughterliness is never overcome. When the intuitive captivity in the patriarchal uroboros leads to the loss of the earth—that is, to a loss of relationship to concrete reality—the Spirit-Father often appears as a sorcerer who negatively fascinates the

17. Jung, "The Relations."
18. See Hugo von Hofmannsthal, *Die Frau ohne Schatten* (1919), libretto, rewritten later as a prose tale.

woman and holds her prisoner. Simultaneously, however, the hostility of the Great Mother forms an alliance with the woman's captivity in the patriarchal uroboros and with the concomitant loss of her connection to the earth.

The necessary development from the mother-bound stage of Self-conservation to surrender of Self to the patriarchal uroboros also includes a certain degree of hostility to the mother, for the transition to a new phase always has to contend with the resistance of the phase to be overcome, a resistance determined by the inertia of the psyche. Consequently the tenacious power of the mother, who now appears terrible, works against the transition to the patriarchal uroboros. But like all corresponding resistances that arise due to the archetype of the phase to be overcome, this does not lead to illness but rather to conflict. However, if a fixation characterized by the dominance of the patriarchal uroboros develops in this phase, there now appears, alongside the negative figure of the father as sorcerer, also a negative form of the Great Mother, who avenges the daughter's betrayal. The figure of the Great Mother regresses to that of the mythological witch who, for example in fairy tales, casts a spell over the daughter and imprisons her.

In the phase of Self-conservation, woman can fully function in a feminine and natural way dominated by the bond to mother, the unconscious, and the body. With the invasion of the patriarchal uroboros, she enters not only a new phase of experiencing herself as a woman but arrives at the experience of the spirit. But if she falls under the sway of the patriarchal uroboros, she becomes spirit-possessed and so estranged from herself that she loses even her physical relationship to her femininity.

For woman the positive bond to the Great Mother is also always the prerequisite psychologically for becoming a mother, for being fertile, and for having a healthy relationship to her own body and to the earth. On the other hand, being estranged from the Great Mother leads to the inability to develop the maternal and fruitful qualities of her feminine nature and consequently to the typical symptoms of hysteria, of estrangement from body, indeed even of sterility.

Often a woman's neurotic animus-possession is the expression of her inability to differentiate her Self from the Masculine. The woman becomes the victim of her tendency to identification and alienates herself from her own nature by over-developing the masculine, animus side. This identification with the spiritual and Masculine can find expression in truly tragic conflicts. By identifying with the transpersonal Masculine that takes the place of authentic surrender and devotion, the woman relinquishes her own earth nature[19] and thus becomes a helpless victim of masculine powers. This danger, which may lead even to psychosis, is also occasioned by the fact that in her extreme surrender of Self the woman never gets to the point of assimilating the masculine side, which lives not only in her partner but in her own psyche, and hence never develops an autonomous personality in her own right.

Nature has granted the mystery of the Feminine its fulfillment both in the primal relationship and in pregnancy, a fulfillment that ever and again comes to pass

19. In this connection, consider the problem of the "negative spirit" in my "The Mythical World and the Individual" (see above, n. 10).

even without consciousness and even if it is not expressed in ritual; the male mystery is the deed and something to be earned.[20]

Although woman's Self-discovery as feminine is an original condition in contrast to the male's experience, the woman who wants to become conscious must also attain to the experience of otherness and dissolve her original totality. Otherwise she would remain "only" herself and would never experience the Masculine, the conscious side of her personality, and her human development.

When we speak of consciousness, we mean a consciousness centered in the ego and largely separated from the unconscious, whose archetypally masculine, independent development we have presented elsewhere. But his form—which has been manifested in patriarchal consciousness, the basis of occidental scientific thinking— is an extreme case. Beside it we find living transitions between the unconscious and consciousness, such as matriarchal consciousness, especially characteristic for women.[21]

For women, relationship to the whole is normally never replaced completely by conscious relatedness. In addition to identifying her ego with the midpoint of consciousness, woman always experiences the female Self—representing a point of view embracing the totality of the psyche—as powerful and convincing at a feeling level, while the male more fully identifies ego with consciousness, and his awareness of the primal relationship falls largely into the unconscious.

20. *Origins and History*, especially Part 1, "The Mythological Stages in the Evolution of Consciousness."
21. See below, essay II.

Hence the male tendency leads from dissolution of the bonds of the primal relationship toward the establishment of the archetypal Masculine as his authentic element. By contrast, female development, leading away from the primal relationship toward consciousness, takes place initially by way of the male "Thou," which plays the role of the redemptive consciousness for the woman, whether it is experienced transpersonally or personally, externally or internally.

Consequently in the life of a woman, her relationship to the Masculine is decisive, but in a way different from a man's relationship to the Feminine. Aside from certain modern vicissitudes, woman's development of conscious and assimilation to culture is most closely associated with the archetypal Masculine. Affiliation with the patriarchal form of our culture has made it possible for woman to separate herself from the state of nature in the primal relationship and has led to her relationship to the Masculine as father and husband, animus and guide.

To exaggerate: for woman, the Masculine characteristically presses forward; for man, the Feminine characteristically holds back. (Both find expression in the process of individuation in the second half of life.) For woman, the Masculine signifies redemption to consciousness; for man, the Feminine means redemption from consciousness. Woman's seemingly greater neediness in her relationship to a man and the Masculine and the man's seemingly greater independence from woman and the Feminine are related to this basic situation, even if the projection of a woman's masculine side onto a man plays a greater role in the development of her consciousness than does the man himself.

25

Although woman's consciousness differs in nature and emphasis from that of man, woman is forced into Self-alienation in the service of the development of consciousness. She is compelled to develop the masculine side, too, without which cultural achievement is not possible.[22]

In the mythological prototype of psychological processes, the liberation of the Feminine from the power of the patriarchal uroboros is the task of the male hero, who must redeem the captured virgin from the dragon. In contrast to the patriarchal uroboros, the archetypal Masculine now appears in individual and personal form and conducts the Feminine—as woman or as anima liberated from the powers of the patriarchal and of the matriarchal uroboros—into his own domain, that of the patriarchate.

Aside from the countless examples in the fairy tales of all peoples, we find this mythological constellation in, for example, the story of Perseus' victory over the dragon and the liberation of Andromeda, or Siegfried's liberation of Brünhilde. In the latter instance, the fixating power is characterized by two symbols. One is Wotan, who as patriarchal uroboros spellbinds his captive; the other is the *Haberlohe*, the wall of flames, that, as uroboric circle, surrounds the sleeping Brünhilde, which the hero must overcome.

The hero, the liberating Masculine, is both an "external" and an "internal" force. This means that the process can run a course in which a "real" man and partner assumes the liberating role of the light of consciousness

22. Jung, "The Relations"; Emma Jung, "On the Nature of the Animus," in *Animus and Anima* (Analytical Psychological Club of New York, 1957); M. Esther Harding, *The Way of All Women* (New York, 1933).

and dissolves the old form of captivity in the unconscious or, alternatively, it can be an "inner" Masculine, a force of consciousness in the woman herself, whose act of liberation is successful. Usually both take place simultaneously in that the woman's own inner quality of archetypally masculine consciousness is at first projected on an external man. But in any case, for the woman's ego this masculine "agency" appears as something "external," "stronger," and independently autonomous. The female ego has the absolute and, in a certain sense, correct conviction that it cannot accomplish this act by the strength of her "own ego" but is dependent on the help of archetypally masculine power. Just as the woman depends on the intervention of the Masculine to "open her" psychically in the death-marriage with the patriarchal uroboros and physically in the actual marriage with a man, so too her liberation to consciousness is bound to the person of the hero. Only in later and higher forms of development can this archetypally masculine force be experienced and known for what it is, as something inner, to the degree that the woman attains to her "autonomy," i.e., to a relative independence from her external male partner.[23]

In the transition from the phase of the patriarchal uroboros to that of the patriarchate, the masculine hero therefore appears to be necessary and a step forward for the development of consciousness. The development of consciousness presented in *The Origins and History of Consciousness* takes place within a tension of opposites created by the ego and the unconscious through which the ego can grow stronger, the conscious system can be

23. See below, pp. 56f.

formed, and the personal sphere can be delimited from the impersonal. This is why in this confrontation there is a devaluation of the archetypal Feminine which, from the masculine viewpoint, appears to be bound to and identical with the powers of the unconscious. The patriarchal development from moon to sun mythology—just as the shift from the position of the Feminine as goddess by whom the earth and the fertility of living things are sheltered to that as spouse who governs only the narrowest family circle, as well as the change from the predominance of the female in the group to the male state—cannot be achieved unless the Masculine places a negative accent on the Feminine.

Mythologically this process corresponds to the phase of the hero's battle with the devouring uroboric monster; sociologically and politically it is expressed in the development of a patriarchal culture and leads, in the relationship between men and women, to the patriarchal marriage as the basis of the family and of patriarchal life.

The patriarchal line of the development of consciousness leads to a condition where patriarchal-masculine values are dominant, values that are often conceived in direct opposition to those of the archetypal Feminine and of the unconscious. This development, directed by the archetypally conditioned cultural canon and impressed upon the development of every male or female child in Western cultures, leads to the separation of consciousness from the unconscious, to the evolution of the independent conscious system with a masculine ego as the center, to a suppression of the unconscious, and to its greatest possible repression from the ego's field of vision.

We are using "patriarchal" and "matriarchal" as psychological terms that are to be applied only secondarily to political conditions, spheres of influence, etc. Hence a "patriarchal" culture and its values stand in opposition to the values and attitudes valid for a "matriarchal" consciousness which itself is a "primary" form of all consciousness and whose preferred representative is woman. In this sense, it is a step forward in development when a patriarchal replaces a matriarchal consciousness. But when one knows of the psychological weaknesses and dangers of patriarchal culture, whose extreme form in the contemporary West has led to a crisis endangering the whole of humankind, one will avoid the error of regarding "matriarchal consciousness" as only an archaic legacy and the archetypal Feminine as "relatively undeveloped."

However, we can penetrate the complex problem of modern occidental consciousness in its patriarchal form only when we have recognized the necessity for the development of consciousness to the "patriarchal extreme" and its opposition to "matriarchal consciousness." Only then can we also grasp the significance of that which, symbolically described as "masculine" and "feminine" psychology, determines the normal as well as the abnormal development of modern persons of both sexes.

As we discuss in the next essay, for the woman the central figure of matriarchal consciousness is the patriarchal uroboros as moon that compels her Self-surrender, that is, her renunciation of Self-conservation in the primal relationship to the mother. But while this Self-surrender brings woman to her own experience of a deep level of the Feminine, the "hero's liberation of the captive," her liberation from the dominance of the patriarchal uroboros by the man, nevertheless again endan-

29

gers her essence in spite of being a necessary development. This is the danger of loss of Self.

Regardless whether the patriarchy is primitive or highly civilized, when woman is integrated into it and subordinated to its values, the male becomes the representative of consciousness and of the development of consciousness for woman. This grants the male a psychological preponderance that determines the "phenotype"[24] of the patriarchal marriage as much as it does woman's place in life.

Marriage in the patriarchal era, which for the sake of brevity we shall call "patriarchal marriage," embraces a number of psychic situations in which the sexes relate to one another. Under the guise of patriarchal forms, a multitude of emotional complications are concealed in these marriages, complications that lie at the root of a great number of modern difficulties in marriage and in child-rearing.

The fact that the varieties of patriarchal marriage have preserved their form for millennia proves that, in a certain way, they offer emotionally viable ways of life both for men and for women. Although the patriarchal marriage presents a not inconsiderable danger for the woman's development, her chances of realizing her inner necessities within it—even if secretly—are great enough. For this reason the patriarchal form of marriage has not been obviously shaken until modern times. Often enough, however, it turns out that, on closer inspection, the patriarchal appearance constitutes only the external form, so

24. In this context, "phenotype" refers to the external appearance, in contrast to "genotype," which designates the actual psychic structure.

to speak the persona, of a marriage behind which are concealed forms of marital relationship that deviate from or even directly oppose the patriarchy.

Patriarchal marriage is a collective solution in which man and woman, Masculine and Feminine, unite in a state where each props up the other, so that they achieve a symbiosis that forms the backbone of patriarchal culture. Preservation of this more transpersonal institution—i.e., that of patriarchal culture, and the security of the individual embedded in it—stands as a transpersonal meaning above the relationship of the parties involved. Mythologically the stability of patriarchal culture is reflected in the relationship of heaven and earth in their mutual interdependence, the certainty of which assures the continued existence of the world. Marriage partners are supposed to correspond to this constellation, the man symbolizing the sky or heaven, woman the earth, as not only myth but rite also clearly reveal in countless marriage customs. In order to make this symbolic identification, each of the partners must surrender his or her natural psychological bisexuality, whose existence in modern persons is shown, among other things, in that the man's feminine side constellates as anima and the woman's masculine side constellates as animus.[25] The male's identification with the structure of consciousness and of the ego, leaving his feminine side unconscious, psychologically facilitates this sort of one-sidedness.

The male's connection to woman is now determined in a characteristic manner: his *purely masculine* consciousness relates only to the femininity of woman upon whom

25. Jung, "The Relations."

31

he projects his own unconscious femininity in the form of the anima. Likewise the woman consciously relates as *purely feminine* to the man's masculinity and projects onto him her own unconscious masculine side in the form of the animus. The fact that this division of roles appears in myth signifies that the patriarchal culture canon, according to which every boy and girl is reared, gives central position and special honor to this limited range of the possible archetypal modes of relating. This sacred, archetypal background imparts to the social institutions erected in accord with it the self-evident inviolability necessary for its continued existence. This means that a "feminine" man and a "masculine" woman—contrary to the actual psychic structure of a multitude of individuals—are now regarded as repulsive forms of human existence that are suppressed from early on, and these individuals themselves strive to conceal their own deviant natures as best they can.

The result of this situation is a polarization of the Masculine and Feminine, man and woman, that appears to create an unequivocal situation. This unequivocalness leads to the feeling of security regarding the orientation of consciousness within patriarchal culture in which Masculine = man and Feminine = woman, and which demands as its ideal that man and woman identify themselves in terms of this unequivocality.

This symbiotic structure forms the foundation of the family and of patriarchal culture, for it guarantees not only security and unequivocalness but also an inherently fertile tension of opposites between the Masculine and the Feminine, man and woman. However, thanks to this collective solution that may well have been originally supportable for a relatively great number of people, all those components of the individual's "bisexual" nature not corresponding to the requisite ideal type are repressed or suppressed. Yet this means that all these components generate an increased tension in the unconscious and, similar to the shadow elements repressed by the prevalent morality,[26] constitute the potential psychic "reserves" that chaotically shape the face of events in times of unrest and revolution.[27]

However, when a great number of persons have developed toward individuation to the point that they can no longer suppress the "equivocalness" of their original human nature in favor of an archetypally based collective ideal, a crisis occurs in the patriarchal marriage and the patriarchal structure of culture.

But in every case, the cultural symbiosis of the patriarchal marriage works out much less favorably for the Feminine and for women than it does for the Masculine and for men. Due to the circumstance that women are compelled to embrace an unequivocal femininity while the values of consciousness in a patriarchal culture are masculine, women remain undeveloped in this domain and are continually dependent on the aid of men. But this is why men consider themselves superior and see women as inferior.

26. Neumann, *Depth Psychology and a New Ethic*.

27. The significant part that "perverse" men and women play in revolutions, insurrections, etc., derives from these types on the periphery of patriarchal society—its fellow travelers, with great suppressed "reserve powers." Countless examples can be found in the French, Nazi, and Russian revolutions. We should not, of course, fail to recognize the often "heroic" and positive character of the revolutionary for this reason.

The negative effects of the patriarchate for the Feminine and for women constitute a vicious circle in which men (forcibly) limit women to the strictly feminine domain but thereby make it impossible for her to participate authentically in patriarchal culture and force her into a role where she is regarded as second-best and inferior. Men, however, base their justification for devaluing women and the Feminine, and women base their supposedly "natural inferiority," on the fact that this attitude places the woman in a role in which the man must treat her as though she were an underage daughter. A situation of this sort cannot but have catastrophic consequences for the girl child who must come to accept these patriarchal values as well as her own Self-devaluation. The daily morning prayer of the Jewish male who thanks God that he wasn't created a woman, just as Freud's female psychology based on "penis envy," are extreme expressions of this patriarchal situation and of the danger to which the Feminine and women are exposed in the cultural symbiosis typical of the patriarchy.

But where this symbiosis does function and woman in the patriarchy suppresses or surrenders her own nature, she becomes the prisoner and marriage comes to resemble a harem. Psychologically this means not only that her patriarchal consciousness remains undeveloped in this sort of marriage, but also that she surrenders the matriarchal consciousness unique to her as woman because it does not correspond to the patriarchal values or is opposed to them. Identification with the patriarchal values that she has not acquired through her own effort but only parroted leads to a slothfulness and crippling of consciousness that endangers woman's psychological development. She persists in a form of daughter-psychology under the protectorate of the patriarchy, a form in which the male carries the projection of the father archetype and the woman remains subordinate to him, infantile and daughterly.

Despite being endangered, however, this filial woman is not the creative person who emerged in relationship to the patriarchal uroboros. In the patriarchal world, men and the Masculine arrogate both paternal and maternal qualities to themselves; the male gives the woman security and is not only the begetter and carrier of spirit or consciousness but also the protector and provider.

This is the way in which the patriarchal wife suffers the limitation, indeed the atrophy, of the Feminine. Leaving behind the earlier stages—the primal relationship to the Great Mother that formed the basis of the female sense of Self, and the patriarchal uroboros that established her relationship to the transpersonal realm—is meaningful if it guarantees the living, dynamic interplay of forces that constitutes progressive development. But making the woman prisoner of the patriarchy arrests further development. Her life and interests are reduced to what is merely personal, indeed to the most restricted material realm; and now, parroting men and the Masculine, an "animus psychology" appears, a symptom of her having fallen under the power of men and of the Masculine that indicates deterioration in place of the matriarchal spiritual generativity inherent in the Feminine and in woman.

Despite all this, however, we must speak of a cultural symbiosis in the patriarchy, for when we analyze the situation more deeply, we find the image of the "power" of men and of the Masculine compensated by a far-reaching reversal of the "power relationship."

The male's external dominance and his psychology finds its complement in the projection of the man's anima onto the woman and in the regression accompanying this "loss of soul." In the patriarchal situation the anima—the symbolic figure of the contrasexual, archetypally feminine powers of the psyche in the man himself—is repressed into the unconscious; but this sort of constellation necessarily leads to the projection of the repressed element (i.e., the anima) onto the external world, which, in this case, is the woman. In this way the man "loses" his soul and hence unconsciously himself to woman. This loss makes the man emotionally infantile, moody, unstable, touchy, and dependent on the woman in terms of his feelings.[28]

A constellation of this kind leads to the dominance of the Great Mother—that is, to a regression to an earlier stage of consciousness in which the man relates to the woman as a child or a youthful lover.

This situation manifests in different forms in the introvert and the extravert. On the lowest level, this loss of soul turns the man into the hen-pecked husband who lives with his wife as though she were his mother upon whom he is solely dependent in all things having to do with emotions and the inner life. But even the relatively positive case where the woman is the mistress of the inner domain and mother of the home who simultaneously has the responsibility for dealing with all the man's questions and problems having to do with emotions and the inner

28. Jung, "The Relations."

life, even this leads to a lack of emotional vitality and sterile one-sidedness in the man. He discharges only the "outer" and "rational" affairs of life, profession, politics, etc. Owing to his loss of soul, the world he has shaped becomes a patriarchal world that, in its soullessness, presents an unprecedented danger for humanity. In this context we cannot delve further into the significance of a full development of the archetypal feminine potential for a new, future society.

This kind of reversal in the psychological relationship of power and dependency between men and women certainly can occur behind the facade of a patriarchal marriage and within a "successful" cultural symbiosis. Indeed, the strength of the patriarchal symbiosis becomes only the greater through this sort of unconscious interlocking of man and woman. Extraordinarily often the clever wife knows how to conceal her dictatorship from the eyes of the world, and certainly from those of her husband. For the more patriarchal and tyrannical her husband's persona is, the more he is ruled from within by his anima.[29] In the patriarchate, whenever a woman other than the wife carries the anima projection that rules the man—and if this woman cannot be included within the patriarchal framework that, as a matter of fact, is fundamentally polygamous both officially and unofficially—dissolution of the stable patriarchal marriage ensues, along with a transition into a later, more complicated, and more conscious stage of the man-woman relationship.

Another form in which men lose their souls to the

29. Ibid.

Feminine and to women within the patriarchal symbiosis is expressed quite oppositely in men's fanatical adherence to the patriarchate that continually devalues the Feminine. Thus the male relates to the female tyrannically to the point of sexual sadism and patriarchal highhandedness so that woman, as is typical under patriarchal law, no longer exists in her own right but is man's property. But even in this situation the ruling male's psychic dependency upon the woman he dominates hovers in the background. His dependency finds expression in, for example, the predominance of the mother archetype, which can often be demonstrated in the dominance of the personal mother or of the wife as mother of the children, as in the patriarchal, Jewish marriage. Paradoxical though it may seem at first sight, another form in which the mother archetype can dominate the man manifests as his dependency on woman as a sexual object. For the fact that he is dominated by sex corresponds to the Great Mother's domination of the son-lover, who for her is actually a tool serving the collective aims of the species.[30]

Since the patriarchal symbiosis is based on a psychic split—that is, on the isolation of a one-sided consciousness from the unconscious that opposes it—here, too, the danger of psychological illness arises. As long as the persons thus endangered continue to be engrossed in and held captive by a collective solution—e.g., by the values of the patriarchal cultural canon—the danger is collectively allayed. This takes place according to the old ethic

30. In its transpersonal aspect, Don Juan's "mother complex" is an example of this. See the chapter "The Great Mother" in *Origins and History*, pp. 39-101.

with the help of scapegoat psychology,[31] which, in this case, leads patriarchally informed cultures such as the Judeo-Christian, Mohammedan, and Hindu to "recognize" the Feminine and women as evil. Therefore the Feminine and women are suppressed, enslaved, outwardly eliminated from life, or even, as in witch trials, persecuted and done to death as the bearer of evil. Only the fact that men cannot exist without women has hindered the otherwise so popular extermination of this "evil" group of human beings who have to bear the projection of the maleficent unconscious.

When a collective valuation such as the patriarchal can persist no longer owing to the progressive individualization of humankind, collective scapegoat psychology is no longer possible either. While formerly woman was held to be the root of all human and earthly evil, today scarcely anybody considers her to be the cause of the World War. The collective mind now regards ideas or images as agents, as forces of fate. It blames all our ills on capitalism or bolshevism, on religion or its lack, on sociological conditions or astrological constellations—i.e., the conditions on earth or in the heavens—called, for example, "the times," but never on the reality of the individual.

But if a psychic split persists and no collective solution can overcome it, it must be experienced individually to a greater degree than in earlier times and must lead to individual illnesses—to neuroses. The presence of neurosis is frequently the indication that we are dealing with a modern person whose individual development no

31. Neumann, *Depth Psychology and a New Ethic*.

longer fits into the old, collective pattern and who, consequently, has fallen ill or is compelled to find new forms of relationship.[32]

The woman who forfeits her own intellectual or spiritual vitality through projection of her animus onto the male in the patriarchal symbiosis regresses to pre-patriarchal stages of psychic development. This can lead, typically, to a reinforcement of the mother archetype in the woman and to her identification with it. The primal Demeter-Kore relationship is revived, and if she herself is not able to assume the role of mother, the character of the supposedly patriarchal marriage is then determined by the wife's family. In the extreme case, the man's mother-in-law—his wife's mother—assumes control. But in the matriarchal situation the maternal brother, as the real authority, can also govern the life of his sister more than her husband does.

Another form of regression is the return to the patriarchal uroboros. At the personal level this manifests as an increase in strength of the father imago to which the woman "returns." For example, following a brief period during which her husband is forced to carry the patriarchal-paternal role, the values, opinions, and attitudes of the woman's father again become decisive for her and undermine her relationship with her husband. For another type of woman on another level of development, the patriarchal uroboros may be projected onto a transpersonal content. A woman's personal relationship to her husband can be completely or almost completely

32. Vice versa, the individual's inability to adapt to the modern canon of collective values can lead to an "atavistic" illness.

40

reduced to nothing when she gives her allegiance to and is fascinated by a movement, group, sect, great man, or such. Although she frequently maintains contact with her children, in extreme cases those relationships can also crumble thanks to her regression. When this happens, the dragon of regression has succeeded in devouring her "body and soul," a phrase aptly characterizing this archetypal situation.

Complications arising from the patriarchal symbiosis, and the attempts at escaping this collective situation and attaining individual solutions and relationships, give rise to a not inconsiderable number of modern marital problems. Before we outline additional, more individualized phases of woman's development, let us consider a dream that illustrates how the problem of one modern woman's captivity in the patriarchy was constellated.

The dreamer, a Jewish woman in the first half of life who resided in Israel, met an Arab who wanted to marry her and promised her a magnificent life, but on the condition that she give up her religion. After some doubts she agreed and began to live a paradisiacal life in the Arab man's palace. But her life in paradise was disturbed by one phenomenon that her dream described this way: Every night an owl came and tore apart an eagle, and every morning she was forced to see the eagle's remains, nailed to the wall. The dream ended as the dreamer began to write a letter to her grandmother in which she apologized for having given up her religion.

Let us attempt to interpret this dream. Her marriage to the Arab created a situation in which the woman's relationship to the man conformed exclusively to the pleasure principle in an infantile and impersonal way.

The woman paid for this sensual paradise of the unconscious with the renunciation of her religion.

Since the dreamer was not religious, the dream did not seem to be dealing with anything essential that she had surrendered. But abandoning the side of herself that differentiated her from the Arab was not without consequences. The drama being acted out took place at a deeper, impersonal level between powers that, at first, appeared to have nothing to do with the dreamer's consciousness and life. Every night an owl mangled an eagle. The eagle is an archetypally masculine symbol of the sun, the heavens, and the spirit; the owl, on the other hand, symbolizes night and the archetypal Feminine. Moreover, as a symbol of the wisdom of the nocturnal, the owl in itself is not associated with any negative symbolism. The owl is she who sees in the dark, i.e., her intuition,[33] which functions by comprehending the dark, unconscious processes. As the principle of feminine wisdom, the owl is just as positive a symbol when it appears as Athene's bird as it is negative when it appears as the bird of the witch, who uses the same wisdom in the service of evil.

The archetypal Feminine, so submissive and well-behaved in the harem by day, wreaks its revenge as the nocturnal owl on the archetypally masculine eagle. While the eagle governs day and consciousness, the owl must hide. But at night she not only rules but destroys the archetypally masculine principle—which, of course, awakens to new life each morning with the sun.

The symbolism of the dream reveals not only the re-

---

33. Jung, *Psychological Types*, CW 6, Definition 35.

versal of the position of patriarchal dominance to which we have referred where the "inner side" is represented by the nocturnal world of the owl, but also the undermining effect that the repressed archetypal Feminine exerts on the archetypal Masculine. The patriarchally reinforced opposition of Masculine and Feminine, day and night, consciousness and the unconscious, leads to a concealed but deadly battle of the sexes that storms beneath the surface of patriarchal domination and male-female symbiosis in the nocturnal depths of the unconscious relationship.

The woman's seemingly innocent acceptance of the harem paradise and her agreeable readiness to subjugate herself to the man has concealed but terrible consequences.[34] In its regression to the matriarchal hostility toward the male, symbolized by the owl as the Great Mother, the archetypal Feminine takes revenge on the archetypal Masculine that has humiliated it and misused it as an object of pleasure. The good archetypal Feminine regenerates the Masculine by night and enables it to be reborn with the new day; here, however, the evil Feminine dismembers the Masculine just as Penelope every night resisted her hated suitors by destroying her day's weaving.

At the subjective level—that is, referenced to the dreamer's psyche—the owl's deed signifies more than the destruction of the archetypally masculine spirit principle and more than the activated possibility of nocturnal

34. It is extremely illuminating that in Apuleius's tale of Amor and Psyche, Psyche's life in Eros's sensual paradise leads to the same mortal consequences. Only there, the invasion of the hostile feminine power is represented not by the owl but by Psyche's sisters. Cf. Neumann, *Amor and Psyche*.

(i.e., unconscious), instinctive, archetypally feminine life. For her marriage to the Arab the woman paid the high price of the sacrifice of her religion, a spiritual principle belonging to the dreamer that is indeed collective but nevertheless represents a higher form of consciousness than does the dominating, alien, instinctual side represented by the Arab. In this sense the owl also represents a negative, regressive aspect of the Feminine principle in the dreamer herself that, every night, repeatedly slays the archetypally masculine side of her own consciousness, the eagle.

Submissiveness to the patriarchate and the sacrifice of her own spiritual side determine the dreamer's consciousness. This bears two consequences: one is the sensual paradise of instinctive life; the other is the drama of the owl and the eagle in the collective unconscious. Interpreted at the objective level where it occurs between the dreamer and her husband, between the Feminine and the Masculine, the drama of the owl and the eagle means this: the revenge of the Feminine against the Masculine, regression to the level of matriarchal hostility toward men—i.e., defeat of the Masculine with the help of its own vulnerability to instinct. This is the Samson and Delilah pattern: the Great Mother's nightly defeat, castration, and dismemberment of the archetypal Masculine with the help of the drives to which the Masculine is vulnerable.

But at the subjective level where owl and eagle are attitudes of the dreamer herself, the dream means this: her readiness to sacrifice her own spiritual possessions, the collective relationship to the spirit-father (religion), in exchange for an unconscious life of pleasure leads to the catastrophic dominance of the Terrible Mother, who makes one unconscious and brings pleasure but who also annihilates all connections with the masculine principle, with consciousness, and with the spiritual side of the psyche. In modern women this regression is expressed negatively, both internally and externally. In practice this damages her husband and her relationship to him just as much as it damages her own development, which can remain neither without consciousness nor only nocturnal and owl-like.

In contrast to the dismembering owl,[35] which is the instinctual aspect of the archetypal Feminine hostile to the day, the dreamer's grandmother is the human aspect of the Great Mother. The process by which the dreamer will become conscious of the faulty situation and be redeemed from captivity in a world that makes her unconscious begins with her letter of apology to her grandmother. The grandmother as Great Mother is the Self, which protects the individual and the consciousness-affirming values of the archetypal Feminine necessary for the development of wholeness, and which, when the time is ripe, determines the life problems, particularly of the second half of life, through which wholeness is to be realized in the process of individuation. But the process of individuation belongs to a phase of woman's development that has already overcome the symbiosis of patriarchal culture.

While the problems already mentioned are played out within the cultural symbiosis of the patriarchy, the fe-

---

35. Here the owl, a positive symbol of feminine wisdom, is negatively regressive because it tears apart the eagle "in an unnatural way."

male outsiders of the patriarchate no longer belong to its particular territory. As outsiders they are, to a great degree, "forerunners." Of course, those women who remain fixated in the primal relationship as eternal daughters of the Mother, or as eternal daughters of the patriarchal uroboros (i.e., caught in pre-patriarchal stages of development), cannot attain a patriarchal marriage and the patriarchal symbiosis. But for the "unredeemed" of the patriarchy—that is, for those women in whom woman's disappointment with the patriarchy is becoming apparent —the situation is different.

The necessity and the readiness of the Feminine to let the hero redeem it from pre-patriarchal phases of development is connected with the fact that archetypally the Feminine experiences the Masculine as solar and transpersonally spiritual. The Masculine is identified with activity, will, consciousness, and the development toward masculine spirit just as it is in the development of patriarchal consciousness in which the Masculine itself assumes this identification. But whenever the woman experiences the individual man as a merely collective representative of these values—that is, when he corresponds to them only so far as he has traversed the archetypal stages of conscious development, but as a person and an individual does not fulfill them in any vital manner —she is disappointed in him since he corresponds only collectively but not individually to the archetype of the redeeming hero. In this case the woman suffering from a patriarchal husband who fails as an individual partner anticipates inwardly the phase of "confrontation" that is characterized by the meeting of two individuals.

Since the patriarchal marriage is almost as old as our

historical knowledge—knowledge, like history, being possible only with the predominance of a patriarchal consciousness—the complications that the canon of patriarchal culture entails for the Feminine are also very old. Hence we find these sorts of situations and their solutions already prefigured in mythology. This is particularly noticeable in Greek mythology,[36] which to a great degree is the precipitate of fundamental conflicts triggered by the clash of the pre-Greek, matriarchal mentality and the invading patriarchal Greek peoples. Thus the tragedy of Jason's encounter with Medea lies in this: although Jason did indeed save Medea from the dragon and free her from the world ruled by her father, he failed when he should have developed an individual relationship with her. He abandoned her because he was no match for her obviously dangerous individuality and passion that could not be contained in a patriarchal marriage. Left with the disillusionment of her partner's failure, Medea regressed to the Terrible Mother who murders her own children and drives off in the dragon chariot. This signifies that redemption by the hero—seemingly accomplished through Jason's victory over the dragon and his abduction of Medea—remained incomplete.

We find the same problem with Ariadne and Theseus but in a different form. Theseus also frees Ariadne, who had aided him, from the power of her father, and he too then forsakes her. But in this case no regression to the Terrible Mother ensues; rather, she takes the much more

36. The origin of individual myths, their overlapping stratification, the new interpretations given them, etc., have nothing to do with this psychological constellation that represents a part of those powers, a constellation that edits and revises the myths as such.

positive, progressive step toward the patriarchal uroboros, a step that reveals itself as a transition in her development. Dionysus finds Ariadne and sets her free. Failure of the personal, earthly hero—Theseus—is eclipsed by her relationship to the transpersonal Masculine that is able to redeem the Feminine.

In the development of a modern woman this would signify that her disappointment in a personal partner indeed leads to surrender of the personal relationship to a particular man or to men in general, but that the same disappointment flows into the emotional and spiritual development of a redeeming relationship to the transpersonal, for example of a religious form. In this case we must not speak of a regression to the patriarchal uroboros but rather should regard the patriarchal, uroboric figure of Dionysus as a progressive symbol of feminine development.

In contrast to this sort of positive encounter with the patriarchal uroboros we find other meetings in mythology in which its power is regressive and destructive. For example, we find the catastrophic outcome of this sort of situation in the Greek myth of the daughters of Minyas. Following their tendency to remain good spouses and faithful wives—that is, by fulfilling the canon of patriarchal culture—they refuse to let Dionysus break in upon them when he triumphantly passes by in their vicinity. But the approach of an archetype—that is, of a transpersonal power that, like Dionysus, signifies death, redemption, and transformation, especially for women —is fateful, and its overwhelming power cannot be excluded from life unpunished. Hence for these women the artificially imposed constrictive tendency of the "good wife" not to admit pressing transpersonal energies leads to insanity in which they perish.

Even today women's mental illnesses can be determined by attitudes of a traditionally "faithful" and constrictive patriarchal psychology. The lively development occasioned by the invasion of the transpersonal is excluded in these cases and turns negative. In this sense the endangerment, indeed the collapse, of the patriarchal, symbiotic marriage may constitute one of several elements necessary for a woman's development. Wherever the encounter of woman and man is necessary—and here we mean the relationship between two individuals—a marriage defined solely by the patriarchal symbiosis and its collective character must be shattered, a contention borne out not only by the large number of divorces but also by the healing of many neurotic illnesses in modern women and by their development.[37] "Fidelity" is a central problem especially in the psychology of woman, for all too often fidelity is not the index of a vital relationship to her partner but rather is only the expression of psychic lethargy and hampers the developmentally necessary progression to a new phase of life. Breaching fidelity can then be a necessary symptom of the hero's struggle in which a taboo that has become worthless must be broken. "Fidelity" is then reversed, being precisely the attitude that does what fate requires, even if that does not correspond to a traditional canon of transmitted—i.e., collective—values. In this case fidelity to individuation—that is, to one's own destiny and to one's own necessary development—is more meaningful than faith-

37. See Neumann, *Depth Psychology and a New Ethic*.

fulness to a pre-individual attitude. However, truly deciding a conflict of this sort, regardless how it turns out, is fateful and never subordinate to a collective judgment coming from outside.

In contrast to the collective, patriarchal marriage that, ultimately, is contracted by clans and families, the problem of individual relationship—that is, of encounter—becomes evident where relationship becomes a question of individual love rather than of being propelled by external collective forces such as groups or of inner collective energies such as drives. The individual relationship that takes its place as love-marriage beside the traditional patriarchal marriage[38] can, however, still exist within the collective norm of the patriarchal marriage.

This situation has changed only in modern times when the entire relationship between the Masculine and the Feminine, men and women, has become problematic. This change finds expression not only in the relationship between husband and wife but also within the psyche itself, since the man's relationship to his own unconscious feminine side, the anima, and the woman's to her unconscious masculine, the animus, begin to enter consciousness.

Here the psychology of the patriarchate ends, and the psychology of encounter, of surrender and devotion to the Self, of individuation, and of the discovery of the feminine Self begins. These are the two last and highest phases of the psychological development of the Feminine. To describe them exceeds the limits of our sketch, for the problems of this phase embrace nearly all the problems of

38. The archetypal prototype of this individual love situation is found in Apuleius's fairy-tale myth of Amor and Psyche.

the modern woman insofar as she is really "modern," i.e., not just living in our times by accident. Both phases presuppose an inner victory over the symbiosis of the patriarchate. It is equally possible, in the process, for woman's development to be played out within a marriage that began patriarchally and symbiotically, or for the process to lead to the break up of marriage and into a new relationship. But every transition from one phase to the next can come to pass only through psychic conflict, and the entire personality must be engaged.

A crisis of this sort, even if it is to take place within a marriage, must involve both partners because, for a woman, a change in the relationship between man and woman also always presupposes a corresponding trans-formation of her male partner. An extremely common cause of marital conflicts and divorces lies in the fact that the development toward a new phase of relationship, vitally necessary for one partner, is tragically doomed to failure owing to the other partner's lack of understanding or inability to participate in the development.

In contrast to the collective polarization of patriarchal symbiosis, a genuine "encounter" brings about a relation-ship in which man and woman are related to each other as conscious and as unconscious structures, i.e., as whole persons. In *The Psychology of the Transference* Jung dis-cussed this form of relationship as an archetypal quater-nio, i.e., as a fourfold relationship in which consciousness and the unconscious of both partners are in contact. This comprehends the whole nature of each person, hence in the case of the man not only his patriarchal masculine consciousness but equally his feminine anima side. But now this is not unconsciously projected so that the man appears both to himself and to his female counterpart as purely masculine; rather, man and woman must consciously relate equally to the man's feminine and masculine sides. In human terms, this produces a plenitude of complications and problems, since the man's feminine anima side is emotional and he is initially unaware of it, so that only circuitously and through suffering does he come to experience essential parts of his own nature, facets that he first experienced in his partner as something foreign and Feminine. However, these problems demand the greatest effort not only from the man himself but equally from the woman, who, for her part, must witness the collapse of her image of ideal masculinity as she becomes conscious of the man's feminine side.

With similar complications the same holds true for the woman's animus-psychology and her growing awareness of it. This process, too, places the greatest of demands on both partners' mutual understanding and tolerance. Consequently in this phase of encounter the complicated multiplicity of psychic relationships between man and woman is in fact incalculable.

Fulfilling the demands of this sort of situation, however, not only guarantees a vital relationship and a tension of polar opposites but at the same time lets the unique and individual essence of both partners enter into the relationship. Since a person's unconscious and his or her wholeness both are caught up in the process of transformation of the personality, the conventionally collective semblance of personality must be surrendered and the distinctive and singular uniqueness of the human being starts to work its effects undisturbed by the persona.[39] Only then, however, do two persons attain to a true encounter. Where the deepest levels of the personality are included in the living *Auseinandersetzung*, the merely individual qualities of the one's personality form the starting point for experiencing the transpersonal in oneself and in one's counterpart. This form of encounter is the highest possible form of a real relationship between man and woman.

At first the intimate form of relationship, symbolized in the transference quaternio and encompassing the unconscious, seems to the man to be difficult and unwelcome as a kind of "captivity," and to agree with the feminine tendency to form relationships of identity. Of course, this tendency to create relationships of identity constitutes the foundation of the community-forming nature of the Feminine that, in *participation mystique*, attempts ever and again to re-establish the primal bonds and ties of humanity. For woman, it is not acting but being in community that bears the sign of life. For her it is not table talk but the shared meal, not discussion and conversation but being together side by side, that is decisive.

Wherever it truly happens, wordlessly knowing one another is a form of togetherness more complete and more essential to the Feminine than the Masculine face-to-face stance that, ego to ego and consciousness to consciousness, more often divides than binds together.

A multitude of conflicts in marriage and love relationships rests on this sharp contrast between feminine and

39. See Jung, "The Relations."

masculine nature rendering the constellation between man and woman so extraordinarily complicated that even between anima and animus all the antithetical relationships appear that archetypally distinguish the Masculine from the Feminine. True to her feminine nature, the anima, independently of the man's distance-seeking masculine ego, tends to create an emotionally colored relationship of identity corresponding to the primal relationship. By contrast, in her femininity the woman indeed does have the conscious intention of being together, of being one in *participation mystique*, but pursued by the archetypally masculine animus side of her nature, she can refrain neither from having separative and irritating "viewpoints" nor from making critical observations, etc.; subsequently she is hurt and wounded when this disturbs the spiritual union she so ardently desires with her husband.

Hence for both participants—man and woman—the phase of encounter holds extraordinary difficulties. Fundamentally these difficulties arise from the fact that the problem of relationship proves to be inseparably tied to the problem of individuation, of the development of one's wholeness. Creation of a "quaternary" relationship such as described in *The Psychology of the Transference* does indeed take place to a large degree in the unconscious with only concomitant or completely absent participation on the part of the ego. But in reality, the "quaternary relationship" is played out between the totality of both persons, i.e., between the wholeness of both that embraces consciousness and the unconscious. If each person's own contrasexual psychic element, anima or animus, is included in the process of integration that again establishes the primordial bisexuality of each individual psyche, then orientation to the patriarchal world of values must be relinquished. But this compels the individual to find his or her own path, a task with which collective precepts can no longer offer any help.

This again highlights a contrast between men's and women's problems, a contrast—having consequences for modern woman's adaptation—that leads easily to the development of neuroses. Assimilation of the feminine side is indeed a decisive problem in a man's individuation, but it remains his "private affair" since our patriarchal culture not only does not demand individuation but tends actually to reject it in the male. Assimilation of the archetypally masculine animus side of woman's nature, however, is a different matter. In modern times patriarchal culture, which no longer oppresses her and hinders her cultural participation, motivates woman to develop the opposite side of her psyche from childhood onwards. This means that women are forced into a certain degree of Self-estrangement for the sake of conscious development. Initially more is demanded of them than of men. From woman both femininity and masculinity are required, while from him only masculinity. We are speaking here of one of the complications but also one of the opportunities inherent in woman's situation for our culture that has led to there being such a high percentage of women involved in the development of modern psychology, actively through their collaboration and passively through their conflicts.

However, a further consequence of the fundamental situation of women is that, to the extent "conscience" is formed by the patriarchal culture's valuations, it awakens no wholehearted response in women, since it often stands in opposition to the values of the female Self as an expression of patriarchal culture. Woman never feels that she is quite her "herself" when she identifies her ego with patriarchal consciousness. Often it seems to the woman that she is estranged from herself in becoming conscious because she suffers the conflict between the symbolically masculine structure of her consciousness and the feminine structure of her wholeness as though it were a disorder. But her suffering is legitimate, and her "duality" is a disorder only when measured against the naïve totality and unequivocality of the primal situation that must be surrendered.

Just as men and women are naturally compelled by the archetypal masculine energy in themselves to abandon the primal relationship and find their path to ego and to consciousness, both are also forced by their inherent archetypal feminine energies again to surrender this position and press on toward a wholeness that embraces Masculine and Feminine. In the case of woman it is the psyche itself that forces her out of the patriarchal world and into what is properly hers; for man it is the anima, and behind the anima ultimately also the wholeness of the psyche, that drives him to give up his purely masculine identity. For both, becoming whole stands at the center of the individuation process, the psychic development of the second half of life.

As the highest phase of woman's development, individuation leads to woman's discovery of Self. Now the encounter with the Masculine takes the form of an inner encounter in which woman experiences her own archetypally masculine energies. Woman now becomes conscious of the psychic agencies that previously were experienced in projected form in the outer world. All the symbols and contents characteristic of the first phase of development reappear, but now they stand under the sign of the integration of the complete personality and of a development having its center not in the ego but in the Self as the center of the unified psyche.

The meaning and significance of an archetypal constellation depends on the phase of life in which it appears. While an archetypal fixation on, or a regression to, any one of the individual developmental phases is almost always negative during the first half of life, the reactivation of these early phases usually has a progressive—i.e., decisively positive—significance for woman's development in the second half of life, although the phases still contain disturbing and seemingly negative aspects. Hence a fixation on the patriarchal uroboros in the first half of life constellates an incapacity for relationship on the woman's part in the sense of discontent with her husband, frigidity, and withdrawal into a neurotic fantasy existence.

But the same constellation often plays an entirely different role in the process of individuation. When the patriarchal uroboros now intrudes it can have a redeeming function and lead the woman out of the constriction of the purely personal realm toward the experience of the transpersonal.

Interpretation of the following dream of a modern woman may serve to illustrate this point. The dreamer's current situation was the result of a long-standing conflict between two men: she experienced the relationship to her husband as unsatisfying and untenable while the relationship with her friend was not only sexually very positive but was also full of spiritual and emotional life. The richness of the relationship found expression in various ways, including a sense of mutuality extending to reciprocal telepathic empathy in the sense of *participation mystique.*

The dreamer finds herself in her childhood home where there were three rooms in a row: her own, the middle room, and that of her father. In this dream the dreamer had wanted to make a choice in favor of her husband and against her friend. She wanted to return to her own room but first, as if drawn by magic, she had to enter her father's room by passing through the middle room where her friend was.

She saw a young girl standing at her father's writing table, but this young girl was a ghost, a shade. When, full of fear, she cried out, "What do you want from me?" she suddenly felt herself stabbed as though with a needle and poisoned. "Something horrible happened." When she wanted to return to her own room, her friend discovered her in the middle room and thought that she was coming back to him. Just as he was embracing her, he became enormous and wound himself about her more and more tightly. "The needle stabs me terribly; he winds about me; I see parts of a gigantic snake; whispering he asks if I will remain with him for ever." As the dreamer nods assent, she is seized with grief at the loss of her relationship with her husband and loses consciousness. Thus ends the dream.

To understand the dream we must mention that the dreamer was strongly attached to her father who, she believed, had not loved her. Nevertheless she appeared somehow to have embodied his anima figure, and he had been in the habit, suddenly and without transition, of making her his personal confidante. Her relationship to her mother was very negative.

What happens in this dream? It is impossible for her to get away from her friend and return to her own room because the female figure in her father's room magically attracts her. This spectral shadow-figure next to the writing table who poisons her is she herself in her unconscious relationship to her father. The unconscious father-bond—whose nature is not personal but transpersonal, i.e., archetypal, and which we have yet to explain—also determines her relationship to her friend, a relationship that completes her unsatisfactory marriage not only sexually. Precisely this unity of mystical and sensual elements is characteristic of the relationship to the patriarchal uroboros.

The dangerous and overpowering aspects of this relationship, which consists in a covert regressive bond to the dreamer's personal father complex and to the archetypal figure of the patriarchal uroboros, become apparent in her attempt to free herself from her friend. The transformation of her friend into the great serpent-dragon of the patriarchal uroboros reveals the poison of her spectral, spiritual bond with her father. Her dragon-friend's embrace is only one more expression of the way in which the overpowering archetype poisons her. The transformation of her human friend into this transpersonal, inhuman creature is a clear expression of the efficacy of the archetypal background, which determines both her unconscious relationship to her father and her relationship to her friend. We have already pointed out that the male

59

dragon in relation to a woman is often the symbol for the patriarchal uroboros.[40] What is particularly significant here is the way the transpersonal overlaps the personal.

A picture she had painted of this scene amplifies her condition of having fallen under the power of the dragon and friend who whispers to her that now she will remain eternally with him. It is characteristic of this picture, in which her friend in snake-form embraces her, that neither looks at the other. Both seem to fix their gaze on some distant point, as if to make it clear that both are fascinated by something different from the actual other whose reality neither perceives.

We recognize the figure of the man with snake's body, for example, in the Greek myth of the Titans and Giants, the lower part of whose bodies were depicted as earth serpents. The Titan who in myth endeavors to lay hold of the powers above him, including the higher Feminine, represents a lower level of development corresponding to the more highly developed centaur, in which the male has the body of a horse rather than a serpent. The centaur also kidnaps the woman and tries to overpower her, i.e., make her unconscious, and carry her off to Hades, etc.

In the myth only the intervention by heroic powers can break the superior power of the patriarchal uroboros manifesting in its chthonic lower form. The heroic powers appear as Theseus and as the Lapithae on the earthly level, for example, and as Zeus and the Olympians on the heavenly level, and both symbolize the patriarchal side of consciousness. In the history of humanity

40. See Neumann, *Amor and Psyche*, and also the reference to the death-wish in Neumann, "The Psychological Meaning of Rituals" (see above, n. 10).

this solution corresponds to the displacement of the patriarchal uroboros in its assaulting anonymity by the patriarchy and by the individual male. This is what the dream would have meant for the dreamer had she been in the first half of life and found it impossible to form a relationship with a partner because of her bond with the patriarchal uroboros.

But here we are confronted with something different. Since she is a grown woman involved in the individuation process, she must become conscious of the figure of the patriarchal uroboros and the danger that it represents for her, independently of the manner in which her relationship to a male partner takes shape. This means that she must come to the point in her inner development where she, as the solar hero, liberates herself from the dragon's embrace or suffers the death-marriage with the dragon in conscious surrender and devotion so that— together with the dragon—she can emerge transformed. Here again the oft-cited tale of Amor and Psyche is paradigmatic. With her acceptance of the patriarchal uroboros and the transformation it brings, a spiritual realm of a transpersonal nature reveals itself to the woman in the second half of life, a realm belonging most profoundly to the spiritual side of her own feminine nature, a realm that makes her inwardly independent of the values and judgments of the patriarchal, archetypally masculine spirit whose essence is foreign to her nature.

Centroversion, which intends individual wholeness, breaks through during individuation, the developmental phase when woman attains the Self.[41] Now a process of

41. See *Amor and Psyche*.

personality transformation begins that leads to a new synthesis of the components of the personality, one in which the center of gravity shifts from the outer world—and from the external relationship—to the world within.

C. G. Jung has so often discussed the transformation processes generally valid for individuation that we need only refer to his writings.[42] Moreover, it is not possible to work out the features specific to woman's individuation in our present outline. For only extensive case material could elucidate the connection between woman's individuation and the stages preceding it. Hence we must content ourselves with a brief summary of some of the problems most significant in this process.

In the course of individuation the woman withdraws to a certain extent from her relationship with an outer partner and experiences within herself and on a higher level the authorities or agencies that she had to relinquish at the beginning of her development. Thus she comes to a renewed experience of the archetypally masculine side of her own nature, which at the beginning she had experienced for the most part externally in projection as hero and as patriarchal uroboros. The transformation process leads to confrontation with the inner masculine divinity on a higher plane: the birth of the divine child and all the developments that, for example, we find portrayed in the myth of Amor and Psyche. But now the primal relationship reappears in a new and higher form: as the encounter of the woman's ego and her female Self. Now development is completed and forms a unity with the beginning

42. See Jung, "The Relations"; *Psychology and Religion: West and East*, CW 11; and "Concerning Rebirth," "A Study in the Process of Individuation," and "Concerning Mandala Symbolism," all in CW 9,i.

when the woman reconnects with the Great Mother as Earth Mother, Sophia, and Feminine Self. With the emergence of the higher uroboric image of the Self, in which the figure of the Great Mother and that of the patriarchal uroboros or the Great Father are united, the woman attains to an inner renewal, to a form of spiritual and emotional fruitfulness specific to herself, and to the highest experience she can have of the totality of the psyche.

Thus, beside the stages of male development described in *The Origins and History of Consciousness* there stands an independent series of stages corresponding to woman's nature that the woman must traverse if she is to attain to the Self in individuation. Neither of these two series of stages, however, is a self-contained course of development in which the male becomes masculine and the female feminine. Again and again the principle of relationship with the other is the decisive element in both. Although coming to one's Self stands as the goal of individuation at the end-point of the development of consciousness and of the personality, the fateful interdependence of man and woman as partners extends through all the stages of man's and woman's development. From the lowest to the highest stage, from containedness in the unconscious to re-attainment of the Self in transformation, one experiences what is one's own in and through the other. And always the "wholly other," opposed to what one is in the polarity of man and woman, Masculine and Feminine, proves to be the mysterious numen from which development toward one's authenticity catches fire and into which it ultimately flows when "otherness" is conclusively overcome.

II

THE MOON AND MATRIARCHAL CONSCIOUSNESS

I

In the history of the rise of consciousness[1] a stadial development can be traced in which the ego separates from containment in the unconscious, the primal uroboric[2] situation of the beginnings, and stands at the end point of the process as the center of modern occidental consciousness vis-à-vis the unconscious as a separate psychic system. In this development that leads to liberation from the superior power of the unconscious, the symbolism of consciousness is archetypally masculine, that of the unconscious archetypally feminine, to the extent that the unconscious stands in opposition to this emancipation of the ego, as mythology and the symbolism of the collective unconscious also teach.

The phase in which ego-consciousness is still childlike

"Über den Mond und das matriarchale Bewusstsein," *Eranos Jahrbuch*, special volume, 1950; republished in *Zur Psychologie des Weiblichen*. Translated by Boris Matthews.

1. Neumann, *Origins and History*.

2. The uroboros is the snake holding its tail in its mouth, the symbol of a closed, self-contained unconscious psychic situation, the original unit. See ibid.

in its relationship to the unconscious (i.e., relatively lack-
ing in independence) is represented in myth by the archetype of the Great Mother. Like the forms in which it is
expressed and projected, we call the constellation of this
psychic situation "matriarchal"; in contrast to this, the
tendency of the ego to free itself from the unconscious
and to dominate it is what we designate as the "patriarchal accent" of the development of consciousness.

Hence "matriarchate" and "patriarchate" are psychic
stages characterized by various developments in consciousness and the unconscious, but especially by various
stances of the one toward the other. "Matriarchate" therefore signifies not only the dominance of the archetype of
the Great Mother, but more generally a total psychic
situation in which the unconscious and the Feminine are
dominant, and consciousness and the Masculine have not
yet attained autonomy and independence.[3] In this sense,
therefore, a psychic stage, a religion, or a neurosis, but
also a developmental stage of consciousness, can be designated matriarchal; and patriarchal does not mean the
sovereign sociological authority of men but rather the
dominance of an archetypally masculine consciousness
that achieves a separation of the conscious and unconscious systems and that is established relatively firmly in
contrast to, and in its independence of, the unconscious.
For this reason the modern woman must also pass
through all the phases of development that lead to the

3. "Masculine" and "feminine" are used here as symbolic terms and
are not to be identified concretely with "man" and "woman" as the
bearers of specific sexual characteristics. Man and woman are psychologically bisexual since in the unconscious both have contra-sexual
"authorities," the anima in the man and animus-figures in the woman.
Cf. C. G. Jung, "The Relations."

formation of patriarchal consciousness, which is typical of and taken for granted in occidental consciousness and is dominant in patriarchal culture.

However, beside this "patriarchal consciousness" there exists a "matriarchal consciousness" whose mode of functioning is hidden but significant. Matriarchal consciousness belongs to the matriarchal level of the psyche, the culture-building level operative at the dawn of human history. Prior to and following the modern woman's acculturation to patriarchal consciousness, it is characteristic of woman's mentality; but it also plays an important role in the life of the man. That is to say: wherever consciousness has not yet or is no longer patriarchally separated from the unconscious, matriarchal consciousness rules—in the dawn of humanity as it does ontogenetically in the corresponding phase of the child's life, and in the man's emotional crises and creative processes, e.g., when his anima, which represents the archetypically feminine side of his psychology, is more strongly activated.

The brief outline of the stadial development of woman presented elsewhere[4] provides the necessary complement to understanding matriarchal consciousness, the unique features of which form a sharp contrast to male stadial development. That aspect of archetypally feminine consciousness associated with the patriarchal uroboros is what we call matriarchal consciousness, a consciousness that—just like the ego at this stage—is not developed to the same degree of independence as is the ego and consciousness in the patriarchate. But the same archetypal

4. See the preceding essay in this volume.

symbol is characteristic for the patriarchal uroboros and for matriarchal consciousness: the moon.

The symbol of the moon is so polyvalent that at first it appears impossible to demonstrate its unequivocal relation to the Feminine, for it appears as both feminine and masculine as well as hermaphroditic. In myth we find the sun as the wife of the moon; more often the moon is the wife of the sun. The new-moon phase can be seen as the death of the female moon in the sun's embrace as well as the death of the moon-man in the embrace of the evil sun-woman; it is interpreted as the death of the Feminine following the fulfillment of giving birth and as death of the Feminine after sexual abuse, but also as the revivification of the famished (male) moon by the sun-woman who nurtures him. When the sun and moon are siblings, the moon can be male one time and female another, and their movement first away from each other and then closer again is interpreted as the longing of the male moon for the female sun-sister or also as the yearning of the sun-brother for his moon-sister; but equally it can signify the female moon's flight from the pursuing male sun and the female moon's desire for the male sun.[5]

There is a variety of associations: in one instance the moon is regarded as the Masculine relating to the Feminine, and in another as the Feminine relating to the Masculine; but this variety is also expressed in the circum-

5. It would be easy to amass evidence for each of these mythological stages and for many others, but that would be superfluous here because we are interested in interpreting the phenomenon, not in amassing material to amplify it. See Hans Kelsen, *Society and Nature* (Chicago, 1943); Robert Briffault, *The Mothers* (3 vols., London and New York, 1927); and Oskar Rühle, *Sonne und Mond im primitiven Mythos* (Tübingen, 1925).

stance that in its different phases it can be regarded as masculine (as the waxing and waning moon-sickle) or as feminine (as the full moon).[6] This leads to the widespread mythological notion that the moon is hermaphroditic.

Even if we try to recognize a pattern in these seemingly arbitrary associations, the richly scintillating moon symbolism teaches us that no symbol is "absolute" but rather can be interpreted only in reference to a greater, all-encompassing symbolic world. But the order of the greater, all-encompassing world is determined by the developmental phase of consciousness in which it appears and to which it is related. Therefore we must distinguish whether the moon symbolism belongs to a matriarchal world governed by the archetypal Feminine and the unconscious or to a patriarchal world ruled by the archetypal Masculine and by consciousness.

As we do this, we must free ourselves from the familiar notion that the moon receives its light from the sun, because astronomically in all its phases the light of the moon is only reflected sunlight. This state of affairs, first appearing among the Greek pre-Socratics and still discussed by Augustine,[7] is not what has always been taken for granted. The relatively late astronomical recognition of the moon's dependence on the sun is the expression and the symbol of the moon's humiliation in the patriarchal world, in which sun and day, like human consciousness in its archetypally masculine expression, have

6. René Spitz, with W. G. Cobliner, *The First Year of Life: A Psycho-analytic Study of Normal and Deviant Development of Object Relations* (New York, 1965).

7. See Hugo Rahner, "Mysterium Lunae," *Zeitschrift für katholische Theologie* (Innsbruck) 58 (1939).

assumed sovereign authority. Here the moon is female and the sun male, but at the same time the solar Masculine is the creative, the light-giver but the lunar Feminine is the dependent, receptive light-borrower. Likewise the many identifications of female deities with the moon (for example in Hellenism) are expressions of this patriarchal revaluation. It is almost always a question of granting secondary or subordinate status to the "consorts" who are ruled by the sun god, but the histories of these goddesses frequently reveal quite different relationships to males and to the sun.

For the world of the dawn of time, every phase of the moon is essential; it manifests the essence of the moon, just as each phase of life manifests the nature of a human being. The changing psychic constellations that are characteristic of woman, or in which woman experiences her relationship to men, are projected onto the moon.

In the late patriarchal phase, the sun can be male and the moon female; as siblings, both can assume either sex, or the moon may, as at the matriarchal level, be regarded as male; but always the sun-moon relationship is mythologically apperceived as a noteworthy celestial phenomenon and, above and beyond that, is often experienced as a symbolic depiction of the relationship between the sexes. The kind of relationship, however, is dependent on the psychic level at which it is played out. The patriarchal world order is the precise inverse of the earlier matriarchal order in which the Feminine predominates. In this regard it makes no difference whether the moon is assigned to the night as a male deity in the matriarchate but at the same time is her child and son—often even, as the new moon, her dying son—or whether the sun and day

69

appear as newborns. In both cases (whose differences we must ignore in this context) the dependency of the Masculine upon the birth-giving motherhood of the nocturnal Feminine is emphasized. At this stage, as is frequently the case in the Orient,[8] the moon has the character of the upper world and of life; the sun, however, carries the character of the underworld and of night. Nevertheless, the Feminine, dying as the new moon and in death impregnated by the sun, is the ruling principle.

The light arising from the sun's embrace is not engendered by the sun nor even borrowed but rather only aroused and ignited by it, for the same holds true for the matriarchal femininity of the moon and for the female wood that, by its very nature, contains the fire within itself which the male fire-drill only releases through boring but does not procreate in it.[9] On the matriarchal level this means that the phases of the moon are understood as phases of female being independent of the sun, even though the female moon dies in the new moon and enters into a life-death contact with the sun. The phases of pregnancy,[10] for example, are also understood in this way. For one of the typical "equations" between the moon and the Feminine rests on its character of swelling up and of shrinking connected with fertility, to which the Masculine possesses nothing comparable.

8. A. Jeremias, *Handbuch der altorientalischen Geisteskultur* (2nd ed., Berlin, 1929; orig., 1913), p. 240.

9. All this will be presented in detail in my proposed study, *Psychologie des Weiblichen*. [Neumann did not later publish what would apparently have been an extended work on the psychology of the feminine, though he touched on the theme of the fire-drill in *The Great Mother* (B.S. XLVII, 1955), pp. 225, 310-11. See also Jung, *Symbols of Transformation*, CW 6, index, s.v. fire-boring.]

10. See Kelsen, p. 45.

In the matriarchal phase the emphasis lies on the phenomena of the night sky—i.e., this phase represents a nocturnal and lunar psychology. The solar day-world of consciousness is less emphasized because, interpreted psychologically, humanity in this phase still lives more in the unconscious than in consciousness, and because the development that reaches its zenith in the patriarchal act of consciousness's awareness of consciousness has not yet come to pass. Although a male moon is often associated with the earlier matriarchal stage and a female moon with a later patriarchal one, it would be too great a simplification to assert that the male symbolism of the moon is later replaced by a female symbolism.[11]

But independent of the stage of conscious development and also regardless whether it appears as the dominant factor in the psychology of a woman or of a man, in its essence the moon is bound to the archetypal Feminine. In every case it belongs among the central symbols of the Feminine whether as male moon it symbolizes the arche-

11. The compensatory relationship of the moon and the consciousness principle—such that an archetypally masculine moon-animus compensates an archetypally feminine matriarchal consciousness, and a moon-anima belongs to a masculine-patriarchal consciousness—does not hold true without exception. For example, at a matriarchal stage the phase nature of the moon can be conceptualized as archetypally feminine, as we have seen. Vice versa, in the patriarchal psychology of Judaism the male can experience himself as a feminine moon vis-à-vis a superior masculine divine solar principle if the man's religious consciousness identifies with the feminine moon-anima. The identification of Jacob and the moon in the Jewish midrash is characteristic of this. Similar examples are found in the Kabala. Analogous symbolic relationships are collectively valid in the identification of the church with the moon (see Rahner, above, n. 7) and individually where, as in mysticism, the individual soul assumes a receptive moon character vis-à-vis the deity.

typally masculine components of a woman's life at the matriarchal level or as female moon it symbolizes the archetypally feminine components of a man's life at the patriarchal stage.

Perhaps the diversity of the male, female, and hermaphroditic nature of the moon was most beautifully stated in the hymn to the moon god of Ur, where we read:

> Mighty Bullock with thick horns, perfect limbs, with
>   lazuline beard, full of strength and exuberance,
> Self-generated Fruit, of high stature, magnificent to
>   behold, of whose exuberance one cannot see one's
>   fill,
> Uterus, Womb of the Universe, who occupies a
>   resplendent dwelling among living creatures,
> Merciful One, Gracious Father, Who holds the life of
>   the entire country in His hand.[12]

"Mighty Bullock with thick horns, perfect limbs, with lazuline beard, full of strength and exuberance"—this image of the moon as steer and fructifier, as a phallic, Dionysian force that intensifies life, and that—as youthful lover and as husband, as bringer of pleasure and procreator—stands at the center point of archetypally feminine matriarchal life, still belongs to the phase of the Great Mother and to her fertility ritual that was intended to guarantee the elemental needs of humanity, particularly for food. As lord of both the cosmic-heavenly and the earthly-female periodicity (whose twenty-eight-day

12. A. Ungnad, ed., *Die Religion der Babylonier und Assyrer* (Jena, 1921), p. 165. [Cf. also a virtually identical version, from a tablet found at Nineveh, tr. F. J. Stephens in *Ancient Near Eastern Texts*, ed. James B. Pritchard (Princeton, 2nd ed., 1955), p. 385.]

rhythm is analogous to its celestial rhythm), the moon—whose waxing, waning, and return has been for humankind since time immemorial the most impressive of heavenly phenomena—is the most visible, lower, terrestrial correspondence to an upper, heavenly process. The areas subject to the moon are manifold and, as we shall see, by no means restricted to the psychological domain.

As the symbol of the waxing and waning self-transforming heavenly body, the moon is the archetypal lord of water, moisture, and vegetation, i.e., of everything growing and living. It is lord of psychobiological life and hence lord of the Feminine in its archetypal essence, the human representative of which is earthly woman. With its dominion over the psychobiological world of moistness and growth, all waters of the deep, streams, lakes, springs, and living juices are subject to it. This world is the primeval world of the "alimentary uroboros" of the dawn of time, in which life as food and fertility is humankind's central concern.[13] The fertility of game animals, herds, fields, and the human group, stands at the midpoint of this world, which consequently to a great extent is the world of the Feminine, of giving birth and nurturing, i.e., the world of the Great Mother over which the moon holds sway.

The fertility ritual as humankind's attempt, with the help of magic, to influence the numinous powers upon which depend all nourishment and hence life itself has from the very beginning been part of the fertility that humanity has revered in woman as the mistress of the fertile womb and the nourishing breasts, of blood and of

13. See *Origins and History*.

73

growth. Consequently fertility depends to a great extent upon the magical activity of woman,[14] over whom the moon stands as the guiding transpersonal power. Enchantment and magic, but inspiration and prophecy too, belong equally to the moon and to woman who is shamaness and sibyl, prophetess and priestess.[15] Briffault's researches demonstrated that the moon and moon mythology played an overtowering role at the dawn of human history, but in the context of our discussion, his evidence of the dominant significance of the Feminine in primeval history and of the subordination of the moon to it (as the masculine principle)[16] is at least equally important.

First of all, we can list the following as archetypally masculine features of the moon found throughout the entire world: the moon is regarded as "Lord of Women"; he is not only their lover but even their real husband next to whom the actual earthly man appears only as the "co-spouse." The moon is the lord of female life in its uniqueness that begins with the onset of menstruation, the monthly bleeding. Menstruation, however, is caused by the moon, who assaults the woman and, so to speak, "spiritually deflowers" her.

As the archetypal wisdom of the unconscious justifiably maintains, spiritual deflowering is the decisive moment of fate for woman. Through menstruation the maiden becomes woman—naturally, as we would say; or

14. See Briffault, above, n. 5.
15. Ibid., vol. 2, pp. 502ff.
16. See M. Esther Harding, *Women's Mysteries, Ancient and Modern* (New York, 1935; rev. 1955), with whose conclusions I agree only in part.

by the deity, the moon, as people used to say. By comparison, anatomical deflowering plays a subordinate role. Among primitive peoples, sexual intercourse resulting in anatomical defloration often begins during childhood; in many cultures defloration accompanied by bleeding is regarded as magically dangerous and consequently as negatively sacred, and is performed by sacred agents, priests or strangers, i.e., not by members of the group who could become infected by the act. Not until woman was regarded as patriarchal property—or more precisely, as a means to acquire property—did the intact virgin and hence anatomical defloration attain a positive significance, and thus indirectly also become an important event for woman upon which her future life as a woman depended.

In every case—i.e., independent of the respective cultural valuations and revaluations—menstruation as spiritual defloration determines the life of woman. As we know, fertilization and fertility were not at first associated with sexual intercourse. This is understandable, for sexual intercourse commences before the epoch of fertility begins and continues after it has already ceased. Marriages remain childless, and unmarried women that no one would believe a man would have intercourse with (e.g., the mentally retarded, mentally ill, misshapen, etc.) have children. While sexual activity is by no means obviously linked with fertilization, the connection between the onset of menstruation and the possibility of fertilization, just like the connection between pregnancy and the interruption of menstruation and the cessation of menstruation and the end of fertility, is self-evident to the primitive mentality.

75

But psychologically the fact that the moon, the lord of menstruation and of fertility, is regarded as the fructifier of woman means that sexual intercourse with flesh-and-blood men is experienced at a different level of significance and meaning than is menstruation, pregnancy, and birth. It is typical for the matriarchal level of woman's psychology that emotionally a total or relative unrelatedness of woman to man prevails. Here woman experiences sexual intercourse not as a special, individual phenomenon related to the personal husband. In early cultures with their general or periodic sacred promiscuity, demonstrable in many places even if it might not represent the original sexual situation, woman experiences sexual intercourse as changeable and ephemeral, and as pleasurable or passionate play. The absence of the individual love relationship and the predominance of the social situation in regard to contracting marriages explain that, at the matriarchal level of woman's psychology, the experience of an objectless sexuality and the experience of menstruation, pregnancy, and birth—just as later the relationship to the child—are bound much more firmly to woman's inner experience than is her relationship to a man.

The basic situation at this level—that the relationship to the man manifests more as a social than as an emotional/spiritual phenomenon—leads to a condition not infrequently encountered in the neuroses of modern women: her inner experiences associated with sexual life are not linked with the earthly-personal husband and partner and related to him but rather are projected into the distance, to a transpersonal and impersonal figure, and experienced as coming from that figure, just as though from the "moon." Hence as lord of inner defloration the moon is lord of women, since menstruation commences after she invisibly sleeps with him; he is the fructifier and "real" father of children, but he is also lord of ecstasy and of intoxication and thus becomes the lord of the soul and of its orgiastic inspiration.

This means that woman belongs to the moon in the manner of a typical *participation mystique*; it arises from woman's unconscious identity with the moon. Woman knows herself to be bound to the moon and identical with it in all essential experiences of her existence, dependent on and merged with it. Woman's relationship to the moon is represented in the relationship of the moon to the Earth and to life. As Bachofen noted,[17] the fact that the moon is regarded as the celestial earth and that earth goddesses are extraordinarily often also moon goddesses points to the multileveled quality of the female psyche that depicts itself in the Earth and the moon and in their mutual relationship. Regarded from the solar-masculine point of view, the "sublunar world" is the despicable matriarchal world." But to a great degree the content and the symbolism of matriarchal consciousness rest upon this unitary character of the Feminine, for which the night sky and the Earth form the great egg-circle of the matriarchal uroboros, in the center of which stands the moon that, as silver egg, represents and illuminates the dark egg orbiting it at a higher level.

"Self-generated Fruit," "Uterus, Womb of the Universe," oddly enough, here a terminology is applied to the moon that belongs profoundly to the self-awareness of the

17. [Cf. *Myth, Religion, and Mother Right: Selected Writings of J. J. Bachofen*, tr. Ralph Manheim (B.S. LXXXIV, 1967).]

matriarchal level in which woman recognizes and celebrates herself as the source of life. "Uterus, Womb of the Universe, Self-generated Fruit"—that is the appeal to the Great Goddess of the dawn of humankind, the Goddess who, as the night sky, is also the moon itself to which she gives birth as something male.[18]

The relationship of woman to the moon, therefore, extends far beyond the biological—i.e., phallic-chthonic —fertility aspect. We have already emphasized that the moon is also lord of enchantment and of fertility magic, but the significance of the moon as spirit is not restricted to woman's sacred, selective relationship, it is a significance she possesses as prophetess and as sibyl.

Essential constituents of humankind's early culture were created by woman and her inventive spirit. Such fundamental accomplishments as preservation of fire, preparation of food and intoxicating beverages, making clothing, spinning and weaving, as well as making pottery, etc., form part of woman's primeval domain. They were not originally "technical" achievements in the sense patriarchal consciousness uses the term, but rather rituals steeped in symbols. They should be called primary mysteries because they have to do with mysteries of an unconscious, symbolic activity, not yet with mysteries involving cognition.

But with startling consistency, here, too, woman's ac-

18. The bisexuality of the moon finds expression as late as Plato's myth in which men originate from the sun, women from the [planet] Venus, and hermaphrodites from the moon. This bisexuality belongs to the primal situation of the uroboros, which contains feminine and masculine. [Cf. *The Symposium*, 190b, where, however, women are said to be descended from the earth.]

tivity is outshone by that of the moon, for the moon appears as the spinner and weaver, as lord of baking, potting, and weaving, the inventor of clothing and physical adornment, and here too proves to be the lord of female life.[19]

Even if only externally at first, this is the point where we can most easily grasp what is of greatest interest to us: the significance of the moon as spirit. The most fundamental spiritual activity of the unconscious is the sudden appearance of something "falling into" consciousness with "moody,"—i.e., moonlike—unpredictability; this is closest to the unsystematic spiritual or intellectual productivity of original humankind and of the Feminine, and originally belongs to that primeval spiritual activity. The sudden thought and the intuition are expressions of the spiritual force of the unconscious, of the *lumen naturae*[20] of the archetypally feminine night world, whose darkness suddenly becomes bright, as if by inspiration.

This numen is experienced in projection onto the moon, that spirit symbol of the unconscious centrally bound to the Feminine, which, for this reason, we regard as the central figure of "matriarchal consciousness." Hence in the language of analytical psychology we would seem to be able to say that the moon is the archetypal midpoint of the female world of the spirit-animus. This formulation does not suffice, however, when we differentiate the concept of animus more highly than heretofore, a task we shall now undertake.

19. See Briffault, *The Mothers*, pp. 624f.
20. "The light of nature is an intuitive apprehension of the facts, a kind of illumination." Jung, "Paracelsus as a Spiritual Phenomenon," CW 13, par. 148.

We distinguish three levels or layers of the animus world that are coordinated with three different developmental stages of woman's psyche: the patriarchate, the matriarchate, and the uroboric level. The transformation that seizes woman's psyche when she develops out of her containedness in the maternal uroboros toward the matriarchate and later out of this stage toward life in the patriarchate also informs and shapes the part-structure of psyche that we designate as animus, the archetypally masculine, spirit-side of woman. These stages can be demonstrated both in the collective projections of the mythic world and in the individual projections of modern woman.

The most superficial and most recent layer of the animus world arises from the patriarchate. This animus world expresses itself in opinions and assertions that, on closer inspection, prove to be property of the archetypally masculine, patriarchal spirit. They arise from the world of male consciousness and of the masculine spirit that is extrinsic and foreign to woman and the Feminine. They express the patriarchate's inner rulership over woman. This is why this level of animus actually belongs not to woman's nature but to male culture.

The highest form of the animus in the patriarchal world is the guide of souls, the psychopomp, that forms the transition to the next, deeper layer into which he "initiates." For behind or beneath this patriarchal world of the animus we find the animus-spirit level with which the Feminine and woman is linked in a more ancient way. We designate this animus-spirit layer as patriarchal uroboros. Here the Masculine is transpersonal and numinous; it has divine, daemonic, and divine-human character and represents a kind of nature spirit that nothing can make rational and close to consciousness but in which feeling and emotion, the daemonic, wordless musicality, and eroticism are dominant. We find this animus-world present wherever woman dreams, wishes, fantasizes and is internally "with herself." This world is ruled by roving and orgiastic, daemonic and divine, loving creatures in whose being earthly and heavenly, super- and subhuman qualities, angelic features as well as aspects lying outside morality, are bound together in a completely irrational manner.

It would be wrong to see the captivation exerted by this forest-, island-, and moon-world only as negative, although its fascination often plays a dangerous role in women's neuroses, coaxing the woman away from reality and real relationship. In spite of everything, this secret inner world is a creative spirit-world of female life, and when one succeeds in annexing this matriarchal psychic stage with its animus-world to a woman's life, the result is a decisive enrichment of productivity. (Here we shall not discuss the deepest level, the level of the uroboric animus, in which the Divine Father and the Divine Mother are united.)

2

Before we attempt a deeper psychological understanding of "matriarchal consciousness," let us indulge in an "etymological interlude on the moon" that will inform us as to the particulars of its archetypal structure. It turns out that the psychological aspect of the archetype provides a virtual unifying point for the inner cohesion of roots that heretofore have been regarded as linguistically independent.

Etymology[21] attempts to distinguish two roots: one is the "moon"-root, which with Greek μην, moon, Latin *mensis*, month, and the word measure belongs to the root *mā* and to the Sanskrit root *mâs*; the other is the Sanskrit root *manas*, Greek μενος, Latin *mens*, mind, etc., which represents the "spirit"-root par excellence.

A richly ramifying growth of essentially spiritual meanings arises from the Sanskrit root *manas*: Greek μενος, spirit, heart, soul, mettle, ardor; μενοιναν, to think of something, meditate, wish; μεμονα, to have in mind, intend; μαινομαι, to think, but also to be lost in thought and to rave or rage, to which μανια, possession, raving, madness, frenzy, and μαντεια, prophecy, also belong. Other branches from the same spirit-root are μηνις, μενος, anger, μηνυω, to announce, inform, reveal, μενω, Latin *maneo*, to remain, tarry, and the Sanskrit *man*, to hesitate, linger, await, remain firm or steadfast, μανθανω, to learn, *memini*, to recall, and *mentiri*, to lie. All these spirit-roots arise from the one original Sanskrit root *mati-h*, thought, intention.

Now, without any justification, we find the moon-root μην, moon, *mensis*, month, *mâs* (belonging to *mā*, to measure) juxtaposed to this root. From it arises not only *matra-m*, measure, but also μητις, cleverness, wisdom, μητιεσθαι, to meditate, to have in mind, to dream. To our

21. Cf. these etymological dictionaries: J. and W. Grimm, *Deutsches Wörterbuch* (1852ff.); M.P.E. Littré, *Dictionnaire de la langue française* (1863-1872); E. Boisacq, *Dictionnaire étymologique de la langue grecque* (1916).

surprise we ascertain that this moon-root—which supposedly stands in opposition to the spirit-root—has been
derived from the Sanskrit root *mati-h*, measure, knowledge, just as has the spirit-root.[22]

Therefore the unitary archetypal root of these meanings is moon-spirit, which is expressed in all these linguistic ramifications and reveals its essence and original
meaning to us in this way. Here an emotional movement
intimately bound up with the activity of the unconscious
emanates from the moon archetype as moon-spirit. In an
active eruption it is fiery spirit, courage, anger, possession,
and madness; it is the activity of revelation that leads to
prophecy, to thinking things out, devising and conceiving, and to lying, but also to poetizing. But this fiery
productivity is accompanied by another, "more measured," stance, which is associated with meditating,
dreaming, awaiting, wishing, hesitating, tarrying, and
with memory and learning, and flows into measure, intelligence, and meaning.

We have already spoken of the sudden emergence into
consciousness (German *Einfall*) of an idea as an original
spiritual activity of the unconscious. The penetration into
consciousness of spiritual contents, endowed with the
character of intuitive cogency, and their capacity to dominate it, is probably the original form in which the spirit
appeared to humankind. While an expanding consciousness and a strengthened ego introjects these emerging
contents and understands them as an internal manifestation of the psyche, they originally appear to the ego "from
outside" as sacred revelation and as numinous messages

22. Cf. Boisacq, *Dictionnaire.*

83

from the powers or the gods. Even if it calls them intuitions or inspirations, the ego that experiences these contents coming from without assumes a receptive stance
vis-à-vis the spontaneous phenomenon of spirit, a stance
characteristic of matriarchal consciousness. Today it remains as true as ever that humankind receives the revela-
tions of the moon-spirit more easily during the night
with its enlivenment of the unconscious and the attendant introversion than in the light of day.

It is obvious that matriarchal consciousness is not restricted to woman; it exists equally in man to the extent
that his conscious is an anima-consciousness. This holds
true especially for the creative person; yet people in general are dependent on the activity of the unconscious for
inspiration and intuition, as well as for the functioning of
the instincts and for providing consciousness with "libido." But all this is governed by the moon; for this
reason it is necessary to remain in harmony with the
moon and to attend to it, i.e., to maintain its cult.

The significance of the moon as chronometer stands in
the foreground of the moon cult. The moon guides primitive humankind's orientation in time; for all of humanity, calculating the moons, months, and lunar year derives from the moon. Moon-time, however, is not the
abstract, quantitative time of the scientific, patriarchal
consciousness. Rather, it is qualitative time: it undergoes
changes and in changing assumes various qualities. Moon-
time is rhythmical and periodic, waxing and waning,
favorable or unfavorable. As the time governing the cosmos, it rules the Earth, living things, and the Feminine.

The waxing moon is not only a chronology but a symbolic quality of the living world and of humankind, ex-

84

ternally and internally, just as are the waning moon, full
moon, and the dark of the moon. We best do justice to the
moon figures of lunar time when we call to mind their
archetypal character as bodies that emanate radiations.
They are centers of vibration, waves, currents, and power
that permeate the world and pulsate throughout psychobiological life from within and from without. Moon-time
determines human life. New moon and full moon are the
earliest sacred times; the dark of the moon as the victory
of the night-darkness-dragon is the "first" typical time of
obscurity and trouble. But also sowing and reaping,
growing and ripening, and beyond that the weal and woe
of every undertaking and activity depend upon the constellations of cosmic moon-time.

The efficacy of moon-time is not limited to the life of
the primitive world and to early cultures; rather, it extends into the late epochs of Greek history, for example,
when the Lacedaemonians (or Spartans, as they were also
known) were not able to arrive in time for the battle of
Marathon because they were not permitted to fight during the first half of the month. This pattern continues
into modern times where—in the form of the sacred year
and the liturgical year based on the seven-day week—
cosmic moon-time still orders and governs our life with
feast days and days of rest.

But the preeminent place where the moon and its
periodicity manifest is, of course, woman and the Feminine, which men and the Masculine therefore ever and
again identify with the moon. Woman is not only bound
to the moon's periodicity in her monthly changes—
although her inner lunar period has made itself independent of the external moon—her entire "mentality," too,

is determined by the moon, and the manner of her spirituality is informed by the moon archetype as the essence of matriarchal consciousness.

Ernst Cassirer[23] speaks of biological-cosmic time and of the feeling for phase inherent in the mythical time concept, without, however, recognizing the former's dependence upon the experience of the moon and its intimate relationship to the Feminine. What is involved is not only that humankind experiences sacred times and its own existence as a sequence of phases (moreover, based on seven); it is important to see that this experience of the moon is a fundamental category of matriarchal consciousness and hence of the archetypal feminine spirit.

The periodicity of the moon with its nocturnal background is the symbol of a spirit that waxes and transforms in connection with the obscure processes of the unconscious. Moon-consciousness, as one could also call matriarchal consciousness, is never separated from the unconscious, for it is a phase, a spiritual phase, of the unconscious itself. The ego of matriarchal consciousness possesses no free and independent activity of its own; rather, it awaits passively, attuned to the spirit-impulse that the unconscious brings to it.

"Favorable" and "unfavorable" is a chronology in which the spirit-activity dependent upon the periodicity of the unconscious turns toward the ego, becomes visible, and reveals itself, or turns away, becomes obscure, and vanishes. It is the task of the ego at the matriarchal level of consciousness to await and to be on the lookout for

23. See Ernst Cassirer, *Philosophie der symbolischen Formen*, vol. 1 (Berlin, 1923), p. 138; cf. *The Philosophy of Symbolic Forms*, tr. Ralph Manheim, vol. 1 (New Haven, 1953).

favorable and unfavorable times, to place itself in agreement with the changing moon and to establish a harmony, a unanimity with the oscillations emanating from it.

In other words, matriarchal consciousness is dependent upon the mood, the agreement-in-mood with the unconscious. One can place a negative valuation on this moon-dependency as lack of constancy and as capriciousness, but regarded positively, it provides consciousness with a background that works as a sounding-board and as such represents a special and most positive peculiarity of matriarchal consciousness. There is something strongly musical about this character of mood and of congruency of moods in its dependency on rhythm, on the times and tides of waxing and waning, of crescendo and decrescendo. Precisely in their emphasis on rhythm, music and dance therefore play a significant role for the attitude and the establishment of matriarchal consciousness and for the unanimity between the ego, the Feminine, and the moon-spirit that sets the tone for matriarchal consciousness.[24]

24. It is not by chance that the precinct of the Muses—i.e., of the feminine powers who rule over all "musings," music, rhythm, dance, prophecy and divination, and, in general, everything creative and artistic—is associated with the moon in its relationship to the numbers nine and three (see C. Kerényi, "Die orphische Kosmogonie und der Ursprung der Orphik," *EJ 1949*). Likewise associated are the figures of Musaeos, of his son Eumolpos, and of Orpheus, who have become so important for carrying forward matriarchal consciousness in the Orphic and Eleusinian mysteries (J. J. Bachofen, *Das Mutterrecht* (orig. 1861), 3rd ed., vol. 2, pp. 849, 856ff. [The work cited in n. 17 above does not contain these passages.]). Further we might mention that in China the origin of the theater is traced to the moon. An emperor who had visited the moon, the legend recounts, was so enchanted by the singing and dancing fairies there that after his

Even if musical quality is not a general characteristic of the "patriarchal uroboros," it is still a feature very often encountered in it. Music's intoxicating, orgiastic nature belongs to the deepest fascinations and exaltations of the female essence. Here an emotional feeling, driving one to the point of dissolution, and the irrational spirit-experience of harmony combine to work together according to an invisible inner law. The experience of being seductively transported and carried away extends from fascination with the sound of the Pied Piper's voice and flute to the ecstatic music of Dionysus, from the disintegrative force in the music of the orgiastic ritual to the effect of music on the modern woman.[25]

If we construe the moon as the spiritual side of the unconscious—the way it often appears in the unconscious of modern persons—it seems initially incomprehensible why we would associate this with periodicity and the phenomenon of time. But this connection, too, is most informative.

A multitude of facts support the view that, independently of the conscious system and in its own right, the unconscious psychic system (which we call the collective unconscious) is active and animated at certain times and at others quiescent and at rest, i.e., that it possesses an

---

return to Earth he taught youths these songs and movements and thus founded the Chinese theater. (See Juliet Bredon and Igor Mitrophanow, *The Moon Year: A Record of Chinese Customs and Festivals* (Shanghai, 1927).

25. In this regard, of course, music is not only one specific art existing in time; rather, the whole of moon symbolism, the concept of qualitative time, of rhythm, of phases, etc., is decisive for its basic structure—and by no means only in primitive music.

inner periodicity. This phenomenon commences with the alternation of day and night, which is linked with an alternation within the psychobiological system and with an alternation between consciousness and the unconscious. Therefore the psychic system and the relationship between the psychic subsystems of consciousness and the unconscious are subject to a psychobiological periodicity. A periodicity of this sort has been partially demonstrated in the doctrine of male and female periods.

But the dependency of psychic life on the life of the more encompassing season of the year also belongs in this context. Psychologically, not only do autumn and spring influence the outbreak of psychoses, whose greatest numbers fall in these seasons, sexual life also stands in conspicuous relationship with spring, whose character as "the season of love" is confirmed by the increase in conceptions, sexual crimes, and suicides in the spring.[26]

But since sexuality is a central locus for symptoms of psychic life in general, we may infer from this the extent to which our psyche depends upon cosmically determined periods, probably right down to the details of our lives. In this regard it makes no difference at all whether we conceptualize this effect as controlled by hormones or in some other manner.[27]

It is well known that creative persons and their capac-

26. See Willy Hellpach, *Die geopsychische Erscheinungen: Wetter, Klima, Boden, und Landschaft in ihren Einfluss auf das Seelenleben* (Leipzig, 1917).

27. Here we can only allude to the psychology of astrology, whose doctrine derives the whole of human typology as well as the course of fate from the cosmic conditionalilty of the time of pregnancy and birth.

ity to produce is greatly subject to periodicity. Here the effects of periodicity extend over many years. But whenever we observe the conformity of developments in similar directions among cultures existing independently of each other in a certain period of history, developments that have either been objectively ascertained or at least made probable, then some of this conformity seems to support the notion that analogous developmental series arise spontaneously in the collective unconscious of humankind in general. To mention only one example: it is noteworthy that certain cultural developments of consciousness in Sumer, Egypt, India, China, and Middle America took place during the same period of time, which, measured against the developments of the preceding thousands of centuries, we must frankly designate as fully contemporaneous, and which are inexplicable in terms of any external influences.[28]

Even if we disregard all interpretations of these facts, it is understandable that observations and experiences of this sort have led humankind to regard the world and fate as a periodic course of events such as we find, for example, in the million-year epochs of the Hindus, the Platonic year, and finally in Nietzsche's "eternal return." Hence there are good reasons for the assumption that a guiding cosmic and psychobiological periodicity exists and that the collective unconscious is one among several of its areas of manifestation. But then this sort of periodicity determines not only the world, but also the history of the development of the mind and its products; it constellates

28. See Rudolf Otto, "Das Gesetz der Parallelen," in *Vishnu Narayana: Texte zur indischen Gottes-Mystik* (1917), pp. 132f.

contents in human collectivities as well as in the "Great Individuals"[29] that represent them, contents that forcefully manifest in the productivity of the individual and of the group, and that then must be worked through in the course of time, often spanning generations.

The times in which one lives and the phase of the supraordinate course of fate in which one's personal lifespan is embedded is not only individually fateful; *time* itself is fate and its course is what determines humanity. Humanity has always experienced it thus, and the deities of fate are deities of time, i.e., at first preeminently moon deities.

Initially the anonymous group member has neither personal time nor fate. He shares the fate and the time of the group. Personal fate separates out from the fate of the collective only with progressive individualization that takes place in the wake of the Great Individual who was the first to have a personal fate and time. Only now is the generally decisive world epoch and cosmic season reshaped into individuation-time, in which the individual's present belongs irrevocably to him as does his ego, his wholeness, and his destiny. Only in individuation-time does the moon become an "inner moon" and the increasingly visible totality of the Self become an encompassing and simultaneously guiding center that is perceived, a center to which, in a certain sense, even the moon is subordinated. But, viewed from the perspective of a matriarchal consciousness, it is still a long way indeed to this final stage.

29. [See Neumann, *Origins and History* and *The Place of Creation* (Essays, vol. 3), indexes, s.v. Great Individual.]

Matriarchal consciousness, or moon-consciousness, stands at the beginning of the development of human consciousness; here we are concerned with that, not with its recurrence in the psychology of individuation, which is a reappearance at a higher level, as is always the case where, in the course of normal development, we again encounter something already experienced.

Yet the connection among time, the unconscious, and the moon-spirit belongs even more profoundly to the essential nature of matriarchal consciousness than has become evident in our discussion up to this point, and only when we adequately grasp the spiritual character of the moon archetype can we understand what matriarchal consciousness and "feminine spirit" means.

The attacking and raping quality that grips the personality and transports it to ecstasy, madness, poetry, and wisdom through seizure by the sudden idea, by inspiration and intoxication emanating from the unconscious, is one side of the spirit activity. On the other side we find dependency and reliance upon matriarchal consciousness. This is the reliance of every intuition and inspiration upon the emanations from the unconscious that emerge whenever, wherever, and however they will, in a mysterious manner scarcely to be influenced. In this sense all shamanism, extending all the way to prophecy, is predominantly a passive suffering: its activity is more that of conceiving than of deliberate doing. The ego's actual achievement lies in one's readiness to accept the emerging contents of the unconscious and to bring oneself into accord with them. But the moon appears so frequently as the universal symbol of the unconscious because this emergence is autonomous and independent of consciousness and has the characteristic of all unconscious contents.

The fact that the moon is lord of time and that this relationship between the moon and time is one of the essential features of matriarchal consciousness becomes clear only when we trace the moon's temporal significance beyond the realm of cosmic-mythological processes to its effects in individual psychology.

The development of patriarchal consciousness culminates in a relative liberation from the unconscious and in an independence in which the ego has at its disposal a differentiated system of consciousness, with a certain quantity of available libido experienced as free will. We must understand the significance of the patriarchal form of consciousness even if we reject the illusionistic self-deception inherent in the notion of an absolutely free system, which this form of consciousness considers itself to be. Patriarchal, archetypally masculine consciousness is a most significant and, as the development of *Homo sapiens* shows, exceedingly successful organ of adaptation and information processing. One of its advantages lies in its ongoing readiness to react, and in the extraordinary rapidity of its reaction and adaptation. Even though the instinctive reactions mediated by the sensory organs are prompt, the achievements of the modern human being's consciousness in its specialization are still extraordinarily superior to the rapidity of instinct. The rapidity of conscious reaction (which we cannot pursue in this context) is increased by all those processes that have led to the freeing of patriarchal consciousness from the unconscious.[30]

30. See *Origins and History.*

As the most recent step in this course of development we find the processes of abstraction, with the help of which concepts can be freely moved about and applied; in the differentiated thinking type, this leads to the manipulation of abstractions—e.g., as numbers in mathematics and as concepts in logic—that possess a maximum of abstract unemotionality in the psychological sense.

While patriarchal consciousness is by nature quick-moving and overtakes the long processes of transformation and development in nature with the arbitrary action of experimental calculation, matriarchal consciousness stands under the sway of the moon's growth time. Its luminescence and its light-knowledge is bound to the course of time and to periodicity, as is the moon. For this form of consciousness time must ripen, and with it, like the seeds sown in the earth, knowledge matures.

In rite and cult, "having to wait" and "waiting for" are identical with procession and circumambulation. As in many other fairy tales, the wife in the marvelous tale "The Nixie of the Pond"[31] must wait until the moon is full again. Until then she must silently circle about the pond, or she must spin her spindle full. Only when the time is "fulfilled" does knowledge emerge as illumination or enlightenment.

Likewise in the primordial female mysteries[32] of cooking, baking, fermenting, and distilling, the processes of maturation, readiness, and transformation are always bound by a period of time that must be waited out. The ego of matriarchal consciousness is accustomed to re-

31. *Grimms' Tales for Young and Old*, tr. Ralph Manheim (1977), no. 181.

32. See above, pp. 78f.

maining still until the time is propitious, the process has run its course, the fruit of the moon-tree has become as ripe as the full moon, i.e., until knowledge is born from out of the unconscious. For always the moon is not only lord of growth but also the growth itself as moon-tree and tree of life: "Self-generated fruit."

That the processes of matriarchal consciousness are through and through uniquely and specifically different from those of patriarchal consciousness commences with the act of "understanding." Here understanding is not, as for patriarchal consciousness, an act of the intellect as a rapidly comprehending organ that perceives, works through, and organizes;[33] rather, it means "conceiving." Whenever something is to be understood, it must "enter into" matriarchal consciousness, and in all respects this is to be understood in the symbolically sexual sense of a fertilization, i.e., of a conception.

But this female symbolism of matriarchal consciousness goes still further, for what has "entered into" must now "rise up," *Aufgehen*. With linguistic genius, *Aufgehen* —the act of "arising," "rising up," or "sprouting"— captures the twofold aspect of matriarchal consciousness for which the light of knowledge "rises up" just as the sprouting seed does.[34] But once something has "entered

33. In this and in what follows, we regard thinking only as the clearest example of a differentiated function whose dominance is characteristic for patriarchal consciousness. See Jung, *Psychological Types*. CW 6,65 and Neumann, *Origins and History*.

34. [The verb *aufgehen* has a number of shades of meaning. First, it means to rise, ascend, as does the sun or moon. Second, used with plants or seeds, *aufgehen* means to come or spring up, germinate, sprout, shoot up. When referring to buds or blossoms, *aufgehen* means to open or unfold. It is the verb used when speaking of dough rising.

into" (*eingegangen*) and has "risen up" or "sprouted" (*aufgegangen*), this "something" lays claim to the entire psyche that now is permeated by the matured knowledge that the psyche seeks—indeed, is compelled—to realize with its totality. This means that with the act of understanding-conceiving, matriarchal consciousness experiences a personality change. The whole person is gripped and moved by the content, in contrast to the experience of patriarchal consciousness in which an intellectually "understood" content is often only filed away in one of the pigeonholes of the systematized mind. Just as it is difficult for a patriarchal consciousness to actualize something rather than only to "magnificently understand it," a matriarchal consciousness finds it hard to understand something if it cannot make it real. But here, "making something real" means "carrying it to fruition" and relating to the content in the manner of the relationship in which mother and embryo reciprocally alter each other during pregnancy.

Matriarchal qualitative time is unique and singular as gravid, pregnant time in contrast to the quantitative time of patriarchal consciousness. For the patriarchal ego-consciousness, every segment of time is the same, but in moon-time matriarchal consciousness experiences the individual time of the world, even if not of the ego. The unique and unforgettable quality of time comes into view precisely for the eye schooled in perceiving living growth, an eye that experiences and realizes the fullness of the

---

Figuratively, *aufgehen* occurs in the expression "Mir gehen die Augen auf," meaning "I see the light," "It dawns on me," "I understand." In business or political parlance, *aufgehen* translates as "to merge." These nuances all resonate in Neumann's use of the word in this context.—Tr.]

moment, its readiness for birth. In the fairy tale a treasure emerges from the deep once every hundred years, on a certain day, at a certain hour, and belongs to him who finds it at the right moment of growth.[35] Only a matriarchal consciousness, attuned to the processes of the unconscious, recognizes this individual temporal element, while a patriarchal consciousness, for which this moment is one of countless identical moments in time, is fated to let it slip away. In this sense, moon-consciousness is more concrete and closer to the reality of life, the patriarchal more abstract and more distanced from actuality.

Hence, symbolically, matriarchal consciousness is usually not situated in the head, but rather in the heart. Here "understanding" also means an act of feeling that comprehends, and often enough this act—as, for example, in the creative process—is accompanied by an intense participation of affect so that something can burst into light and illuminate consciousness. In contrast, the process of thinking and abstraction typical of patriarchal consciousness is "cold," since the "cold-blooded" objectivity demanded of it necessitates establishing distance that presupposes a cool head.

Assigning moon-consciousness to the heart is generally true for that part of humanity in whom the head has not yet become the center of patriarchal consciousness, separated, as it is, from the unconscious. Just as in Egypt the heart was regarded as the source of thought and of the creative spirit, in India the heart—cosmically assigned to the moon—is believed to be the locus of a psychic and spiritual organ called *manas* (related to the word root

35. Characteristically, it is often said that the treasure "blossoms."

men), and is the place where the highest, self-revealing god manifests. The same holds true for China. "*Dö* (in ancient times written simply with the character for 'heart,' i.e., spiritual or intellectual capacity, and with the character signifying what lies directly in the line of vision) originally meant the radiating, magical power; then the mystical power of the heart; moreover, power, usefulness in general; and finally virtue."[36] This heart-center of matriarchal consciousness that is referenced to the qualitative time of the moon remains the valid orientation for all processes of growth and transformation. It is also typical for the creative, spiritual process in which contents are constellated in slow developments in the unconscious more or less independently of consciousness and stream towards a non-systematized, open consciousness ready to be expanded.

To mention only one consequence of this symbolism, the fact that the heart and not the head is the seat of matriarchal consciousness means that the ego of patriarchal consciousness—our familiar head-ego—often knows nothing of what goes on in the deeper consciousness-center of the heart.

For it is essential that the processes of matriarchal consciousness, too, are related to an ego and hence are not to be labeled unconscious. The activity of the ego in matriarchal consciousness is, to be sure, of a different sort than that of the ego in the patriarchal system of con-

36. *Lau-Dse: Führung und Kraft aus der Ewigkeit*, tr. Erwin Rousselle (new ed., 1952). [Rousselle's translation of the *Tao Teh Ching*. According to Dr. Rudolf Ritsema, Neumann evidently chose this version rather than that of Richard Wilhelm because Rousselle focused upon a feminine and matriarchal aspect of Lao-tse.]

sciousness familiar to us; nevertheless this ego and its activity participates in the processes of matriarchal consciousness. Its presence constitutes the difference between early human functioning at the matriarchal level and a totally unconscious existence.

The usual identification of our ego with the patriarchal "head"-consciousness and the corresponding extensive unrelatedness to matriarchal consciousness often lead to a condition in which we know nothing of what is actually happening to us. For example, we later discover that things, situations, and persons have made a deep impression on us, an impression of which our head-ego has taken no notice whatsoever. Vice versa, however, one can observe a seemingly blunt lack of reactivity in an individual—often enough a woman—whose head is not capable of an immediate reaction but whose heart-consciousness has perceived. That something has "hit home" and been realized is evidenced in the subsequent fruitfulness of personality changes. Here Heraclitus's remark holds true for matriarchal consciousness: "Nature likes to hide."[37]

The moment of conception is hidden and mysterious; the ego of matriarchal consciousness suffers it, often without the head-ego having noticed anything. But deeper introspection that takes into account dreams, images, and fantasies reveals that this point in time and what then transpired was recorded in matriarchal consciousness, i.e., it did not run its course without the participation of some sort of consciousness.

37. Heraclitus of Ephesus, fr. 123, in K. Freeman, *Ancilla to the Pre-Socratic Philosophers* (1948).

This dimming or darkening of the existentially decisive moment of conception is absolutely meaningful, for growth needs quiet and seclusion, not commotion and brightness; it is not by chance that our patriarchal consciousness is symbolically a sun- and day-consciousness. That this law holds true as much for spiritual-emotional as for biological growth is confirmed by a line from Nietzsche, that great connoisseur of the spiritual-emotional creative processes: "When pregnant, we conceal ourselves."[38]

The creative process takes place not under the burning rays of the sun but in the cool, reflected light of the moon when the darkness of the unconscious is great: night, not day, is the time for begetting. Darkness and stillness, secrecy, remaining mute and veiled, are a part of it. For this reason the moon as lord of life and of growth is opposed to the death character of the devouring sun. The nocturnal moistness of the moon-night is the time of sleep, but also that of healing and recovery. Therefore the moon-god Sin is physician, and, as a cuneiform inscription states, the healing herb "is cut after sundown and before sunrise when one has veiled one's head and made a magic circle of flour around the healing herb."[39]

In addition to the symbolism of the magic circle and the flour we find "veiling" as a mystery symbol that belongs to the moon as well as to night and to its secretive character. The precinct of healing and of the healer, of the healing plant and of the growth that heals, find their

38. Nietzsche, *Nachgelassene Werke*, vol. 11:2 of *Nietzsche's Werke* (Leipzig: Naumann, 1901), par. 385, p. 305.

39. Jeremias, *Handbuch*, p. 242, n. 7 (see above, n. 8).

place in this context.[40] It is the regenerative power of the unconscious that does its work during sleep, in the darkness of the night or in the light of the moon, as a mystery and in mystery, from out of itself, from nature, without the influence of consciousness and without the help of the head-ego. This is why the healing pill and the healing plant are assigned to the moon, and their secret is protected and preserved by women, or better, by the Feminine, which belongs to the moon.

Growing vegetation is to be understood here in the broadly symbolic sense embraced by every symbol as the synthesis of both inner and outer realities. The power of sleep that regenerates the body and its wounds and the restoration that runs its course in darkness belong to the night domain of the healing moon, as do the happenings in the soul that let a person "grow beyond" an insoluble crisis through the dark processes perceived only by the heart.

That green is regarded as the moon color[41] is due not, as people have supposed, to the fact that in the Near East the moon often looks green but rather to the connection between its essence and that of vegetation of which it has been said: "When Sin's word descends upon the earth, green springs up."[42]

The green of Osiris, of Khidr, of the Shiva sprout, and

40. See C. Kerényi, *Asklepios: Archetypal Image of the Physician's Existence*, tr. Ralph Manheim (B.S. LXV:3, 1959; orig., 1956), pp. 78f.; and C. A. Meier, *Ancient Incubation and Modern Psychotherapy* (Evanston, 1967; orig., 1949).

41. Here we will not consider the symbol of silver that belongs to the moon and Hesiod's "Silver Age of Man" associated with it.

42. Jeremias, p. 248, n. 3.

of the green stone of alchemy is the color not only of physical but also of emotional-spiritual development. As lord of matriarchal consciousness, the moon is connected with a specific body of knowledge and a particular kind of knowing. It is concealed consciousness, spirit as something hidden, light as birth from the night.

The act of knowing as fruit belongs to the essence of matriarchal consciousness, for which Nietzsche's word is valid: "Everything about woman is a puzzle, and everything about woman has its solution. It is called pregnancy."

Time after time the tree of life is a moon-tree and its fruit the precious fruit of the full moon. The drink and the pill of immortality, the highest knowledge, enlightenment, and intoxication, are the radiant fruits of the moon-tree of transformation through growth. For the moon is also King Soma of India; it is the intoxicating liquid, the quintessence of sustenance, of which it is said: "As King Soma, as the Self of nourishment, I revere him."[43]

The moon is lord of fertility and of fertility magic. The magic associated with matriarchal consciousness is above all the magic of growth that must be intensified or assured in contrast to the goal-directed magic of the will, to the active feat of casting a spell that—as, for example, hunting magic—belongs to the actively masculine, patriarchal consciousness. Transformative processes, which is what growth processes are, are subject to the Self and are mirrored in matriarchal consciousness that supports and accompanies them in its particular way. Formative pro-

43. Paul Deussen, tr., *Sechzig Upanishads des Veda* (Leipzig, 1897), p. 53.

cesses, however, in which the initiative and activity rest
with the ego, belong to the domain of the masculine,
patriarchal spirit.

Carrying a perception or realization to full term and
letting it mature, as is typical of matriarchal consciousness, also signifies an act of "taking into and unto one-
self." This sort of taking to oneself—the typical form of
female activity that must not be confused with a passive
surrender or with letting oneself be forced or propelled
—still underlies the concept of "assimilating a content."
That the ego of matriarchal consciousness is more passive
when compared with the patriarchal is due not to its
incapacity for activity but rather to the fact that it is
delivered over to a process in which it cannot "do" anything but must "let" it happen.

In all decisive situations of her existence, woman is
exposed to or, better yet, "left to the mercy of" the numinous in nature and to its workings to a far greater
degree than is the man who is only masculine. For this
reason woman's relationship to nature and to the deity
partakes of greater familiarity and intimacy, and her
bond with the anonymous-transpersonal dimension exists earlier and works more deeply than does her relationship to her personal male partner.

Although matriarchal consciousness is common to all
human beings and also plays a significant role in the male,
and most assuredly in the creative man, it is nevertheless
woman who is the real representative of this form of
consciousness, even if today she commands a patriarchal
consciousness and if the conflict between her two modes
of consciousness belongs to the fundamental conflicts
of the modern woman. From the beginnings of time

woman has had the fundamental receptive-accepting attitude of matriarchal consciousness; by nature that is something she takes for granted. It is not only during the menstrual period that woman must place her agreement with the moon ahead of the willing and planning of a masculine ego-consciousness if she is to live wisely. Pregnancy and childbirth bring about a total psychobiological alteration that demands and presuppose both a stance and a change of attitude that have existed in her for years. The unknown nature of the child, its uniqueness, its gender (of decisive significance in many matriarchal and patriarchal cultures), the state of its health, its destiny— in all these things woman is dependent upon the mercy and power of the deity and condemned, as an ego, to non-activity and to being unable to intervene. Similarly in a later phase, woman is handed over to the superior power of a love relationship in a different way than a man is. This is why the male's unquestioning patriarchal belief in ego and consciousness is foreign to woman; indeed, it even seems to her a bit ludicrous and childish. This is the origin of woman's deep skepticism and, in a certain sense, lack of interest in patriarchal consciousness and in the masculine world of the spirit associated with it, especially when woman, as is often the case, confuses spirit with the world of consciousness. The male is a captive of the ego and of consciousness and has intentionally freed himself from his relatedness to nature and to fate, in whose depths matriarchal consciousness has its roots. But the patriarchal accent on ego, will, and freedom contradicts woman's experience of the predominance of the powers of the unconscious and of fate, and of life's dependence upon the non-ego and on the Thou.

In contrast to the activity of the head-ego, the pre-ferred attitude of an observing consciousness at the ma-triarchal level also corresponds to this muted activity of the ego. Here it is a question more of an attentive perceiv-ing than of an intentional thinking or judging activity of consciousness. The observing matriarchal consciousness is to be confused neither with the sensation function of masculine ego-consciousness nor with the distance of masculine consciousness that leads to science and objec-tivity; the observing matriarchal consciousness is guided by concomitant feelings based on half-conscious pro-cesses and accompanying intuitions with the help of which the ego orients itself in the presence of strong emotional tendencies.

Matriarchal consciousness reflects the unconscious pro-cesses, summarizes them, and directs them inward; that is, it assumes a stance of "waiting for," without deliberate ego-intentions. For matriarchal consciousness it is a ques-tion of a kind of total perception in which the entire psyche participates and in which the ego has more the task of directing the libido toward the observed life pro-cesses or events and intensifying them than that of ab-stracting from them and hence arriving at an extension of consciousness. Typical for this observing consciousness is the act of contemplation where energies are guided to-ward a content, process, or midpoint while the ego estab-lishes a participation with the emotionally colored con-tent and lets it impregnate and permeate it. This differs from the extremely patriarchal consciousness that dis-tances and abstracts itself from the content.

The observing nature of the moon-spirit that is con-nected more to the *Gemüt*, the totality of the soul's innermost sensibilities and feelings, is referred to in German by the root-word *Sinn*, which has a range of related meanings in English: feeling, inclination, disposition, tendency, temper; mind, wit, understanding; sense, faculty, organ of perception. A number of compound words derive from *Sinn: sinnieren*, to be lost in thoughts, brood, ponder; *im Sinn haben*, to have in mind; to meditate, muse; *sich besinnen*, to recollect, remember, call to mind, think of; but also *Besinnung*, recollection, consideration, consciousness; *Sinnesart*, character, disposition; and *Gesinnung*, disposition, sentiment, way of thinking; as well as *sinnlich*, material, physical; sensuous; sensual, voluptuous; sentient. And last but not least we must mention the *Eigensinn*—the obstinacy, stubbornness, headstrongness, and willfulness—that men generally ascribe to women. The brooding and circumambulating mental activity of matriarchal consciousness does not have the goal-directedness of the *act* of thought, of inference, and of judgment. What corresponds to the mental activity of matriarchal consciousness is circumambulation about a center or consideration (which Jung once interpreted as "making full as in pregnancy," *trächtig machen*), not the bull's-eye directness of masculine consciousness and the knife edge of its analytic power. Matriarchal consciousness is more interested in the sensory-sensual-sensuous aspect (*Sinnhaftigkeit*) of phenomena, situations, or persons than in facts and figures, and, in accord with organic growth, is oriented more by teleology than by the causal-mechanical or the causal-logical point of view.

Because for moon-consciousness knowing is a pregnancy and its product a birth—i.e., a process in which the totality of the personality participates; the epistemological act lies beyond statement, justification, and proof. As an inner possession realized by the personality and intimately bound up with it, moon-consciousness has a kind of intuitive cogency that easily tends to evade discussion because the inner experiential process inherent in this way of knowing cannot be adequately verbalized and is scarcely communicable to another person who has not gone through the same experiential process.

To a dull masculine consciousness the manner in which matriarchal consciousness "knows" appears uncontrollable, arbitrary, and—especially—mystical. And in the positive sense this does in fact capture its essence. What mysticism and the authentic mysteries have come to know are indeed of this sort—i.e., not communicable truths but experienced transformations that therefore of necessity have validity only for those persons who have the corresponding experiences. Here Goethe's warning applies:

> Tell it no one, only sages,
> For the crowd derides such learning.[44]

This means that the knowledge of matriarchal consciousness does not exist independent of the personality that has it; this knowledge is neither abstract nor stripped of emotion, for matriarchal consciousness preserves the connection to those realms of the unconscious out of which its knowledge arises. Therefore it can often stand in opposition to the knowledge of patriarchal consciousness that consists ideally of isolated and abstracted con-

44. [Goethe, *West-Eastern Divan* (tr. J. Whaley, Munich, 1979), p. 27.]

tents of consciousness from which all emotion has been extracted and which is generally valid independent of the personality.

The fundamental direction in the development of occidental humanity tends toward extending the domain of patriarchal consciousness and feeding it with whatever it can possibly incorporate. In spite of this, matriarchal consciousness is definitely neither an antiquated mode of functioning nor a range of contents that, simply out of lethargy, have not been developed to the level of patriarchal consciousness. For the most part the insights and knowledge of the moon-side of the psyche cannot be grasped by the natural scientific consciousness, at least not by our contemporary psyche. These are insights into life of a general sort that have been the object of the mysteries and of religion since time immemorial, and that belong to the domain of wisdom, not to that of science.

The moon-spirit always brings culture, too, but its significance does not lie in having led historically to mathematics and astronomy via observation of the heavens and astrology. It brings culture as the heavenly prototype, as the "Self-generated Fruit," as victor over death, and as the one who brings rebirth. As the lord of the spirits and of the dead, the moon-spirit from the waters of the deep over which it holds sway is the one who commands the nature- and spirit-forces of the unconscious to rise up when their time has come, and thus it gives the world of humankind not only growth and bread, but also prophecy, poetry, wisdom, and immortality.

Matriarchal consciousness experiences the mysteriously unknown process of the coming-into-being of an insight or of knowledge as an activity in which the Self as a whole is at work. This is a process running its course in the dark. The Self is dominant as the moon, but above and beyond it the Self rules as the Great Mother, as the unity of all things nocturnal and of the nocturnal realm. The very relationship of matriarchal consciousness to growth presupposes that matriarchal consciousness never surrenders its connection to the matrix of all growth, the Nocturnal Mother herself, as the masculine ego does on principle and with heroic decisiveness. Hence in the symbol of the moon the efficacy of the masculine moon often overlaps that of the Great Mother. The participation of the matriarchal ego with the moon goes yet further, as is true also of the Great Mother herself, who is the partner of the moon-lover and almost achieves identity with him. The hermaphroditic nature of the Great Mother is revealed in two ways: first, she receives the moon-spirit, her lord and beloved, not only as a woman from outside herself (as she believes, both rightly and wrongly); and, second, in the fact that she carries the moon-spirit within herself as her own masculine side, a deity who is simultaneously son-lover, father, and child.

The ego of matriarchal consciousness experiences the fructifying power of the moon as the fructifying side of the unconscious, i.e., as part of the uroboric Great Mother. This is why, in its non-separation from the whole that confronts it in the image of the Great Mother, the ego of matriarchal consciousness experiences itself in her likeness. Like her, it surrounds what it has received and like her also knows him who procreates as one born of herself, as her son and fruit of her own growth.

Thus the moon manifests in male form as the center of

the spirit-world of matriarchal consciousness, but also in female form as the highest expression of the female spirit-Self, as Sophia, divine wisdom. This wisdom, however, refers to life in its indissoluble and paradoxical unity of living and dying; nature and spirit; time and destiny; growing, dying, and overcoming death. For this female figure of the wisdom of life, order is not based on unrelated, abstract laws where dead heavenly bodies or atoms orbit in empty space; rather, it is a wisdom that is and remains bound to the earth, to organic growth on earth, and to experiencing the ancestors in us. It is the wisdom of the unconscious and of the instincts, of life and of relatedness.

Consequently the wisdom of the earth, of peasants, and, to be sure, of woman corresponds to matriarchal consciousness. The teachings of China, especially those of the *I Ching* and of Lao-tse, are an expression of this matriarchal consciousness that loves darkness and hidden things, and that has time. Renunciation of speedy success, of prompt reactions, and of visible effects belong in its domain. Facing the night more than the day, matriarchal consciousness tends to be more dreamy and contemplative than alert and active. By no means does it love the brilliance, clarity, and sharp focus of the light of day to the extent desired by patriarchal consciousness, which, in its aversion to the moon-side of life, is all too glad to disguise the dependency of its existence upon the darkness of the unconscious. Its wisdom is the wisdom of paradox that does not extricate and juxtapose opposites with the clear separation of patriarchal consciousness, but rather binds them together with a "both—and."

In this sense—which must not be misunderstood—

matriarchal consciousness is relativistic, for it is referenced less to the absolute unequivocality of truth than to a wisdom that remains embedded in the cosmo-psychic system of continually changing forces. Often this relativization even appears as the hostility of matriarchal consciousness vis-à-vis the "absolute," if we are permitted to label as hostility what in fact is a difference in nature and a tendency to relatedness.

Matriarchal consciousness depends upon its moon-spirit partner and upon coinciding with the moon's phases, and this contains an element of eros, of dependency upon the Thou who, as moon-lover, is partner. This fundamentally distinguishes matriarchal consciousness—as a consciousness of relatedness and relationship —from patriarchal consciousness. Where the patriarchally liberated and unattached consciousness is able to do and think whenever, however, and whatever it will and is self-satisfied—or better, ego-satisfied—in its removed, abstracted manner, and is ruler within the circle of its conscious contents, matriarchal consciousness is not independent since it is related and referenced to the moon and to the unconscious upon which it knows itself to be dependent and which govern it.

This is why Moon-Sophia does not have the abstractly non-individual and generally absolute character of spirit that the patriarchal male declares to be the ultimate, which he reveres as the day-heavens-sun-spirit and superposes above the moon-world. The moon-spirit of matriarchal consciousness is "only" moon-spirit, only soul and eternal Feminine. But instead of having the quality of the "distant" deity, matriarchal consciousness preserves the milder and non-blinding light of a human spirit. Female wisdom is non-speculative, for it is close to life and to nature, bound to fact and to living reality. Its illusionless eye for reality may shock an idealistic male mentality, but on the other hand it is bonded to this reality through nurturing and helping, consoling and loving, and it leads this reality beyond death to ever new transformation and birth.

The moon-wisdom of biding one's time, of accepting and ripening, absorbs everything into its totality and transforms what has been taken in and itself as well. It is always concerned with wholeness, with giving form and actualizing—that is, with creating—and let it never be forgotten that by its very nature creating is bound to matriarchal consciousness, not because consciousness is creative but rather because the unconscious is, and because every creative accomplishment presupposes all the attitudes of pregnancy and relatedness that we have recognized as characteristic of matriarchal consciousness.

But while the cultural achievement of the creative person—at least in its highest expression—is always a synthesis of the matriarchally receptive-gestative and the patriarchally form-giving consciousnesses, woman's predominant attachment to matriarchal consciousness and to its wisdom holds fundamental dangers in addition to all its blessings. That remaining silent and making real are more important than formulating and making conscious is a significant and wise part of the moon-spirit and of growth. But in the case of woman, the tendency toward making real, which is one of the creative elements inherent in matriarchal consciousness, easily gets caught up in what is merely natural creativity.

In the phase of self-conservation,[45] the stage in which woman may naturally remain in the custody of the Great Mother without damage, the matriarchal ego is completely unaware of being dominated by the unconscious. But even if woman's ego attains to a level of self-awareness that distinguishes it from matriarchal consciousness, it continues to cling to the basic conditions of the existence it has hitherto led—i.e., of being undivided. Even when woman must move from self-conservation to self-surrender (as we have discussed elsewhere), she demands to be totally seized by emotion. Woman is not satisfied, as is man, with fulfilling a part-structure of the psyche, for example with the accomplishment of the ego's differentiation of consciousness. Woman wants to be gripped and moved as a whole. At the spiritual-emotional level that means realization, actualization.

But here one of the "tricks" of woman's nature often comes into play, and instead of realizing and actualizing she concretizes and, via the natural process of projection, she displaces the creative process of pregnancy onto an external object.

This means that woman takes the phase of matriarchal consciousness and its symbolism literally and falls in love, gets pregnant, gives birth, nurses, cares for, etc., and is feminine outwardly but not inwardly. Woman's fewer visible creative intellectual accomplishments, the absence of a creative opus (as compared to that of man), may possibly arise from this tendency. To be the origin of life through pregnancy and birth and to shape the proximate

45. See the preceding essay.

reality that belongs to this life appears to woman adequately creative.[46] And is she wrong? Matriarchal consciousness is "written in woman's flesh," and with her body she lives in external reality everything that, for a man, must take place as a spiritual and emotional process if it is to be realized. In this respect man is a step ahead of woman in his development toward patriarchal consciousness, for by his very nature he can experience the phase of matriarchal consciousness only as a spiritual-emotional stage, not in a physically concrete way.

If, for reasons we have elaborated elsewhere, humankind must attain to patriarchal consciousness and to a separation from the unconscious, matriarchal consciousness like the matriarchy—and with it the moon—signifies something negative to be overcome. For every stage and development that presses toward patriarchal consciousness—i.e., toward the sun—the moon-spirit becomes the spirit of regression, the spirit of the Terrible Mother and the Witch. Whether experienced as feminine or masculine, this negative moon is now the symbol of the devouring unconscious. Especially as the black moon it becomes the bloodsucker, child murderer, and cannibal[47] and symbolizes the danger of being inundated by the unconscious as moodiness, somnambulism, and insanity. The English term, to moon—to be listless, to fritter away

46. As if in answer to the penis-envy that men ascribe to women, one woman's psychoanalytic theory maintained—not without justification, and in any case not without humor—that the male's entire cultural achievement is only a compensation for his inability to give birth concretely and hence arises in a way from his "uterus-envy." [The allusion is to a theory posited by Karen Horney; cf. her early papers republished in *Feminine Psychology* (New York, 1967).]

47. Cf. Briffault, *The Mothers.*

one's time—shows that "being distracted" can also mean being attracted by the moon and the dangerous pull of the unconscious.

Here as everywhere it is a question of the significance of a psychic phase within a developmental stage. Moon-consciousness or matriarchal consciousness is creative and productive as beginning and as end. The light of the moon is the first light that illuminates the dark world of the unconscious, out of which light is born and to which it is bound; and everything growing, creative, and feminine remains faithful to this connection with and indebtedness to the moon-spirit.

But as development continues, clinging to the unconscious becomes antithetical to whatever may be called progress. As the new and superior value, the sun-world comes into opposition to the moon-world as do the patriarchy and the matriarchy, both understood as psychological stages. Only in later stages of development, when the patriarchy has attained fulfillment or gone to absurd ends and lost its connection to the maternal ground, does a reversal take place in the phase of individuation. Now patriarchal sun-consciousness is reunited with what has preceded it, and along with the regenerative powers of the primordial waters matriarchal consciousness—closer to the primordial matrix—and its central symbol, the moon, rise up out of the depths to celebrate the ancient *hierosgamos* of moon and sun at a new, higher plane in the human psyche.

In conclusion let us once more recall the phases of woman's development. In the phase of self-conservation the primal relationship is completely dominant, the male is subordinated as a tool or as a child. To the extent that woman's ego has experiences, it does so in the context of the archetypal Feminine and of motherhood; Kore is Demeter; that is to say, the ego experiences its identity with the totality of the psyche completely without division. The principle of opposites is undeveloped and consequently consciousness is meager.

A new development is discernible in the phase of the patriarchal uroboros. Men and the archetypal Masculine are experienced as overwhelmingly different, and by giving up herself and surrendering to the transpersonal Masculine, woman experiences herself as female at a new level. First she must sacrifice her primal relationship to the mother and to the maternal ground from which the patriarchal uroboros liberates her, and now she experiences men and the Masculine as wife and daughter, not as a mother experiencing something born of her. This constellates a new phase of consciousness, which we have characterized as matriarchal consciousness. In this phase the masculine spiritual component takes its place as the Lord of Women, as the moon; overwhelmed, consciousness receives him and is impregnated by him. In both constellations, cognition and knowledge is not something made by consciousness but rather something that happens to it. The activity rests with the moon-spirit side of the unconscious, that part of the psyche that later becomes the world of the animus. Its mode of expression is a world of emerging recognitions, cognitions, and pieces of knowledge that the ego awaits, accepts, and observes, to a certain extent only as "midwife."

When the moon-spirit aspect appears to matriarchal consciousness in female form as Sophia, this means that the female Self has become visible to the woman's ego. This moon-goddess–Sophia manifestation corresponds to a process of transformation of the archetypal Feminine itself in which its inherent spirit character breaks through. This transpersonal-heavenly archetype of female spirit stands in opposition to the earth-unconsciousness of the archetypal Demeter, who refuses to surrender the Kore-daughter.

Even if this Sophia-stage of female development attains final clarity only in the process of individuation, it first appears in mythological projection in the early phase of the patriarchal uroboros. There the male moon-spirit is experienced as the center of the animus-world, as the son-spirit–progeny of a female-spirit totality. Just as for the male the anima is the daughter of the male spirit-figure who represents totality (the male divinity), the animus in woman is the son of the female spirit-figure, Sophia, the female deity who represents wholeness.

After she has lived out the various stages of the patriarchy and of confrontation, woman overcomes the patriarchy and patriarchal consciousness in the final phase of individuation. Her primal relationship to the Great Mother is restored at a new level, but—to the extent that matriarchal consciousness does not fall into morbid self-alienation—she also experiences an intensified vivification of matriarchal consciousness, which continues actively working its effects in her even when it is outshown by the day-visibility of the newly won patriarchal sun-consciousness.

But even for the male, whose differing course of development presses toward a much greater distancing from the unconscious and from the Great Mother, matriarchal consciousness is far from being an archaic vestige to be overcome. The differentiation that reaches its zenith in modern patriarchal consciousness has also led to making modern humankind neurotic, to self-alienation, and to a dangerous loss of the creative vitality of the psyche. This is why reconnection to the unconscious is of the greatest significance precisely for men. But in the case of the male, reconnection to the unconscious takes place via the anima, his female side, and by his making real and embodying that matriarchal consciousness associated with the anima. The only path that leads to synthesis, to the new knowledge that we may call illumination or enlightenment in contrast to a one-sided consciousness, is man's reconnection to the anima-world of soul and woman's reconnection to the animus-world of spirit.

In Chinese the character *Ming*, illumination or enlightenment, is drawn as a union of the images of sun and moon.[48] For men as for women, wholeness is attainable only when the united opposites day and night, above and below, patriarchal and matriarchal consciousness attain to the generativity peculiar to them and complete and fructify each other.

The Jewish Midrash tells that at the beginning of creation the moon and the sun were of equal size, but that something culpable happened and the moon was diminished while the sun became the ruling heavenly body. God's promise to the moon, however, speaks of the restoration of the original situation in the future:

> In days to come shalt Thou again be great like the Sun; and the Moon's radiance will be as is the radiance of the Sun.[49]

48. See Rose Quong, *Chinese Wit, Wisdom, and Written Characters* (New York, 1944), 14th page (unfolioed).

49. M. J. Bin Gorion, *Die Sagen der Juden*, vol. 1 (Frankfurt, 1913), p. 16.

III

ON MOZART'S "MAGIC FLUTE"

For my Wife

Of the many conflicting interpretations of the libretto of
The Magic Flute, one that is still widely read laments that
Mozart had to work from such an unsuitable and confused text. Critics then usually make the point that the
genius of Mozart's music has more or less managed to
prevail despite the incongruities and banalities of the
libretto.

At first sight, the origins of *The Magic Flute* appear to
confirm this view. The version that Emanuel Schikaneder, the librettist, had assembled from many sources
and versions, and that Mozart had already half set to
music, was suddenly completely reversed and reformu-
lated. Mozart left parts of his composition as they stood;
parts of it he began again; and some critics claim that they
can still distinguish the various layers and contradictions
in its structure.[1] But the essential point, and the one that

---

"Zu Mozarts Zauberflöte," in *Zur Psychologie des Weiblichen*. Translated by Esther Doughty and revised by Boris Matthews.

1. See Otto Jahn and Hermann Abert, *W. A. Mozart*, vol. 2 (Leipzig,
1924); in almost incomprehensible contrast, see Alfred Einstein,
Mozart: His Character, His Work, tr. Arthur Mendel and Nathan
Broder (London, 1945).

concerns us here, is how the deeper layers of meaning carry through at the precise place where these gaps or incongruities appear in the libretto. In a sense, these incongruities can be compared to gaps in consciousness: far from damaging the integrity of the work, they actually constitute the factor that puts it in touch with its deeper levels and evokes an inner meaning that includes its unconscious aspects.

The structure of the libretto was originally based on the fairy-tale situation of the struggle between the good fairy and the wicked magician; this formed the context in which the lovers, in the leading roles, played out their sufferings and development. The transformation of this basic concept—a transformation that probably originated with Mozart himself—rests on the reversal of the polarity of the male and female background figures. The good fairy became the Queen of the Night—presenting the principle of evil—and the wicked magician became the priest of light. In keeping with this shift in values, the mystery symbolism of Freemasonry was then incorporated not only into the libretto but actually became the fundamental content that guided the inner development of the plot. It was only with this transformation that the multilevel mystery drama (for that is how we must regard this late work of Mozart) emerged from the original magical fairy-tale opera.

It was established long since that *The Magic Flute*, like the *Requiem*, was written at the time when Mozart had become aware of his approaching death, an awareness that is clearly expressed in his letters. The transformation of the original fairy tale into an opera of initiation imprinted with the Masonic mystery rites bears witness to

Mozart's consciously Masonic religious and ethical orientation. It seems to us that in the strange libretto Mozart set to music, with its combination of the most diverse spiritual tendencies, we are dealing with something fundamentally other than an accidental grouping of various pieces of text that he had not quite succeeded in integrating. We can grasp the profundity of *The Magic Flute* and its underlying text only when we understand that the many layers of the libretto are analogous to a dream, expressing many levels of consciousness and of the unconscious; and when we also recognize as essential those contents that, beyond the intention of creating a unitary libretto, have to a certain extent slipped in and permeated the text.

Fairy tales and fairy-tale operas always contain an abundance of unconscious symbolism whose living meaning rests on universal human contents that have many nuances and therefore are always open to, and demand, different interpretations. The fairy-tale motifs are motifs of the collective unconscious; they are common to all humanity and are found in remarkable unity of agreement in the most divergent peoples and cultures.[2] By contrast, the "Masonic symbolism" Mozart used in *The Magic Flute* is on the whole allegorical, and thus closer to consciousness. The Masonic symbols are taken by the initiates as indicators of certain conceptually comprehensible contents. Although these contents are not experienced without participation of feeling, they lack

2. See C. Kerényi, Prolegomena to *Essays on a Science of Mythology* (with C. G. Jung; B.S. XXII, 1949; orig. 1942); Hedwig Roques von Beit, *Symbolik des Märchens: Versuch einer Deutung*, 2 vols. (Bern, 1955-1967).

the original quality of a symbol: its content of mainly unconscious and irrational elements.[3] That is, these "symbols" correspond to a differentiated code of morality into which the Freemason is initiated.

As a continuation of Rosicrucianism and late alchemy, Freemasonry has only very distant and indirect connections with the ancient mystery cults. For the person of antiquity, the religious experience of a mystery rite differed from the rationalistic-enlightened emphasis on Masonic allegory as well as from the latter's mystical and rapturous attitude. The ethical-Masonic orientation of *The Magic Flute* conforms to the spirit of Mozart's time—humanist and "progressive," and, in this sense, modern. Nevertheless, fragments of authentic archetypal symbolism remain alive within the Masonic allegory, and in *The Magic Flute* the emotion and passion of Mozart's genius revitalize layers of symbolism that formed the original core of the now-abstract allegory, layers that had been lost in the course of rationalization. In our opinion, it is specifically the strange mixture of fairy tale and Freemasonry that allows archetypal and symbolic elements to come through, without the librettist or the composer necessarily having been conscious of the process.

Our psychological comments on the Masonic aspect of *The Magic Flute* are therefore directed not toward its rationalist-Enlightenment allegory, but rather toward its archetypal-symbolic background. One of the two inner threads of Freemasonry leads to the conscious, rationalist moralizing of the Enlightenment, whereas the other leads to the revitalization of a genuine numinous experi-

3. See Jung, *Psychological Types*, CW 6.

ence through archetypal symbols. Such a revitalization is as characteristic of Mozart's *Magic Flute* as it is of, for example, an incomplete version of Part II of *The Magic Flute* by Goethe, or a number of other Goethesque and Romantic works.

The ritual of Freemasonry consists of an initiation whose process, like that of all patriarchal initiations, stands under the motto: "Through the night to the light." This motto means that the course of events is determined by a sun symbolism, which we recognize in the "night sea journey" of the hero. Dying in the evening in the west, the sun-hero must undergo a journey through the night sea of the dark underworld and death in order to arise as a new sun, transformed and reborn, in the east.

This sun symbolism is the archetypal pattern of every hero and also of every path of initiation in which the hero represents the principle of a consciousness that is to be attained, and that must prove itself in the battle with the dark powers of the unconscious. Furthermore, in his struggle with the forces opposed to consciousness the hero has to set free the treasure of new contents and new life from the night world of the unconscious, and it is through this process that he emerges transformed and "newborn" out of the conflict in which he risked his life.[4] The best-known example of such a mystery rite is the initiation into the Isis mysteries, set forth in the novel of Apuleius, in which the initiate reappears "solified," that is, "illuminated" and illuminating, after he has traveled

4. See Leo Frobenius, *Das Zeitalter des Sonnengottes* (Berlin, 1904); Jung, *Symbols of Transformation*, CW 5; H. G. Baynes, *Mythology of the Soul* (London, 1940); Neumann, *Origins and History*; Joseph Campbell, *The Hero with a Thousand Faces* (B.S. XVII, 1949).

through the underworld and survived the ordeal that led him on a path through the four elements. In this initiation, the initiate becomes Osiris, like the Egyptian king, who likewise, in his "Osirification," represents such an initiation.[5]

The Egyptian symbolism of *The Magic Flute*, like the Masonic symbolism, is in this sense completely "authentic," even if diluted by Rosicrucian and alchemical elements. The recognition of Egypt as the home of the mystery religions, already prevalent in antiquity, is not entirely unfounded, insofar as the Isis and Osiris mysteries are among the few ancient mystery cults of which we have any knowledge at all.

The "prize" won in initiation, its meaning and purpose, lies in the extension of the personality that, since it implies illumination, also includes an extension of consciousness. Thus the symbol of the treasure attained— whether interpreted as a "higher" life, as immortality, or as wisdom, and later as "virtue"—should always be understood in the sense of a transformation of the personality.

We have characterized this model of initiation and of development as "patriarchal"[6] because (as is typical in the West) the attainment of consciousness is bound up with the symbolism of the Masculine, and the forces antithetical to consciousness, represented especially by the instinctual world of the unconscious, are connected with the

5. "Transformation, or Osiris," *Origins and History*, pp. 220ff. [See also Neumann, *Amor and Psyche*.]

6. *Origins and History*, index, s.v. "patriarchate." [And the previous essay in the present volume.]

symbolism of the Feminine. This association inevitably leads to a devaluation of the Feminine, which—for the Masculine and for the sort of consciousness associated with it—represents what is dangerous and negative: the night-side of consciousness. This is not, however, a question of a "voluntary" association but rather of one that is archetypal. This means that, although such an evaluation of the Feminine by the Masculine is objectively false, it will not give way until the psychological self-knowledge of the Masculine (and of those identified with it) has been able to see that it is involved in a projection of archetypal symbols. The Feminine is linked with the unconscious, not only because it is the birthplace of consciousness and hence the Great Mother; above and beyond this, those identified with the Masculine also inevitably experience in the Feminine the "dangerous" instinctuality of their own nature; hence the Feminine (and whatever is associated with it) appears as the danger *par excellence* of falling into the unconscious.

If we look at the libretto of *The Magic Flute* in this light, we can gain an insight into the inner character of the opposing forces represented by the Queen of the Night on the one hand and the priesthood of Sarastro on the other. The Queen of the Night represents the dark side; she embodies what the moralizing masculine conception of virtue experiences as "evil." In the action of the opera she becomes the representative of all the dangerous affects, particularly "vengeance"[7] and "pride."[8] In addi-

7. *The Magic Flute*, I, 19; II, 10. [Citations are to acts and scenes in the libretto.]
8. I, 24; II, 1.

tion, she stands for the power principle of evil which, in the act of murder, takes the form of death,[9] and which sacrilegiously seeks to take possession of the light side and the sun, the "good" principle.[10] Thus the Feminine becomes seductive; by means of delusions, superstitions, and deceptions,[11] it plays out the role of the devil and ensnares the mortal who, mocked by evil, perishes in despair.[12]

Not only the warning of the chorus of priests proves that "death and despair" threatened the endangered hero; as the Queen of the Night herself proclaims, "Death and despair blaze up round about me"; and when she says, "Within my heart hell's vengeance seethes and rages,"[13] she appears to reveal the deepest secret of her nature. As Queen of the Night, in contrast to Sarastro as the principle of light, she symbolizes the underworld and hell, the aboriginal danger that waylays the Masculine on its path to self-realization. That is to say, the Queen of the Night represents the Terrible Mother, the night goddess aspect of the Great Mother,[14] which the mythological hero is to overcome in the dragon fight, one of his ordeals.[15] The point is summed up in this sense with the line:

Protect yourselves from woman's crafty scheming:
This is the Order's first command.[16]

9. II, 3, 10.
10. II, 10.
11. II, 28.
12. II, 4.
13. II, 10.
14. II, 8.
15. "The Hero Myth," *Origins and History*, pp. 131ff.
16. II, 4.

This aspect of the Feminine, which the Masculine experiences as extremely negative, is much more visible in the second part of *The Magic Flute* than in the first, where the "positive" aspect of the Queen of the Night that is characteristic of the original libretto seems to be still partly retained. Of course, these dual aspects can be reduced to a question of "surviving fragments"; but a superficial explanation of this sort will not satisfy everyone, especially when one fully realizes how easy it must have been for Mozart to get an overview of the short text and thus how obvious the actual inconsistencies in characterization must have been to him.

The contradiction between the first[17] and the final[18] self-revelation of the Queen of the Night could apparently be fully explained by regarding the former as "misleading illusion" and conscious deception to which the trusting hero, Tamino, necessarily falls victim.

But this interpretation does not hold up in light of the fact that the strange magical instrument that gives the opera its name, the magic flute, is, like Papageno's glockenspiel, a gift from the Queen of the Night; hence the "evil" nature of the Queen does not lack ambiguity. And another point: the question of the legitimacy of the black-and-white that characterizes the description of Sarastro becomes particularly problematic when one recalls that the action opens with a strange act of violence on Sarastro's part, namely the abduction of Pamina.

The violence of this abduction stands unmistakably in stark and irreconcilable contradiction to Sarastro's otherwise pious and virtue-laden speeches, which are full of

17. I, 9.
18. II, 10.

mildness, wisdom, gentleness, and brotherly love. He explains that he had to snatch the daughter from her proud mother because the gods had destined her for Tamino.[19] However, these words are particularly unconvincing in view of the fact that the Queen of the Night has also promised Pamina to Tamino for setting her free. Here, too, depth psychology finds itself in a position to clarify contradictions in the text, which, like the text of any dream, result not only from a lack of clarity in the ordering consciousness but also are the expression of profound and deep-seated conflicts arising from the unconscious background and constellated by the situation.

The opening situation, the relationship between the Queen of the Night and Pamina, corresponds to the archetypal constellation that appears in the myth of Demeter and Kore and the rape of Kore, and forms a central problem in the psychology of the Feminine, and hence of "matriarchal psychology" in general.[20] The close mother-daughter bond, the rape of the daughter by the Masculine, and the protestations of the bereaved mother still give rise to considerable conflict in the contemporary development of women, a development in which membership in the matriarchal world of the mother, or in the patriarchal world of the father, or in the world of encounter with the beloved is still decisive.

Thus the grief of the Queen of the Night over the loss of her daughter is entirely true archetypally:

> To suffer I have been selected,
> No longer do I see my daughter.

19. II, 1.

20. See Kerényi, Prolegomena (above, n. 2), and Neumann, *Amor and Psyche*.

> With her my happiness was taken;
> An evil fiend escaped with her.[21]

Her mourning continues:

> I still see her shuddering,
> Anxious and trembling,
> Frightfully shaking,
> Timidly struggling.
> I had to watch her be carried away.
> Oh help! was all that she could say.[22]

This description is fully confirmed by the behavior of Pamina, who, in no way reassured as to Sarastro's good intentions, finds herself in his halls delivered over to the power of the wicked Moor, Monostatos.

An explanation which assumes that Mozart left the features of the original version intact (the Queen of the Night as good fairy and Sarastro as wicked magician) and failed to align them with the tendencies of the later version would have to be based on the assumption of a superficial attitude, in fact a complete lack of seriousness, on Mozart's part. On the other hand, even if we do not believe that Mozart wholeheartedly accepted the text with its contradictions, one thing must be said: the intensity and balanced opulence of this latest of his works very consciously embraces the many sides of life with all its contradictions, and therefore we are fully justified in assuming that the "double meaning" of all the elements in the multilayered text cooperated eminently with his genius, even without his conscious awareness.

21. I, 9.
22. Ibid.

Mozart's all-embracing range of musical feeling perhaps comes to expression more fully in *The Magic Flute* than in any of his other works. Elements of the folk song and of comedy stand beside the highest lyricism. Gaiety and horror, sensual instinctuality, and reverent solemnity inspired by death and the beyond follow and alternate with one another. Indeed, every time the work reaches a spiritual and musical climax, we can almost be sure that a counter-movement will immediately begin, an alternation that prevents the emotion and lyricism from becoming "romantic" and the "high seriousness" from becoming tragic. The thirty-fifth year of life—the year when Mozart composed this work—is the typical year of life's "midpoint" and "turning point."[23] Around this time it often seems as though something in the psyche draws together the fullness of the first half of life and looks for the beginning of a new path, which finally manifests itself as the start of a *via nuova* and a way of transformation.

In this sense *The Magic Flute*, in its depiction of an initiation rite, is a typical work of middle age; but at the same time this last creation of the thirty-five-year-old Mozart has the depth and transcendent quality of a work of old age. And thus the uniqueness of *The Magic Flute* lies in (among other things) this very unity of fullness and youth on the one side and maturity and nearness to death on the other. The harmonious union of these opposites is expressed not only in the work as a whole but also in the interrelationship of each detail and in the complementarity of the polar characters, which, in our opinion, constitute the real "unity of character" when taken together.

23. See Jung, "The Stages of Life," CW 8; orig. 1931.

The onesidedness of one element continually finds balance in a contrasting antithesis. The most important example of this play of opposite characters, aside from the relationship of Tamino and Papageno (which will be discussed later), is in Sarastro and the Moor Monostatos, who so conspicuously represents the "dark side" in Sarastro's palace. For the Moor belongs to the positive masculine figure of the priest as his shadow. It is not on behalf of the gods that he has seized Pamina for someone else; he did so entirely for himself and as a sacrifice to his own instinctuality. The remarkable and apparently meaningless statement of Sarastro to Pamina

> For even though I do not question,
> The secret of your heart I see:
> You love another very deeply.
> I shall not force you to embrace me,
> But neither will I set you free.[24]

would appear to be a survival from the old version, in which the wicked magician stole the maiden for himself. But in fact it makes perfect sense when Monostatos is seen to be Sarastro's shadow, just as Papageno is Tamino's and Pagagena is Pamina's.

While on the conscious level the abduction of Pamina was to fulfill the requirements of the gods, Sarastro's original, selfish intention has become unconscious and has been shifted onto Monostatos, whose presence in Sarastro's company becomes meaningful in this way (and only in this way). In recognizing this double meaning of the Sarastro/Monostatos character, one also understands

24. I, 24.

that the grief and anger of the royal mother/Demeter character is no longer so entirely unjustified. For we are looking at a genuine "rape of Kore" in which the Moor Monostatos is as clearly Sarastro's "dark brother" as Hades, the abductor of Kore, is the dark brother of Zeus.

In the case of the above characters the "opposite side" takes on external reality as a separate role in the drama. However, the other side of the terrible Queen of the Night, the good Demeter, is also present, but does not take on a separate outward role. In her case the doubleness is expressed in the alternations in her character and in the archetypal background typical of her appearances in the first and second acts.

The relationship of the Queen of the Night to her daughter Pamina corresponds to the tendency to "hold fast" that archetypally governs mother and daughter during the first phase of the matriarchy. In the important scene between the two that unmasks the terrible aspect of the Great Mother, we see her as the Terrible Mother who actually wants never to give up the daughter. It then becomes clear that her "love" is at the same time the expression of a will to power that does not let the daughter's life achieve autonomy but rather exploits the daughter for its own purposes. "You may thank the power by which you were snatched from me that I still call myself your mother."[25]

This means that if the daughter had left the mother of her own free will, the mother-daughter bond would immediately have been dissolved and nullified. The Queen of the Night talks as if this were self-evident. The Terri-

25. II, 10.

ble Goddess functions according to the all-or-nothing principle; she has no relationship with the personal and individual aspect of her daughter; rather, her connection stands or falls with her requirement of absolute obedience that, however, signifies complete containment of the daughter in the mother. This becomes clear from the decisive second self-revelation of the Queen of the Night in this scene. Here the Queen, inciting Pamina to the murder of Sarastro, says to her:

> Within my heart hell's vengeance seethes and rages,
> Death and despair blaze up round about me!
> If by your hand Sarastro does not perish,
> Then nevermore my daughter shall you be.
> Abandoned be forever, and forsaken,
> Each natural tie and bond be rent asunder
> If not through you Sarastro's life be taken!
> Hark! Gods of vengeance, hear the mother's curse!

Suddenly the ancient mythological figures appear: the Erinyes, goddesses of vengeance, representatives of the Terrible Mother, guardians of the matriarchy. Here again we confront the conflict between the matriarchy, the reign of the Great Mother, mistress of the moon and the night, and the patriarchy, the reign of the father's world, the day and the sun. After thousands of years, the enmity between the masculine principle and the mother's world, afraid of betrayal to the Masculine, breaks through in the Queen of the Night's curse with the same savagery that we recognize in the Amazons, the man-hating mythological representatives of the matriarchy.

All these features are only alluded to, yet it is astonishing how clearly present they are when one remembers that neither the librettist nor the composer could have had any knowledge of the archetypal realities that determine the entire action. By no means does this Queen of the Night let herself be disposed of as Sarastro attempts to do. While he is a priest, she is actually a goddess, and the entire action of *The Magic Flute*, at least in Act I, is determined by her movements, which are more than a match for his. She chooses Tamino as liberator; she assigns Papageno to him as helper; she is the source of the magical instruments; and both the Three Ladies and the Three Boys that later belong to Sarastro's realm come under her law. And anyone who is still not convinced that an aboriginally superordinate female divinity is present in the Queen of the Night should be persuaded by Mozart's magnificent music, which accompanies both of her archetypal appearances.

The meaning of Sarastro's comments on the Queen of the Night and her pride are to be understood in the context of this opposition between a self-determining matriarchal world and a patriarchal world that dominates and feels superior to the Feminine. The patriarchal sense of self, all the arrogance of the patriarchy and of the Masculine toward the Feminine, speak in his words:

> A man must guide your heart aright,
> For by herself each woman tends
> To overreach her proper sphere.[26]

The utterances of the priest, "Woman does little, talks a lot; truly that is woman's lot,"[27] or of Tamino: "Gossip

26. I, 24.
27. I, 19.

women oft repeat" and "She's a woman, has a woman's mind,"[28] are the expression of a presumptuousness of the Masculine and of men which can be demonstrated on every level of the patriarchy, in the pub and the fraternity just as in the onesidedly male way of philosophizing and in the male's psychological evaluation of the Feminine and of women.[29] But this prejudiced attitude in men on the personal level is archetypally determined, and is necessary to the development of the male, and hence psychologically valid. Here we must refer to what we had already begun to develop at the beginning of this essay, namely the patriarchal symbolism of the "way" of the hero, which determines the development of consciousness, and in which the symbols of the unconscious that he is to overcome are projected—although meaningfully and understandably—onto the Feminine and woman. The Masonic way of mystery rites and initiation, which determines Tamino's development, is constructed on the basis of this patriarchal mystery symbolism. Only against this background can the symbolism of "manliness," which plays such an important role in *The Magic Flute*, be fully understood.

The motto of the path of initiation lies in the words of the Boys, who say to Tamino:

> By this path the goal you'll reach:
> But, Lad, win you must by manly daring,
> So harken to these words we teach:
> Be silent, steadfast, and forbearing.

28. II, 5.
29. Cf. Freud's attitude toward women in his *New Introductory Lectures on Psycho-Analysis* (Standard Ed., vol. 22; orig. 1933).

and again:

> Be silent, steadfast and forbearing!
> Consider: just be a man!
> Then you will win by manly daring.[30]

This passage makes clear that the way of initiation referred to is analogous to the young men's initiation rites with which we are familiar from primitive cultures.[31]

We have already seen that overcoming the Queen of the Night—the embodiment of the Terrible Mother—stood for the victory over the affect and instinct side of the unconscious, and that the male hero, in the image of the sun, was to undergo the same struggle. Thus when Tamino has proved himself in the first half of his ordeal, and the stage is therefore also "half dark," we hear:

> The dismal night drives off the sun's rich splendor;
> Soon our Lad will feel new life.[32]

The course of the alchemical way of transformation is analogous to the hero's night sea journey, traces of which can be found in the Masonically colored parts of the work. Oversimplified, the alchemical stages of transformation lead from the black of chaos and the night through the silver of the moon to the gold of the sun. Thus it is not accidental that the Three Boys, messengers of the light, with whose announcement "the serpent disappears,"[33] make their first appearance[34] carrying "silver

30. I, 17.
31. See *Origins and History*.
32. II, 21.
33. I, 12.
34. I, 17.

palm branches" in their hands. In the same way it is said of the grove of palms that appears at the beginning of Act II, the act of initiation, that "the trees are made of silver and have golden leaves."

After the "work" of transformation has been fulfilled and Evil has been thrown into eternal night, the last part of the piece stands under the sign of gold. Hence it takes place in the temple of the sun. Its ending takes the form of Sarastro's victorious motto: "The sun's radiant glory has vanquished the night," and the words of the chorus of priests: "Hail to the initiates! You have passed through the night."[35]

Just as the initiation rites of primitives were intended to strengthen the ego of the initiate or the novice and the purpose of the ancient mysteries was to reinforce the wholeness of the psyche so that it would no longer be vulnerable to the fragmenting effects of any powers of darkness, here the criterion of male development is found in the stability of the male who must prove his invulnerability to the seductive powers of the Feminine. "Manly and patient"[36] is what a man must be; "A steady spirit rules a man; He weighs his words before he speaks."[37]

Here self-control and keeping his own counsel are—as in countless fairy tales and rites—the expression of the strength of consciousness and ego-stability on which everything depends. Seduction by the Feminine—here embodied in the Three Ladies—can consist of women's "gossip" or, equally, of the talk of the "vulgar masses," in contrast to the man's taciturn power of mind steadfast in

35. II, 38.
36. II, 22.
37. II, 5.

the face of temptation. His manliness is expressed as much by the ego-stability of his mind as by his conquest of fear and his rejection of temptation by the instincts in the face of which Papageno shows himself to be so overcome that he is unworthy of initiation. But this whole world of temptation stands under the sign of Maya, whose embodiment is the Great Mother as the Queen of the Night.

We are interpreting the characters of the drama on the subjective level, that is, as intrapsychic aspects of the subject. Thus, for example, the "man-hating female" is also the unconscious within the man. And the "fury of the matriarchy" represents the layer of the male psyche itself that is unconscious and hostile to consciousness, and against which the man's consciousness has to prevail on its heroic journey in the same way as the young men during their initiation, who must demonstrate that they are a match for everything feminine, including its traits within themselves. In this way the lines we quoted earlier take on a new meaning; in the struggle with the "proud Feminine" it is said that:

> A man must guide your heart aright,
> For by herself each woman tends
> To overreach her proper sphere.

Ultimately this, too, is related to the control of the emotional and unconscious side of the man by means of his own consciousness. In this sense, "overreaching her proper sphere" signifies a potential autonomy of the feminine forces in the man that would endanger his consciousness.

It is obvious that this internal situation is experienced

and lived out as an external projection; this is the basis of every "objective" dramatic representation. Insofar as it represents an unconscious outer dramatization of inner and psychic events, the inner psychic constellations are changed into externalized ones. However, this dramatization takes place not only between the upper sphere of the initiation and the opposing sphere of the Terrible Mother, but also between the "upper" and "lower" forces within the individual himself.

The upward movement of the "higher" values is continually being compensated by a counter-movement of the "lower" (and vice versa), a device through which Mozart attains a dramatic representation of the wholeness of life in the unity of upper and lower. In Mozart's superior irony the lower and primitive side of human nature thus always retains its rights alongside the ritual solemnity and the invocation of the "ideal human." Thus, in particular, the character of Papageno with his earthly realism complements Tamino's solemnity of initiation and idealistic otherworldliness in a frankly Mephistophelian counterpoint. Papageno is the primitively sensuous shadow, the child of nature, the "lower," dissenting voice to Tamino's idealistic and emotional "higher" voice. Just as the Basel letters are documents of Mozart's primitive, natural, animal side, so Papageno plays the Sancho Panza–like Mephisto to Tamino's Faust–Don Quixote character, and both are aspects of Mozart's being.

And look what *The Magic Flute* has done with the pair of clowns that carried on their ridiculous antics in the earlier operas! The unity of Tamino and Papageno is one of the best representations of the twosidedness of the human spirit which Goethe described in *Faust* with the words:

> Two souls, alas, dwell within my breast!
> The one wishes to leave the other;
> The one with gripping organs clings to earth
> With a rough and hearty lust;
> The other rises powerfully from the dust
> Toward the region of the great forefathers.[38]

But Papageno does not represent only the spontaneous instinctual side; he has a heart within him and a basic form of humanity, a first foundation from which the higher aspect, Tamino, can begin its ascent. Seen from this perspective, the meaning of otherwise strangely incomprehensible scenes make sense, such as the one where Pamina together with Papageno sings the great song in praise of love that anticipates the core of the initiation rite and the *coniunctio*:

> No greater good than man and wife;
> Wife and man, man and wife
> Reach the height of godly life.[39]

What does the primitive natural man, Papageno, whose version of love is not ennobled by any higher sphere of initiation, have to do with this song? Pamina herself supplies the answer: "The men who feel sweet love's emotion / Will never lack a kindly heart."

When Papageno celebrates the love that works "in the realm of nature," this love, hearty in every sense, is the

38. *Faust*, Part One, scene 2.
39. I, 16.

miracle of nature and the basis of all higher being. For this reason, the counter-voice to the successful initiation of Tamino and Pamina: "Victory! Victory! Noble Couple!"[40] is the song of Papageno and Papagena about the "dear little children":

> It is the greatest of all feelings
> When many, many, many, many Papageno(a)s
> Upon their parents blessings bring.[41]

Unquestionably, the way of initiation in the mystery rites is the way of the hero, but its ascetic and idealistic impetus under the rubric of virtue and wisdom stands in natural contrast to Papageno's anti-romantic common sense upon which the continuation of the material world depends. He represents the natural fearfulness and desire for comfort of the person who shuns all asceticism and striving. Who could remain aloof from Papageno's protestation: "But tell me, Sir, why must I suffer all these torments and horrors? If the gods really have selected a Papagena for me, why do I have to risk such dangers to win her?"[42]

He has no intention, unlike the hero, of going through darkness and mortal dangers for the sake of "higher goals"; in horror, he denies the suggestion that he has "spirit,"[43] but he stands firm by his "heart full of feeling." He says, "To be truthful, I don't demand any wisdom either. I'm just a child of nature who is satisfied with

40. II, 33.
41. II, 36.
42. II, 7.
43. I, 16.

sleep, food, and drink. And if I once could catch a pretty little wife. . . ."[44]

And when he answers the scornful pronouncement: "However, you shall never experience the heavenly pleasures of the ordained" with the words: "Anyway, there are more people like me in the world,"[45] he certainly has the majority of people with healthy common sense on his side. Yet in spite of his naturalness and primitivity, Papageno does experience, even though on a lower level, the initiation, the way of the hero, that Tamino has to undergo on a higher plane in full consciousness and willingness.

The experience of death forms part of a genuine initiation, and in the mystery of *The Magic Flute* the danger of initiation is also pointed out more than once.[46] Although in the opera itself the ordeals, like all the dangers, are only hinted at or alluded to, the solemn and ominous mood of the music at these points[47] vouches for the genuineness of what is said and felt. And just as in the suicide scene Pamina has to experience death as a genuine living out of her love,[48] the same happens to Papageno. Even though Papageno's suicide scene is full of rich humor from beginning to end, it still remains true that his lament,

> Now I'm sick and tired of living.
> Death will put an end to love
> Even though my heart's still burning,[49]

44. II, 3.
45. II, 25.
46. II, 1, 3.
47. II, 1, 3, 23, 31.
48. See below, pp. 147f.
49. II, 34.

in fact forms the comic counterpart to Pamina's suffering. In both scenes the same experience is expressed, though on different levels. Hence the Three Boys come to rescue Papageno as well as Pamina.[50]

Earlier we made use of Bachofen's discoveries[51] in our interpretation of the text; in this connection we will now bring Papageno's bird aspect into the interpretation. Papageno is a bird-man, and as such he belongs obviously to the realm of the Queen of the Night. As we have known since Bachofen, a fundamental division obtains in the symbolic realm of birds. There are higher "birds of the spirit," whose home in the air is the predominant feature. We need only remember the eagle and its significances: "the Masculine," "the spirit," "the sun." But besides this group there is another male-related group of birds that belong more to the region of water and marsh. These birds—including the stork, with which we are most familiar, but also the gander, the swan, and the drake—have a phallic/masculine character, and their fertilizing function comes under and remains subject to the rule of the Feminine.

The bird-man Papageno belongs with this "lower" kind of masculine bird; he is not capable of sharing Tamino's lofty flight of the spirit, but settles for the lower realm of nature. Even in his transformation—and he, like all the active characters in *The Magic Flute*, undergoes a transformation—he does not overstep the lower sphere in which he belongs; but he reaches his fulfillment on his own plane through his relationship with his part-

50. II, 35.
51. J. J. Bachofen, *Das Mutterrecht* (orig. 1861; 3rd ed., Basel, 1948), vol. 2 .

ner Papagena, just as Tamino does with his, except that for the latter all the action is played out on a higher plane.

It is part of Mozart's greatness to have recognized that the higher mystery of initiation is filled with the same power of love as the lower world of Papageno. Just as the Masonic Temple of Wisdom in the opera stands between Nature and Reason, so his love and wisdom embrace both at the same time. He accepts the wisdom of the higher sphere of love, but he also accepts the lower love and wisdom of the simple natural world, without finding them beneath him.

Just as the Queen of the Night is the unconscious, especially in the aspect of the Terrible Mother, and Papageno is Tamino's shadow, so also Pamina is not only the (external) beloved to be won by Tamino, but also the symbol of his soul to be attained through the ordeal, that is, his anima figure.[52] In Masonic terms, she is an object that we must attain with effort and zeal.[53] Pamina's nature as a typical anima figure, that is, as an inner image of the Feminine that lives within the man, is clearly discernible from the way she and Tamino first meet. The famous "portrait aria"[54] is the typical form of the encounter with the anima, in which the man stumbles on his own inner anima image.

But in the ordeal situation the hero has to prove his steadfastness in the face of seduction not only by the mother but also by his own anima. Tamino keeps the command of silence imposed on him even to the point of running the risk of losing Pamina because of it. Just as

52. See Jung, "The Relations."
53. I, 1.
54. I, 7.

in the matriarchy the world of the mothers demands of the daughter a decision in which she has to oppose the Masculine—even in the form of the man she loves—and adhere to the mother, so the patriarchal world of the father—represented by Sarastro and the priests—requires the hero to opt for it and against the Feminine, even against the beloved woman. (Here we cannot discuss the dangers concealed in these extreme requirements.) Here, too, the text demonstrates its unexpected profundity when the steadfast silence of Tamino throws Pamina into despair.

At the center of the original conception of the magic opera stands the pair of lovers, and here again it is the archetypal task of the hero to set his captured beloved free from the evil powers. Originally this constellation was also retained in *The Magic Flute*, at least in Act I. But the events of Pamina's rescue have moved into the background, obscured by the Masonic way of initiation that Tamino has to follow, which leads from the evil serpent at the beginning to the sunrise at the end. Indeed, it even seems as if the course of Pamina's deliverance has come into conflict with Tamino's development.

But the solution to this problem lies close at hand: it consists of the bond between Tamino and Pamina. In the most ingenuous way, she is simply included in the journey of purification, and instead of one hero we now have two about to go through the ordeal. It can even be assumed that Schikaneder had become aware of this solution in his own mind, and probably Mozart had too. But look what the unconscious—even if only by way of suggestion—has made of this "practical solution"!

While it is typical of patriarchal mysteries that the

145

woman, as bearer of the symbolism of the negative aspect, is excluded from the rites, in the action of *The Magic Flute* we find not just a breach of this basic principle but the introduction of a new mystery in which the *coniunctio*, the union of the Masculine with the Feminine, occupies the highest level of symbolism, beyond a one-sided matriarchal or patriarchal identification.

Undoubtedly this principle of the *coniunctio*, which makes its first Western appearance in Apuleius's tale of Psyche,[55] did play a role, if not the decisive one, in ancient and medieval alchemy.[56] But in alchemy the principle of love between the two initiates never occurred as the essence of the mystery, because the action was always played out in the form of a projection onto material substances in which the union of masculine and feminine potencies was experienced. The appearance of a mystical "sister" in the work of the alchemists, frequent but not emphasized, is undoubtedly the closest precursor of such a two-person mystery rite, which C. G. Jung has introduced to us in one of its modern forms in *The Psychology of the Transference*.

There is a profound and central significance in the fact that the mysteries of *The Magic Flute* are associated with the double figure of Isis and Osiris, one of the highest pairs of gods and lovers, although at first it seems that their inclusion in the opera, like the whole layer of Egyptian allegory and symbolism, is only the product of a typical Masonic veneer that was fashionable at the time.

While the rites of *The Magic Flute* attain an unexpect-

---

55. Cf. *Amor and Psyche.*

56. Cf. Jung's work on alchemy [*Psychology and Alchemy*, CW 12, *Alchemical Studies*, CW 13, *Mysterium Coniunctionis*, CW 14, and *The Psychology of the Transference*, in CW 16].

edly modern significance through the introduction of the
coniunctio principle, it is even more astonishing to see
how Pamina is transformed from a princess awaiting
rescue into an equal partner as worthy of initiation as
Tamino.

The "initiation ritual" through which Pamina proves
herself worthy, but which here takes the form not of a
mere ritual but of a direct experience, is the ritual of the
"death-marriage." For Pamina, as also in Masonic symbolism, death is the "key" to initiation into a higher state
of being. Four years before his own death Mozart wrote
to his dying father: "As death, when we come to consider
it closely, is the true goal of our existence, I have formed
during the last few years such close relations with this
best and truest friend of mankind, that his image not only
is no longer terrifying to me, but is indeed very soothing
and consoling! And I thank my God for graciously granting me the opportunity (you know what I mean) of learning that death is the *key* which unlocks the door to our
true happiness."[57]

The effect of Tamino's silence, by means of which he
had to prove himself steadfast vis-à-vis Pamina as his
anima figure, was to throw Pamina into the loneliness
and despair of her love, which in this situation proved
itself for the first time to be a "love unto death." Half-
insane with despair, Pamina addresses her dagger: "So
you are to be my bridegroom," and, "Be patient, my
Beloved, I am thine; / Soon we shall be united for all
time."[58] If only by allusion we are reminded of the femi-

57. *The Letters of Mozart and His Family*, ed. Emily Anderson
(London, 1938), April 4, 1787 (vol. 3, p. 1351).
58. II, 30.

nine myth of the death-marriage that—extending from
Apuleius's story to Schubert's "Death and the Maiden"—
forms part of the initiation mysteries in which woman
comes to herself as she turns away from her original
connection to mother and surrenders herself to the male
and to death.[59]

The decisive step in the liberation of the daughter from
the mother consists in her leaving the matriarchal world
for love of the man and giving herself freely to him in the
death-marriage. But this submission to the male, although
liberating for the woman, is regarded by the matriarchal
principle as a betrayal. The conflict between these two
archetypal forces, the Maternal and the Masculine, always
form the tragic background of the death-marriage. In
Pamina's intended suicide the dagger symbolizes the
Masculine due to whose (apparent) hard-heartedness she
is about to die. But beyond that, suicide is a regression.
Since the suicide form of the death-marriage is not a
progressive symbol of genuine union with the beloved in
a *Liebestod*, a love-death, the dagger also symbolizes the
negative aspect of the Feminine, the Terrible Mother,
revenging herself on the lovers' betrayal of her. Even this
archetypal characteristic finds expression in *The Magic
Flute*. For Pamina reveals the meaning of her suicide herself when she says: "You, my Mother, make me suffer /
And your curse pursues me now."[60]

Only the intervention of the Three Boys, who always
stand for the principle of grace and mercy within the
principle of light, prevents Pamina's suicide. But the attempted suicide is recognized as a genuine demonstra-

59. Cf. *Amor and Psyche.*
60. II, 30.

tion of love on the part of the Feminine, a genuine death-marriage, and accepted unconsciously—certainly in a way that was completely foreign to Mozart's consciousness—but still validly, as the ritual of initiation. Hence we hear that: "A woman who has death disdained / Is worthy and will be ordained."[61] Since Pamina experienced that death was the key, in the way appropriate to her as a woman, just as Tamino did in his male way, both undergo the ordeal and are initiated as equals and as fully valid partners in their love, as in their full and equal membership in the human race.

It is not by accident that the two divine figures, Isis and Osiris, as the highest symbol of the *coniunctio*, preside over the initiation ritual that the lovers have to go through in the three scenes of Act II.[62] The old "apotheosis motif" of the mystery rites, proclaimed at three places in the opera, is fulfilled in the lovers themselves.

Although externally *The Magic Flute* is divided into two acts, it is actually arranged according to the number three, the sacred Masonic number, which recurs in the three temples,[63] the figure of the pyramid and its number nine,[64] the three appearances of the Three Boys,[65] and also musically in the solemn thrice-repeated motif of initiation in the overture and at the beginning of Act II. Act II actually ends at scene 20, and a third act can, and in a certain sense should, be distinguished from it, to clarify the structure—just as the ending of *Faust* has been accurately described as a "Part Three."

61. Ibid.
62. II, 31-33.
63. I, 17.
64. II, 1.
65. II, 17.

In the last part, which begins with the chorus of priests: "O Isis and Osiris! Sacred wonder! / The gloomy night by light is rent asunder,"[66] Tamino is no longer undergoing the ordeal and the initiation alone; in this "third act" the mystery of the *coniunctio* of Tamino and Pamina is accomplished in the image of the divine couple, which operates as Isis and Osiris above and behind the entire action.

The inner and only barely concealed tripartite division of the work is represented in ascending sequence in the figure of the pyramid, a favorite symbol of Freemasonry, which has a very important function in the structure of the opera. The base of the pyramid is formed by Act I, ruled by the chthonic powers, the Queen of the Night. In Act II, the act of the initiation process and the middle section of the structure, the battle between the dark and the light is presented. The "third act" forms the apex of the pyramid: in it is celebrated the union of the Masculine and the Feminine as the secret of Osiris and Isis. If we accept this sequence, the symmetrical structure of the piece and its correspondences become much clearer. Just as in Act I, scene 9 the Queen of the Night is revealed as the Good Mother, and in Act II, scene 10 as the Terrible Mother, so we find corresponding symmetrical appearances of the Three Boys who bring their assistance in Act I, scene 17 and in Act II, scene 17. Their nature as uniters of the upper and lower realms is clear from the fact that on the lower, magical plane of Act I they bring in the wisdom-and-ordeal motif of the second, and on the higher, wisdom-oriented plane of Act II they bring in the magic instruments of the first. But in the "third" act, too, both

66. II, 21.

the magic flute and the Three Boys play their most significant and, to correspond with the summit, their most
elevated role.[67] And likewise, the three occasions where
the apotheosis motif appears fit into the general three-level
structure of the opera. In the great scene of Act I between
Papageno, the "natural man," and Pamina, the still-virgin
daughter, where they celebrate the love principle in nature,
we hear this motif for the first time: "Wife and man, man
and wife, / Reach the height of godly life."[68]

At the beginning of the initiation scene, under the sign
of Sarastro, the motif is heard again, but now on a higher
plane. We are now concerned with the paradise of Reason, where humanity, returning from the lowest plane,
rediscovers its originally "divine" state:

> When virtue and integrity
> The path with glory have adorned,
> Then is the Earth a paradise
> And mortals equals of the gods.[69]

But the same motif is heard for the third time—and
this time on the highest level—at the beginning of the
last part, in which the mystery of the *coniunctio* of the
lovers is brought to completion:

> O calmness from above descend,
> Enter the human heart again;
> Then Earth becomes a paradise
> And mortals equals of the gods.[70]

67. See below, p. 155.
68. I, 16.
69. I, 26. The entire closing scene of Act I is simultaneously the
prelude to all of Act II.
70. II, 29.

What was acted out in the context of nature in the lowest stage, and in human society in the middle stage, now turns inward to the center of the individual, the human heart. The symbol of this paradise is "blessed peace." This peace, which was among the original inner possessions of humanity and was lost at the "fall," is attained again in the highest stage.

The series of three stages leading to godlikeness is the only clue in the opera to the meaning of the three temples: the Temple of Wisdom between the opposites, the Temple of Reason, and the Temple of Nature.[71] The paradise of the love that is rooted in nature, the paradise of human reason, and the paradise of the wisdom of the heart are the locations of the temples in which the apotheosis of the human being takes place. But of the three, the Temple of the Wisdom of the Heart represents the central, the highest, and at the same time the most inward sanctuary.

However, this holy of holies can be reached only by way of the series of trials that the lovers must go through, which manifests itself as the way of their *coniunctio*. Their journey through the purifying elements stands as much under the sign of death as of rebirth. With the words "No force on earth our lives shall rend, / Even though death may be our end,"[72] both are ready to face their trials and experience their love as well as to die together. They stand side by side as partners on the last stretch of the road through danger; the Feminine is also prepared for death, not just—as is still the case in al-

71. I, 16.
72. II, 31.

152

chemy, for example—the Masculine. While there the Feminine appeared in the transformation process of alchemy as the Terrible Mother in which the Masculine was dissolved, here the anima figure, the female partner as a human companion, has already been set free from the mother figure, the Queen of the Night. But Pamina does not simply stand the test together with Tamino; here again the strange text offers us a new and almost imperceptible surprise: in the decisive moment when they are threatened by the greatest danger of the journey through the elements, Pamina herself assumes the leadership. What empowers Pamina to act under the sign of Isis in this highest mystery of rebirth (the *coniunctio*) is not only the greater connectedness to nature characteristic of the Feminine, which is better able to find its way through water and fire, but also its greater affinity to the love principle that, as the principle of the heart, leads to wisdom, the highest stage.

> Wher'er the path may take us,
> I shall be at your side.
> I myself shall lead you,
> For Love will be my guide.[73]

But the decisive assistance on the way of initiation comes through the magic flute. It too has a very close connection with Pamina. It is not just that Pamina tells Tamino to play the flute: "It guides us on this dreaded course";[74] the flute is ultimately invoked by both of them as a god, in fact as "divine power" itself: "We wander by

73. II, 32.
74. Ibid.

153

sweet music's might / With gladness through death's darkest night."[75]

To understand what this divine power invoked by the anima and identified with love is, we must look at the strange symbol presented in the form of the magic flute.

One of the most striking incongruities of the libretto is undoubtedly to be seen in the fact that the Queen of the Night, supposedly the principle of evil, gives Tamino the redeeming magic flute to which the opera owes its name, and also gives Papageno the glockenspiel. This is particularly puzzling if the Queen of the Night is regarded solely as the representative of the unconscious, instinctual aspect. The fact that the shadow figure, Papageno, comes from her domain confirms this association, but it also attests to the rootedness of Tamino and his "lower" masculinity in this realm of nature.

In determining the place of the magic instruments within the opera, one can disregard Papageno's glockenspiel, since it is a double of the magic flute, with no separate significance. Where it is not used simply to answer wishes, it possesses the same power as the magic flute to transform people's feelings, as in the enchantment of the wicked Monostatos. Of it the Three Ladies say:

> Human passions it transforms,
> The saddest man to smile will learn;
> The coldest heart with love will burn.[76]

The first act of the opera stands under the sign of entanglement in the "lower" world of the Queen of the

75. Ibid.
76. I, 12.

Night; it is she who leads Tamino astray by inducing the emotions of revenge and hostility. The initiation does not come until Act II. And as the structure of Act II is in many respects parallel to that of Act I, so Tamino-Papageno is invested twice with the magic instruments. In Act I, the Queen's Three Ladies bestow the gifts of flute and glockenspiel (I, 17); in Act II—in exact correspondence—they are brought out of Sarastro's palace by his Three Boys (II, 17).

The Orpheus motif of the magic flute—the enchantment of the animals, analogous to the transformation of the negative affects into positive feelings—already plays a significant part in Act I. But the deeper meaning of the magic flute becomes clear in one place in particular, where Tamino plays on it for the first time and cries out:

> If only I could show my thanks
> As from my heart it flows profound,
> Almighty Gods, with every note
> Your honor I would let resound![77]

While on this occasion he draws only the animals to him (that is, reveals the connectedness of his feelings with nature), the flute has a more significant magical effect in Act II. Here its sound tames the lions threatening Papageno (II, 20); the flute becomes an instrument of mastery over the aggressive-animalistic world of the affects.

This function of music and the musical instrument—whether in relation to good or to evil—is an archetypal motif. The Pied Piper of Hamelin, as well as violins, flutes, pipes, and harps, play a similar role in fairy tales—

77. I, 20.

quite apart from the lyre of Orpheus—and have a similar meaning.[78] Inclusion of many such archetypal motifs into an all-encompassing spiritual whole, which takes the form of the mysteries of human development, makes *The Magic Flute* unique. While the Orpheus motif is already crucial in Act I, on the higher plane of the second act the magic flute plays an even more significant role. With its notes Tamino calls to Pamina, and draws her, without knowing it himself, into her own fate. For the encounter that then follows, in which Tamino remains steadfast in the face of her entreaties, throws Pamina into despair and suicide, but then leads her beyond them into the "higher marriage" of shared initiation.

But in the "third act," the *coniunctio*, the magic flute becomes the most important of all the participants. Its sounds enable the couple to pass through the elements that are brought together into the pairs of opposites formed by fire and water. The power of the magic flute to subdue everything in nature is clear on every level of its workings. Like the song of Orpheus, it is the symbol of music itself, which harmonizes the savage and the resistant in nature—the elemental as well as the animal and the human—into a higher unity. But this power of music is at the same time a power of the feelings and of the heart, which, as Tamino said in his cry to the gods, "transforms the passions."

Thus music, which Pamina calls a "divine power" in the scene of the ordeal, becomes a symbol of love and of the highest wisdom, which here stands under the sign of Isis. Just as Isis, the supreme divinity, brings her brother-

78. See *Origins and History*, p. 161; V.C.C. Collum, "Die schöpferische Muttergottin der Völker keltische Sprache," *EJ 1938*.

consort through the valley of death to rebirth,[79] so Pamina on the earthly plane, but by analogy with the act of the goddess, leads her beloved—and herself—to the highest goal, the union of Isis and Osiris, made possible by the love of Isis. For this reason we hear at this point—and only at this point: "Isis' joy is granted us!" and

> Victory! Victory! Noble Couple!
> You have vanquished every peril,
> Isis' blessing now is yours,
> Come! Step into the temple's shrine.[80]

While the Eternal Feminine in *Faust II* still appears in personalized form as the Madonna, she works her effects in *The Magic Flute* as an invisible spiritual power, as music. But this music is the expression of divine love itself, which unites law and freedom, above and below, in the wisdom of the heart and of love. As harmony, it grants humankind divine peace and rules the world as the highest divinity.

From the earliest times, magic and music have stood under the rule of the Archetypal Feminine, which in myth and fairy tale is also the mistress of transformation, intoxication, and enchanting sound. Thus it is quite understandable that it is precisely this feminine principle that bestows the magical instruments. The Orpheus motif of the magical taming of the animal energies through music belongs to her, for as mistress of the animals the Great Goddess rules the world of wild as well as tame creatures. She can transform things and people into animal form, tame the animal, and enchant it because, like

79. See *Origins and History*, pp. 220ff., "Transformation, or Osiris."
80. II, 3.

music, she is able to make the tame wild and the wild tame with the power of her magic. In contrast to Sarastro's patriarchally colored *imago* of her, in which the Queen of the Night simply represents the feminine as the negative, an essentially positive group of qualities of Queen and Goddess of the Night has asserted itself in both text and action in *The Magic Flute*.

We have a rather similar case, even though very diluted, in the assignment of the Three Ladies to the Queen of the Night and of the Three Boys to Sarastro's realm. Not only do the Three Ladies intervene against lying and on behalf of "love and brotherhood"[81] when they bestow the magic flute; the Three Boys, who doubtless belong to Sarastro's realm of light—even musically their classification is unambiguous[82]—are given to Tamino and Papageno by the Queen of the Night as guides.[83] This happens in the same scene in which the Three Ladies bring the magic flute and the glockenspiel as gifts from the Queen of the Night. But this means that Tamino actually begins his way of initiation, his series of ordeals, as a mission for the Queen of the Night.

Just as the hostile goddess Hera in the development of Hercules and the goddess Aphrodite in the corresponding path of initiation of Psyche[84] embody the terrible aspect of necessity without which no development is possible, so there is no night sea journey of the hero without night, no sunrise without darkness, and no series of ordeals for Tamino without the Queen of the Night. Hence

81. I, 12.
82. Jahn and Abert, *W. A. Mozart*, vol. 2, p. 793 (see above, n. 1).
83. I, 12.
84. *Amor and Psyche*.

Apuleius is right in saying that the initiate sees "the lower and the higher gods"; in reality both are necessary to his development and are fundamentally the same.

The patriarchal onesidedness of Sarastro's priesthood may well overlook this basic relatedness, but in the completeness of *The Magic Flute* everything finds its proper place. The night sea journey begins with the snake entering from the left,[85] and while Tamino's journey at first seems to receive the support of the dark aspect, he has to disentangle himself from this dark side and finally overcome it in the development of Act II.

The negative aspect of the Queen of the Night, her matriarchal will to power that uses the Masculine mainly as a means of extending her domain, can be clarified once again by contrasting her relationship to Pamina's father, the consort of the Queen of the Night, with the very different kind of bond between Pamina and Tamino.

We learn nothing about Pamina's father in the version of the opera which is performed today. He is mentioned only in a passage that will soon occupy us—that is, in Pamina's account of the origin of the magic flute. However, in a conversation with her daughter[86] in the unabridged libretto,[87] the Queen of the Night provides some important information about him, his relationship to Sarastro, and the mysterious symbol of the "seven-fold circle of the sun."

This mandala symbol of the sevenfold circle of the sun was inherited by Sarastro and the initiates from Pamina's

85. The "right" and "left" directions in the libretto should be reversed, since they are intended "for the reformers."
86. II, 10.
87. *Die Zauberflöte*, complete version (Reclam Verlag, Leipzig).

father. But thereupon the power of the Queen of the Night "went to its grave," as she states in the conversation. With this transferral of the "mighty circle of the sun" to Sarastro, who wears it on his breast as a sign of his office, the rule of the patriarchal line by the sun-consort of the nocturnal moon goddess is finally established. His comments: "And now no more words; do not seek after things that the female mind cannot grasp. Your duty is to surrender yourself and your daughter to the guidance of wise men," are made entirely in the arrogant "patriarchal style" with which we are already familiar.

We are faced with two problems at this point in the text. Why is the sevenfold circle of the sun said to be "all-devouring"? And why is it precisely the death of her consort that leads to the development of the patriarchy and the "repression" of the Queen of the Night, who, as Sarastro informs us, "wanders about in the subterranean rooms of the Temple, brewing revenge on me and on the human race"?[88]

Just before his great aria, "In these sacred chambers revenge remains unknown," Sarastro says to Pamina in the original text that, understandably, has been suppressed: "You alone shall see how I take my revenge on your mother."

This puzzling juxtaposition of opposite statements is psychologically not only understandable but in fact "correct."

The sevenfold circle of the sun, the symbol of the patriarchal masculine spirit, is not only "all-mighty" but also "all-devouring," i.e., warlike and deadly, aggressive and cruel, vengeful and destructive. Only the masculine

88. II, 13.

mind's misconception of itself overlooks this "burning" aspect of the sun symbol, which appears in corresponding form as the danger of the murderous sun ram in the tale of Amor and Psyche.[89]

In the Egyptian myth this death aspect is represented by the Uraeus snake of the sun disc, originally an attribute of the great Mother Goddess that later became an attribute of the patriarchal god-king. This means that the "all-devouring" power of the sevenfold circle of the sun corresponds to the deadly masculine shadow side of the warlike-patriarchal spirit. This makes possible the interpretation of the second problem: specifically, why the power of the Queen of the Night came to an end with the death of her consort.

So long as there is a love relationship between the Masculine and the Feminine, the subterranean power of the female night-aspect is guaranteed, but at the same time the male power of the sun is not only tempered but, without knowing it, is largely subjected to the rule of the Feminine. (Here, too, there is a striking parallel in Apuleius's story,[90] where Psyche gets the golden locks of the deadly sun-ram when the sun is setting and turning towards the nocturnal Feminine.) With the death of the Queen of the Night's consort, the personal relationship of the Masculine and the Feminine, sun and moon, comes to an end, and its place is taken by an anonymous brotherhood of male initiates with Sarastro at the head. But the appearance of an impersonal patriarchal spiritual order means that the sphere of influence and the power of the Feminine really is broken, and it is precisely at this point

89. *Amor and Psyche*.
90. Ibid.

that the Feminine becomes regressive, hostile to men, and "evil."

In the Queen of the Night's attempt to incite Pamina to kill Sarastro and steal the sun symbol, and in her effort to manipulate Tamino through his love for Pamina and thus reinstate the power of the Feminine, there appears the negative will-to-power of the matriarchy in its unrelatedness to a partner. Pamina's path of suffering and redemption stands in complete contrast to it; her loving relatedness has nothing to do with power; she overcomes the matriarchy in the self-sacrifice of the death-marriage, and in her personal existence of a meeting with another individual outside herself she attains a genuine *coniunctio* of lovers.

With Pamina's separation from her mother, the Feminine has made itself independent in a higher sense and has differentiated itself. Pamina now stands as a genuine mediating figure between the upper feminine world of Isis—where music, heart, and mind come together—and the Queen of the Night's dark magical realm below. As "divine image" she not only is Tamino's anima figure, but also has developed into a person in her own right, a human being who loves and is loved, that is, a genuine partner in the *coniunctio*. An analogous transformation happens to the magic flute itself.

During the final ordeal when Pamina turns Tamino's attention to the magic flute, whose sounds will enable him to overcome the danger, it no longer belongs only to the realm of the Queen of the Night but has attained a higher consecration by virtue of Sarastro's world. For this reason the flute was bestowed upon Tamino a second time so that to some extent it now bears the mark of both the lower and the upper worlds. This dual nature of the magic flute is confirmed by the story that Pamina tells almost at the end of the opera:

My father at a magic hour
Did carve it from the very core
Of th' ancient, thousand-year-old oak
While lightning flashed and thunder roared.[91]

So the actual maker of the magic flute was Pamina's father, the Queen of the Night's husband, of whom we otherwise hear almost nothing, since he—like Osiris, the consort—"has died." This constellation in which the father plays a subordinate role, evidently because of the dominant mother-daughter relationship, is familiar to us from myth as well as from women's inner reality. Here again the Queen of the Night—who is even directly addressed as a goddess—shows her mythological nature as the Great Goddess, the dark side of Isis.[92]

In myth and cult as well as in fairy tales, the "tree" and the "abyss" are symbols under which the Archetypal Feminine is worshiped, and the night hours are dedicated to her honor. These images confirm once again the archetypal-mythological background of this remarkable text.

The hero's deed always consists in his "stealing" something from the depths of the unconscious, whose symbol is the Great Mother, and bringing what he has stolen to the daylight world of consciousness in order to give it recognition or form; and we obviously have such a deed

91. II, 32.
92. *Origins and History*.

in the story of Pamina's father. The magic flute differs from other well-known symbols of this treasure in that not only was something brought out of the realm of the Feminine when it was created, but also this thing was given the power to make music. The silence of the night and the unconscious, the dark realm of feelings, finds a voice of its own in the magic flute, the symbol of music. Those beloved of the Feminine, the Queen of the Night, are the poets and singers, the musicians of the heart, who not only bring the silence of the feminine darkness to the light of rational recognition and illumination but also let it resound and make music.

In the initiation ritual of *The Magic Flute* the devaluation of the Feminine leads the Queen of the Night actually to become the embodiment of evil through the arrogant assertion of her will-to-power. And while it is true that Sarastro's patriarchal male fellowship with its glorification of virtue and friendship remains associated with the sun and its victory, the virtue that he proclaims is expressed more in the tasks and trials that he sets than in the assistance needed to accomplish and endure them. This assistance comes to the lovers from the magic flute, which combines in itself the Masculine and the Feminine. Thus music—the art in which the depths of the unconscious reach their most mysterious fusion with form through the spirit—becomes a symbol of grace. And in the words of the lovers, "We wander by sweet music's might / With gladness through death's dismal night," the music of the magic flute becomes the highest revelation of the union of Masculine and Feminine, under the sign of a wisdom of the heart that points toward the mystery of Isis and Osiris.

IV

THE MEANING OF THE EARTH
ARCHETYPE FOR MODERN TIMES

I

When we talk about an archetype, we should remember in the first place that we are undertaking what is virtually an impossible task. The fact is that we cannot make any statement about archetypes except from the standpoint of our conscious minds, which are subject to certain inherent limitations. Paradoxically, however, the archetype is a power whose intrinsic reality functions beyond the scope of our conscious minds and their limitations. To our conscious minds the archetypal realm appears in terms of the differentiation of groups or symbolic opposites; there is no other way in which we can describe and understand the forms in which it appears to us. At the same time, however, this experience is continually pointing out to us that the mode and manner in which the archetypal realm becomes visible does not correspond to the essential nature of its reality, which is beyond the range of our con-

"Die Bedeutung des Erdarchetyps für die Neuzeit," *Eranos Jahrbuch 1953*. Part 1 has been translated by Eugene Rolfe (based on a draft by Madeline Lockwood, edited by Ruth Ludgate); part 2, translated by Michael Cullingworth.

scious minds and can only be grasped by means of a borderline concept that limits our experience but implies something beyond. It is in terms of opposites and of the multiplicity of qualities that we experience what really exists "in itself" in the form of a unity of opposites beyond all qualities. That is why, when we are talking about one archetype, we are constantly compelled to refer to another archetype, which from our point of view constitutes its opposite; and it is only by making a serious attempt not to lose sight of the unitary nature of the archetype as it exists beyond the differentiation of our conscious minds that we can hope to include our own unitary nature, i.e., the totality of our psyche, within the compass of our enquiry.

It follows that when we speak of the Earth archetype we are always inevitably also referring to the archetype of Heaven and the relationship between the two. Here again, it is our differentiating the conscious mind that first dissolves the uroboric unity of the closely entwined original World Parents, who in the myth are enclosed in the round of the Calabash. It is the intervention of the son-like conscious mind that first separates Heaven from earth, and it is only after we ourselves have taken in hand this separation of what is above from what is below that the coordination is valid, in accordance with which Heaven is connected archetypally with the symbolism of what is above, light, bright, masculine, and active, and Earth, with what is below, heavy, dark, feminine, and passive.

It is only gradually that it dawns upon us that a large number of the ideas that we use to comprehend the world when we are thinking are only the abstract extrapolation of images, whose archetypal nature makes what is by no means self-evident and obvious to ourselves seem to be so.

Thus, for humanity as a whole, to some extent right up to the present day, the symbols grouped around the Earth archetype include not only what is below, dark, feminine, and passive, but also what is of this world, corporeal, tangible, material, and static, while the opposite symbolism of Heaven is connected with what is otherworldly, incorporeal, intangible, spiritual, and dynamic.

When we come to consider the meaning of the Earth archetype and the changes in the meaning of that archetype, we are constantly confronted by the inner congruence of these symbols and concepts that are deeply rooted in the human psyche, and at the same time we have to come to terms with the contradictions between the symbolic groups of Heaven and Earth, Spirit and Nature. The fact is that, with the aid of these opposites in the primordial symbols of the psyche and the concepts derived from them, our conscious minds achieve knowledge that still does not give us any indication to what extent this archetypally conditioned knowledge is adequate to the reality that we experience. This doubt becomes still more serious and disquieting when we see that the history of the development of consciousness is repeatedly marked by a change in the meaning and—what amounts to the same thing—a change in our evaluation of what these symbols represent.

At first sight, our disquiet may seem ridiculous, since to scientifically educated Western man, experience in terms of symbols and archetypal images ostensibly belongs to what, for him, is a long outdated atavism. But even if the modern scientist no longer orientates himself by symbolic categories of Earth and Heaven, can our modern consciousness dispense with concepts such as Nature and Spirit, static and dynamic? And are not these, in the final analysis, only abstracted from the opposite archetypal images of Earth and Heaven? For the depth psychologist, for whom archetypal experience is valid human experience, this problem arises precisely because the discrepancy between the conscious mind's experience of opposites and multiplicity and the unitary reality of the archetypal is one of the almost insoluble problems of the epistemology of human consciousness.

When we speak of the projective character of an archetypal image, we mean that this image is related to the psychic wholeness of the individual, the group or the time that is experiencing in terms of this archetypal image. In this sense the meaning of the image is relative to the psyche in which it appears. This in no way contradicts the fact that the archetype as such always also represents an "objective" truth; that is, it also represents a fragment of the real world. The archetype belongs as much to the experiencing psyche as to the world of reality that is to be experienced; otherwise, orientation by means of it would not be, everywhere and at all times, a redeeming factor; on the contrary, it would plunge us into chaos. Validity and relativity are not mutually exclusive terms. However, as the archetype only leads to knowledge within its relationship to the psyche in which it appears, archetypal experience is always only the individual's own unique experience.

The position of the Earth archetype as an expression of man's relation to the earth is naturally, in the final analysis, an expression of his relationship to his Earth and his

Heaven. We must also understand as an archetypal projection a theological, astrological, scientific, or any other image of the Cosmos that gives us information about mankind, and moreover about what Earth and Heaven effectively mean to man. Only very late, if at all, in the history of mankind, has a world become visible that is no longer overlaid by archetypal projections of the images of the psyche.

During the Middle Ages, the Christian patriarchal image of the Earth was unambiguously negative, while the positive archetype of Heaven was dominant. This means that the Earth, as the dark and feminine, was regarded as the coarse, sensual, tangible, material, this-worldly, and evil body that is a prison and a peril, to be associated with the lowest level of the world, with night and with hell. So far as this world of Earth is experienced as "animated," it is contrasted with and opposed to Heaven, and is only animated as the World of Devil, who is, of course, "the Lord of this World." The link with Earth and everything connected with it, both archetypally and symbolically, is the bond with the seductive spirit whose demonic hostile power as expressed in Nature and this world, as woman and the body, as instinct and joy in the splendor of this world, has to be overcome for the sake of the salvation of the soul. For only the fallen and inferior part of this soul belongs to the world of the Earth; its true essence is the "spirit" and originates from the masculine Heavenly side of "God," or of the Upper World. The medieval conception of human nature in terms of opposites is certainly derived from the images of the Old Testament Creation, from the Heavenly spiritual breath of God into the body of Adam formed out of the earth *Adamah*, but the conception still currently in Judaism of the purity of Created Nature has been reversed in this case. The earthly side has to be sacrificed for the sake of Heaven, because "human" Earth is from the beginning fallen and corrupted Earth. And Earth, the Earth Serpent, Woman and the instinctual world, as represented by sexuality, are evil, seductive, and accursed, and Man, who in virtue of his essential nature really belongs to Heaven, is the one who is only seduced and deceived.

This interpretation of the Old Testament Creation story then becomes the basis for the self-negation of man, which arouses in ourselves not only astonishment but almost horror, in which human nature as earthy, and the earthy, and with it the feminine, are calumniated as being repulsive and poisonously evil.

Perhaps the crassest words are those of Pope Innocent III, in "De contemptu mundi" (On the contempt of this world), where he clearly states about mankind:[1]

> *Formatus de spurcissimo spermate, conceptus in pruritu carnis, sanguine menstruo nutritus, qui fertur esse tam detestabilis et immundus, ut ex ejus contactu frudes non germinent, arescant arbusta . . . et si canes inde comederint, in rabiem efferantur.* — (Formed from filthiest sperm, conceived in the prurience of the flesh, nourished by menstrual blood, which is said to be so loathsome and filthy that after contact with it, the fruits of the fields no longer germinate, the orchards wither . . . and dogs, if they eat of it, become rabid.)

1. According to Johan Huizinga, *Herbst des Mittelalters* (tr. T. Wolff-Mönckeberg, Leipzig, 1931), p. 318. [The English version, *The Waning of the Middle Ages* (London, 1924), omits this passage, though Huizinga presents similar material in chapter 11, "The Vision of Death."]

Examples from Christian, Jewish, Mohammedan, and Indian sources, i.e., from old "pneumatically" patriarchal authorities, with their emphasis on Spirit and Heaven, can be multiplied *ad libitum*, as you are aware. Everywhere an archetypally identical group of symbols has gathered around the center of Heaven or Earth, and the carriers of the projection of this negative symbolism, for example women, suffer the same negative fate. For since body, Nature, and the world belong to the sphere of what is merely earthly and illusory, it is always the task of the heavenly Spirit, especially, of course, that which is alive in man, to withdraw ascetically from the perilous embrace of Earth.

Devaluation of the Earth, hostility towards the Earth, fear of the Earth: these are all from the psychological point of view the expression of a weak patriarchal consciousness that knows no other way to help itself than to withdraw violently from the fascinating and overwhelming domain of the Earthly. For we know that the archetypal projection of the Masculine experiences, not without justice, the Earth as the unconscious-making, instinct-entangling, and therefore dangerous Feminine. At the same time the projection of the masculine anima[2] is mingled with the living image of the Earth archetype in the unconscious of man; and the more one-sidedly masculine man's conscious mind is the more primitive, unreliable, and therefore dangerous his anima will be. However, the Earth archetype, in compensation to the divinity of the archetype of Heaven and the Father, that determined the consciousness of medieval man, is fused together with the archaic image of the Mother Goddess.

2. Jung, "The Relations."

Yet in its struggle against this Mother Goddess, the conscious mind, in its historical development, has had great difficulty in asserting itself so as to reach its—patriarchal—independence.[3] The insecurity of this conscious mind—and we have profound experience of how insecure the position of the conscious mind still is in modern man—is always bound up with fear of the unconscious, and no well-meaning theory "against fear" will be able to rid the world of this deeply rooted anxiety, which at different times has been projected on different objects. Whether this anxiety expresses itself in a religious form as the medieval fear of demons or witches, or politically as the modern fear of war with the State beyond the Iron Curtain, in every case we are dealing with a projection, though at the same time the anxiety is justified. In reality, our small ego-consciousness is justifiably afraid of the superior power of the collective forces, both without and within.

In the history of the development of the conscious mind, for reasons which we cannot pursue here, the archetype of the Masculine Heaven is connected positively with the conscious mind, and the collective powers that threaten and devour the conscious mind both from without and within, are regarded as Feminine. A negative evaluation of the Earth archetype is therefore necessary and inevitable for a masculine, patriarchal conscious mind that is still weak. But this validity only applies in relation to a specific type of conscious mind; it alters as the integration of the human personality advances, and the conscious mind is strengthened and extended. A one-sided conscious mind, such as prevailed in the medieval

3. Neumann, *Origins and History*.

patriarchal order, is certainly radical, even fanatical, but in a psychological sense it is by no means strong. As a result of the one-sidedness of the conscious mind, the human personality becomes involved in an equally one-sided opposition to its own unconscious, so that actually a split occurs. Even if, for example, the Masculine principle identifies itself with the world of Heaven, and projects the evil world of Earth outwards on the alien Feminine principle, both worlds are still parts of the personality, and the repressing masculine spiritual world of Heaven and of the values of the conscious mind is continually undermined and threatened by the repressed but constantly attacking opposite side. That is why the religious fanaticism of the representatives of the patriarchal World of Heaven reached its climax in the Inquisition and the witch trials, at the very moment when the influence of the archetype of Heaven, which had ruled the Middle Ages and the previous period, began to wane, and the opposite image of the Feminine Earth archetype began to emerge.

We have already referred elsewhere[4] to this process, which started about the time of the Renaissance and began to make its way in all departments of Western culture at about the same time. The work of Bosch, like that of his contemporary, Leonardo da Vinci, is typical of this development, although in a totally opposite sense. Bosch looks backwards, molded by the values and anti-values of the Middle Ages, flooded and possessed by the negative and demonic powers of the Earth. His desperate flight through this world, and out of this world, is the flight of

4. Neumann, "Art and Time," in *Art and the Creative Unconscious*, (Essays, vol. 1).

the Prodigal Son, who, like the Gnostic son of the king, has forsaken his father's house, and now wanders homeless and astray through a demonic and evil foreign land. For Bosch, as for the early Christian fathers, "Earth" and "World" are still symbols of the moral "remoteness of God," and it is still true that "the Devil is neck and crop stuck fast in the Earth," and he, like the Earth, is dominated by the "Christian doctrine of the Unholy Spirit," which is the "Spirit of the Earth," the "Prince of this World," who must be driven out by the Holy Spirit.[5]

And yet the overwhelming power and deadly peril of this demonic earthly dimension is so great and almost irresistible, precisely because for Bosch this world is adorned with all the colors of earthly beauty that in this list first enchanted the eye and heart not of medieval, but of Renaissance and modern man.

In contrast to Bosch, Leonardo's anticipatory and forward-looking artistic and scientific work is an expression not only of the beauty of this earth, but also of its new spirit. For him, the liberation and spiritualization of the Earth archetype also liberates the feminine principle, which now, like the Earth itself,[6] reveals its creative and psychospiritual countenance to him. For the new emphasis on the Earth archetype also corresponds to a new "downward" movement, but by no means only that. When Leonardo notes: "You must point out in your treatise that the Earth is a star like the Moon, and thus prove

5. Hugo Rahner, "Earth Spirit and Divine Spirit in Patristic Theology" (orig. 1945), in *Spirit and Nature* (PEY 1).

6. Neumann, "Leonardo da Vinci and the Mother Archetype," in *Art and the Creative Unconscious*. (Essays, vol. 1).

the nobility of our world,"[7] he is specifically concerned to liberate the Earth from its sub-lunar station, where it occupied the lowest and most contemptible place in the hierarchical arrangement of the late classical, early Christian and medieval picture of the world, and was the sewer for the refuse of the rest of the world, and to find it a new place as a star among stars in an infinite cosmos of shining heavenly bodies.

Before the Renaissance, the Earth stood "outside" at the center of the world, and religious events encompassed it, so that the world closed around the Earth like a sphere. This almost hybrid central position of the Earth was balanced by the depreciation of the Earth and of man, who as fallen represented at the same time the "worthless" element in this world system. But with the Copernican turning point at the Renaissance, the Earth fell out from its central position in the world. The closed globe of the world burst open, and the Earth and its inhabitants— as seen from outside—became a whirling particle of dust within an immense cosmic space, which, open and circling in a prodigious dynamic, released an infinite number of worlds, emerging and passing away in unimaginable ranges of time and space.

Yet the psychic compensation to the Copernican turning point, with its outward dethronement of man, was not only the reinforcement of the Earth archetype, but also a corresponding reinforcement of the significance of ego-consciousness and the individual as a "Child of the Earth." These interrelated phenomena are evident in ev-

7. MS. F, fol. 56r, in *Leonardo da Vinci, der Denker, Forscher, und Poet*, ed. Marie Herzfeld, (4th ed., Jena, 1926), p. 59.

ery department of culture, in social events as well as in art, in religion and philosophy, as much as in the developing sciences.

The dominance of the archetype of Heaven and the devaluation of man as a creature fallen with the Earth implies the non-reality of the human standpoint per se, but at the same time the incapacitation of his ego-consciousness and of his individual experience. Revelation and the tradition of revelation were the sole sources of truth; in scholasticism, the principle of deduction was largely dominant, which even in epistemology took the upper world, Heaven, and the idea as its starting point since this was regarded as the sole certainty and looked down to the reality of Earth, if at all, only with a certain lack of respect. The fact that man "fallen," irrevocably "fallen," stood at the center of the pre-modern world-picture involved such a potent theological undermining of man's self-esteem that this terrible shock could only be compensated by some supra-personal act of grace. There is a psychological vicious circle here. The more such an insecure human consciousness is imbued with fear, the more man experiences the jeopardy of his position, and is brought to an ever-renewed confirmation of his "fallen state."

A turning point came with the Renaissance, when man first found himself in a changed world, but in the context of this change, and going beyond it, achieved a completely new and changed experience of himself. Experiment, which was the beginning of modern scientific thought, in which the world was discovered to be a naturally ordered world and was no longer thought of in theological and hierarchical terms, appeared in Leonardo

da Vinci—one of the first pioneers, though by no means
the only one—as the expression of the coming of age of
human consciousness. Leonardo's indefatigable curiosity,
alertness, and reverence, which extended to every department of Nature, like the wanderlust of the more recent
Paracelsus, are an expression of man's new discovery of
his presence on an earth that was still an unknown and
enigmatic homeland. The discovery of unknown conti-
nents at this time was an outward indication of the same
need in man no longer to devalue and misunderstand
Earth as an accursed footstool of Heaven, nor himself as
primordial man fallen like the angels and expelled from
the heavenly paradise. Freed from its curse, the Earth
becomes a star among stars, it becomes nature, a world
awaiting discovery, and appears in all the richness of a
living creature, which is no longer in opposition to a
hostile Spirit-Heaven of the deity, but in which the divine
essence actually manifests itself.

Here again, it was the unique Leonardo whose intuitive vision included what was emerging as a new creation and realm from the unconscious of Western man, in
the archetypal image of the Mother and Sophia.[8] What
he created in his art he also discovered as the basis for his
work in science—the earth, that is as Mother Nature,
who does not abandon man,[9] and "does not break her
laws,"[10] and in whom "the wise source of the law lives
and is poured out in full measure."[11] What C. G. Jung
said of Paracelsus, that scientist who was to such a large

8. Neumann, *Art and the Creative Unconscious.*
9. MS. A, fol. 77r, in Herzfeld, p. 63.
10. R 3, MS. W, AN IV, fol. 163r, in Herzfeld, p. 3.
11. MS. C., fol. 23r, in Herzfeld, p. 12.

extent in the grip of magic, that the authenticity of one's own experience of nature against the authority of tradition was a basic theme of Paracelsian thinking,[12] is true to an even greater extent of Leonardo. The fact that the entire epoch of the Renaissance, Humanism, and the Reformation was occupied with the authenticity of man and hence of human consciousness, is perhaps most beautifully illustrated by the speech of Pico della Mirandola that is appropriately entitled *De hominis dignitate*,[13] "On the Dignity of Man":

> At the end of the seven days of creation, God created man, in order that he might observe the laws of the universe, love its beauty, and admire its greatness. He did not bind him to any fixed place, any specific action, any rigid necessities, but he gave him flexibility and free will. The Creator told Adam: "I have placed you in the centre of the world so that you may look around you more easily and see everything that is therein. I have created you as a being who is neither heavenly nor earthly, neither mortal nor immortal, so that you may be your own free sculptor and the conqueror of your destiny. You can degenerate into an animal, or be reborn as a godlike being. The animals bring forth straight from the womb all that they need to have, but the higher spirits are from the beginning, or become soon afterwards, what they will remain for all eternity. You alone have a development and a growth in accordance

12. Jung, "Paracelsus as a Spiritual Phenomenon," CW 13, par. 149.
13. Jakob Burckhardt, *The Culture of the Renaissance in Italy*, tr. S.G.C. Middlemore (Oxford, 1945), IV, 8, End.

with free will. You have the seeds of an inward life within you."

It is only when one becomes aware of the contradiction between these words and those of Innocent III, that one can comprehend what the liberation from the burden of his guilt and the reconquest of his dignity means for modern man.

However, man's coming of age involves mainly, in the first place, the coming of age of his consciousness; and, as is demonstrated by the evolution of the West, this means predominantly the development of an extroverted consciousness which is turned towards the world. In contrast to the medieval dominance of introversion, which had projected the inner Heaven and the inner hierarchy of images in the form of cosmological order, there now emerges an extraversion that is related to the objective physical world and a function of sensation that records the data of the world by a process of observation and registration. This comment should not be misunderstood. Its one-sided typology is only an attempt to illustrate the case in terms of an extreme position. Just as in the Middle Ages, extroverted people were also creative, so, too, people with an introverted attitude are also contributing to our modern development. But just as in the Middle Ages, the extroverts also played their part in developing the inner world-picture of Christianity, so, too, at the beginning of the modern era introverts have made their contribution to the new experience of the external world. Thus the direction of introverted philosophy, for example in the theory of knowledge, has retained its orientation towards the natural sciences up to the present day—that is, in the final analysis, towards the extraversion of the Western spirit which began with the Renaissance. It was not until the last century that a countermovement set in, which culminated in depth psychology, with an orientation of a very different kind.

There has certainly been a liberation of human consciousness through the decline in the dominance of the archetype of Heaven as the true backbone of western patriarchal culture and the rise of the image of the Earth Mother in opposition to it, but at the same time this has led to an exceedingly grave danger. The man with a Western type of consciousness experiences himself as a "Son of the Earth," and to a great extent orientates himself to this image and bases himself upon it. At the same time, however, modern man has lost something which pre-classical and medieval man possessed, namely an orientation to the spirit.

One of the difficulties in what I am attempting today arises from the fact that we are constantly confronted by archetypal images and the ideas relating to them, which cannot be explained "as we go along." For example, it would be impossible for me to define what is meant here by "Spirit." But those of you who know the relevant Eranos volumes, and Jung's writings on the subject, will have some idea of what it is all about. Nevertheless I will make an attempt to explain the essential point in a few sentences.

The archetype of Heaven is closely connected with the symbolism of the Spirit, in fact it seems at first as though Heaven and the Spirit are archetypally identical terms. This identity is reinforced by the formation of opposites within the archetypal symbolism to which we referred at the beginning of this talk. If everything that moves invisibly from above is symbolically connected with Heaven and everything that resists visibly from below is symbolically connected with Earth, and these things are actually experienced in that way, then there is no positive "Spirit" left over for Earth. And what is nevertheless experienced as "Earth Spirit" in contrast to "Air Spirit" is dismissed as negative by the representatives of the "Spirit of Heaven." It is no accident that the witches of the Middle Ages are also representatives of a Spirit, and in fact their "flying" is a symbolic expression for this; but their spiritual Lord is the Devil.

We shall see later to what extent this conception is objectively justified. Even in the unconscious of modern man, this Earth Spirit is connected with a symbolism that often coincides with the symbolism attributed to the Devil in the Middle Ages. Here again, we have to understand that interpretations that turn out to be false and dangerous at a later stage of development are psychologically necessary at an earlier stage. For example, even for our modern consciousness, the symbolism of the Devil as the Spirit of Earth still retains its validity, but our evaluation is now different and in fact almost antithetical to that of the Middle Ages.

As we have already emphasized, since the Renaissance ego-consciousness has played an increasingly potent role in the development of the consciousness of Western man, while the Spirit of Heaven and the Air has played a more and more insignificant part. We cannot pursue this process now, and I personally would be quite unable to delineate this whole process of evolution, for example in the light of the development of science and philosophy.

But it may perhaps suffice to indicate that the spirit, which from now on will be sought and found, is a spirit of earth and humanity, not a spirit of Heaven and theology, and this quite irrespective of whether our point of view is of the idealistic or the materialistic variety. Even if an idealist wishes to pursue a spiritual plan of development, he will take the materials that he uses to illustrate his thesis from earth by human reality, not from the data of a revelation or from a heavenly spirit handed down by traditions. When we understand the fundamental meaning of this phenomenon, the apparently opposite conceptions and interpretations approach one another very closely, much more closely, in any case, than appears to the representatives of the opposing varieties of idealist or materialist interpretation. Whether they interpret a cultural phenomenon in extraverted sociological or introverted psychological terms, whether they derive it from outer transpersonal conditions of the collective or from inner transpersonal conditions of the collective—i.e., from the collective unconscious—the common ground that remains in spite of all the contradictions of the opposites is that in every case the starting point is the earthly realities of the human constellation. The standpoint of modern man is above all clearly and exclusively determined by this relationship to the actual given reality, that is, to the earth.

Man, as a creature on the earth, humanity in all its diversity, and in all the diversity of its cultures, is alike everywhere determined by the diversity of the earthly environments to which man is adapting—it is always a question of the history of this humanity on earth. If, one hundred and fifty years ago, Greece represented almost the beginning and the Persians already the barbarian frontier of history, and the Bible was celebrated as a primordial glimpse of humanity's earliest revelation, since that time the history of humanity has been pushed back, not by thousands but by hundreds of thousands and even millions of years and more. The earth, which, according to Judaic chronology, was created by God five thousands years ago, has an antiquity, by our reckoning, of the order of thirty thousand million years; the prehistory of man goes back one million years, and that of living creatures, with all of whom we are all connected by history and evolution, can be traced back some twenty thousand million years. Thus we ourselves are connected and infinitely entangled with this earth in a way that we still cannot realize even now. History and archeology, anthropology and ethnology, biology and zoology, and preceding them chemistry and physics, all this is the history of the earth, all this is "we ourselves"; it is the root-stock from which we stem.

The Earth archetype, which emerged during the Renaissance and with difficulty shook off the chains with which it had been banished into Hell by a hostile Heaven, today fills all our horizons. There is nothing beyond it, and the Earth, which above all means deliverance and liberation for Heaven-enslaved man, now itself represents a danger in the immense superiority of its powers.

Just as, before the Renaissance, man had been overwhelmed by Heaven, so now in modern times he is being overwhelmed by the Earth. The embracing Mother has become the devouring Mother, and the descent of man into the underworld of the Earth archetype, though necessary, is still no less dangerous than his earlier alienation from the Earth by Heaven.

It is not easy to describe the psychological "earthing" of modern man, since it is not a question of his having become "materialistic" in the primitive sense of the word, although to a great extent this has actually been the case, and is in fact an integral part of the symbol of his earthing. What is more vital is the drowning of human consciousness in facts and data—the way it is being overwhelmed and inundated by facts in innumerable areas that an individual consciousness cannot possibly coordinate within a unitary scheme, still less assimilate. The situation familiar to us all in which reality has been split up into innumerable disciplines and specializations has led to a state of affairs in which modern man no longer has a unified picture of the world,[14] but contents himself and apparently must content himself with a strange conglomerate of fragments of old philosophies, new insights, unverified conceptions, etc. The immense range of facts discovered, to which every decade and every year adds unforeseen and revolutionary innovations, nowhere allows a comprehensive orientation to appear possible, particularly if every individual is obliged to accept in good faith everything that does not take place in the tiny sector that falls within the range of his own experience.

The orientation of the meaning of the whole has been lost to such an extent that today it is already almost for-

14. The numerous programmatic schemes in which an attempt is made to produce such a picture of the world only demonstrate, by their contradictory nature, that such a uniform picture of the world exists nowhere, except in dictatorships.

bidden to pose the problem of meaning at all; it is the question. There is no religion and no philosophy that can give us a comprehensive answer to the whole of our problems, and the abandonment and isolation of the individual who is given no answer, or only inadequate answers, to his question lead to a situation in which more and more cheap, obvious solutions and answers are sought and provided. As, everywhere and in all departments of life, there are contradictory schools and parties, and an equal number of contradictory answers, one of the most frequent reactions is that modern man ceases to ask questions and takes refuge in a conception that considers only the most obvious, superficial aspects, and becomes skeptical, nihilistic, and egocentric. Or, alternatively, he tries to solve all his problems by plunging headlong into a collective situation and a collective conviction, and seeks to redeem himself in this way.

Evasions of this sort become easier as mankind is more and more reduced to the level of the mass. In conjunction with the growing millions of the human population of the earth, the reduction of the community to the level of the mass does constitute a new factor. Only when mankind succeeds in developing the intelligence and personality hidden in these millions can it also succeed in overcoming the downward trend that automatically accompanies the statistical increase of the mass, and results in a lowering of human standards. All these phenomena together are an expression of what we have defined as the "earthing" of modern man. The individual experiences himself as small and ultimately inferior in the face of an earthly reality that overwhelms and annihilates him in its infinite multiplicity and diversity. His horizon cannot encompass the range and variety of that which always proves to be new and different from the "earth" on which he lives. This horizon, which constricts the individual as a particle of the mass, is supplemented by a collective orientation from above, which reduces and is itself reduced to the level of the mass; what is "above" is in this case not only dictators and dictatorial states, but also the press, radio, films, advertising, etc., irrespective of the source from which these media are directed.

However, if we pronounce "from above" with the distinctness that the sense requires, we may be seized with sudden dread. "Above"—it looks as though this is what we have exchanged for "Heaven," which certainly violated medieval man, but at the same time did give him light. It cannot be denied that in spite of all the further development of Western consciousness in modern times, the overwhelmingly superior power of the earth has almost devoured us. And when we see collective man deprived of spirit and degraded—everywhere, not just on the other side of the river—then we understand the fact that and the reason why the Great Mother was always experienced in mythology as also the devouring and castrating terrible Mother.

Of course, there have been not only individual protestors in the West, but also ideological countermovements, which have tried to halt this "earthing" process. However, they have all been inevitably unsuccessful, as this "earthing," and even the downfall of modern man in and on the earth is an inevitable and irreversible process.

Initially, this situation does not become conscious in the collective, but in the individual, where all future collective problems first announce their presence and compel recognition. In this context we can abbreviate, since we are dealing with a development to which attention has often been drawn, particularly by analytical psychology. The radical turning of consciousness towards the so-called objective external world has led to a progressive splitting off of the conscious mind from the world of the subject, the "Inner World," which has culminated in the isolation of the individual, and the individual and collective neuroticization of modern man. The counter-movement, which began last century, reached its climax in the emergence of modern depth psychology, leading from Freud and Adler to Jung, with its inner way. Here the first rediscovery was what we might describe as an "inner Earth side" of modern man.

Up to now, our approach has been cultural and psychological; it could rely on the evidence of the whole course of culture in modern times. In what follows we shall also try to work out the cultural and psychological aspect, but from now on we shall depend to a large extent upon the manifestations of individuals. This means that from now on our attempt to examine the significance of the Earth archetype will no longer be able to supply us with any evidence about the collective destiny of modern man. But this in no way implies that our findings about the individual may not provide us with indications for the future of the collective; perhaps indeed they are bound to do so.

When the Earth archetype of the Great Mother appears again in the unconscious of the individual, appearing "again" implies that it had emerged before in the history of mankind, for example in mythology and religion. The mythological images of the Great Mother are manifold; manifold too are the stages of the revelation of her being, but the most widespread and well-known form of her manifestation, the form that fundamentally defines her essence, is that of the Earth Mother.

As the Good and Terrible Mother, she shows what we call her elemental character, in which she appears positively as the child-bearing and protectively containing Mother, and negatively as the possessive, imprisoning, depriving, and devouring Mother. This phenomenology takes place in her as the earth and fertility goddess, who determines the elemental life of early man, and of ourselves, insofar as we are natural creatures conditioned by nourishment and in reproduction subject to the meaning of the species. In her elemental character, the Great Earth Mother rules over the collective life of the species, and all individual life is adapted and subordinated to it.

If we turn briefly to the group of symbols which characterizes this Earth Mother archetype in contrast to the archetype of Heaven, we observe with some surprise that in her manifestations the dark side clearly seems to predominate. Only when we grasp the nature of this "darkness" from a psychological point of view can we comprehend the significance of this archetype for the history of mankind and understand why the phenomenon of fear is bound up with it, and finally recognize what it means when we are told that the situation of modern man is constellated by his "earthing" and by "the descent on to and into the Earth."

The purely mythological aspect of the Earth archetype seems at first to be simple and obvious. The earth is the Dark Mother, her womb brings forth all living things, plants, animals, and man, but in her capacity as the Terrible Mother, the Great Mother devours everything that is born, and swallows it back pitilessly into herself. Her womb of death is a devouring maw of darkness, and as the grave, the flesh-devouring sarcophagus, hell and the underworld, she is the inside of the earth, the dark abyss of everything living. That is why, as the Dark One, she is the Goddess of Night who is worshipped and satiated nightly, underground, in caves, with the blood of her victims. But she is not only, as an abyss, the devouring hole of death, she is also savage and greedy as child-bearer and slayer. The symbol of this greed is once again blood, which fertilizes her, with which she gives nourishment, and from which she feeds the life to be born. That is why the earth must be satiated with offerings of living blood. The earth demands blood, and as the drinker of blood, she is the mistress not only of death but of killing in her capacity as the goddess of war and the chase. The instincts of aggression and sexuality, love and the longing for death, are all bound up with one another in her in primordial proximity. The fruitfulness of the living is based not only on the dark instinctuality that drives living creatures to sex, but all life in the realm of the animal world is directed towards nourishment by the devouring and overpowering of prey; i.e., even here, it is again bound up with the shedding of blood and therefore with death.

But why is the Great Earth Mother of Night not only the Terrible Mother of Night of the grave and death, but also at the same time the Mother of Initiation? *Inire* (to go "into") in the sense of initiation means originally, it appears, to go into the earth, and the place of this initiation was the cave, the uterus of the Great Mother, this primordial image of the holy place, the temple, and the house.

At the center of every initiation, whose ultimate creative significance is not our concern in this context, there is always the deadly peril represented by the Terrible Mother. She is the devouring West, the place of death on the hero's path, which is an essential part of every initiation. The confusion of the labyrinth, the devouring monster, the dragon of chaos, death, the underworld, and hell, are only some of the unpropitious symbols that express the darkness of the terrible primordial Feminine. And gathered around this central place of evil fortune are the alluring, captivating, deceiving, misleading, destructively demonic powers, which appear always differently and in new forms as animals, monsters, sorceresses and witches, fairies and pixies, etc., and are the expression of the deadly peril that menaces the candidate for initiation, the hero. But this entire world of uncanny animation belongs to the earth, however strange and improbable it may appear to us at first. The horror of the Christian hell is only a later offshoot of this archetypal situation, in which mankind has animated the earth everywhere with the deadly monstrosities of its fear and its terror. But this animated earth is always an inner world, and the inner world of this humanity has populated with its own inner animation the hollow of the cavern which is hell. Today we call this process the projection of the unconscious, and the dark Earth Mother appears as the unity of the dark life-bearing womb in the psyche of mankind, which as material *uroboros* and as *prima materia* is and brings forth the animated chaos in which living creatures devour and generate each other.

It is the world of affect, of instincts and emotions, the exuberant energy of the chaotic, the demonic, and the evil in the depths and the shallows of humanity, which seems to be released here. He who has been seized with horror at the bloodstained history of mankind, in which races and peoples, nations and tribes, cities and villages struggle to combat and exterminate each other, may be overcome by a still worse horror if he visualizes the world of gods and demons that this humanity has adopted as the highest governing authorities of its existence. And even if a supposedly cultivated humanity populates the world of heaven with less horrible powers, then the face of the repressed opposite side of the world is no less distorted than the world of the Christian hell, which represents the evil side of the earth, sufficiently betrays.

Why must the candidate for initiation descend into this fearful world, and why can there never, at any time or in any place, be anything heroic and enlightened in humanity without a battle and without a fateful immersion in this dark womb of death in the underworld?

One explanation, which remains on the mythological level of projection, is obvious and simple. According to this, it is because of the victory, because of the conquest of evil, which is represented by the Terrible Mother and all the negative symbolic figures assembled around her. The hero must dare the descent into the peril of the dragon in order to prove himself stronger than the apparently overwhelming power of the fearful darkness. Elsewhere we have tried to describe what this means psychologically.[15] If we say in the language of clichés that the hero always represents consciousness and the Terrible Mother the unconscious, that does grasp the basic schema of the situa-

15. *Origins and History*.

tion. But that is all, and it is now our task to fill in this schema psychologically as far as possible.

Why is the "Earth" the dominant symbol of the unconscious? After all, we know that fire, water, and countless other things are also basic symbols of this perilous unconscious! What does the "victory" of the hero mean here, and how, finally, is this constellation connected with the situation of modern man and what we have called his "earthing"?

Here we encounter the obvious but significant phenomenon that in the symbolism of the unconscious, the earth, irrespective of any cosmological theory about it and irrespective too of the forms that man ascribes to it, always occupies a dominant place. What appears here as earth has nothing to do with whether man regards it as part of the so-called "exterior" world, as flat or a cube, a sphere, or an egg. In the symbolism of the unconscious the earth is the uterus of all that originates from her, and is alive in the fantasy of man, that is, in his unconscious. In this symbolism the earth does not count as one element, which occupies as it were a fourth place alongside fire, water, and air, but represents the whole, as in the reality of our symbolic language, when we talk of "our" earth. Fire lives within the earth, water springs from it, and the ocean of air flows around it. Here we reach the basic matriarchal conception of the unconscious, a view of the world according to which the earth is the Great Mother, in opposition to the patriarchal masculine principle. Such a matriarchal symbolism may, indeed must, have in it something dangerously heretical and heathen, for a patriarchal world, particularly when we remember what the accursed earth meant as the quintessence of evil for the patriarchal world that was dominated by Heaven.

So long as the hero could be interpreted patriarchally in the sense that he has to conquer the matriarchal world of darkness and evil, everything is in order. It is true that within this order an irreconcilable split prevails between the higher Masculine good world of Heaven and consciousness and the lower Feminine evil earth, which represents the unconscious. The world and humanity are torn asunder into an upper and a lower part, and there can be no reconciliation between them.

To identify oneself with the upper, heavenly spirit part means to experience oneself as not-earthly and absolute, as though one "genuinely" were pure spirit. Man has fallen into lower matter and is imprisoned in it as in something not genuine, but this earthliness remains "foreign to his nature" and "wholly other," it is evil and accursed even though one suffers from it, and against the intentions of Heaven participates in it. This position becomes extremely clear in the world-picture of Gnosis, but actually it is operative in all radially patriarchal conceptions. The fact that this "evil earth" has been created and exists remains inevitably an insoluble problem for this way of thinking, as is proved over and over again by discussions about the "origin of evil." But if we consider seriously the emergence of the Earth archetype and the transformation of Western man, as we must because it concerns our own destiny and the future of modern man, then we have to admit that an element is announcing its arrival and gaining acceptance here, which we have to experience, consider, and understand in such a way as befits a numinous event. This means that we must relate to it in the "religious" sense, which Jung has summarized as the "careful and scrupulous observation of the numinosum."[16]

But then, no more has been done for modern man in regard to "conquering" the matriarchal world of evil. We are forced to come to terms with this world in a profounder and more perilous way. Undeniably a volcanic fire-spirit, who can also be characterized as the Devil, lives at the center of the emerging earth. He lives as an emotionally explosive element as much in the nucleus of man's psychic earth as in the nucleus of matter itself, and within and without we are caught up in a confrontation with this earth side whose fateful character is absolutely clear. Every patriarchal world is based on banishing back into the primordial maternal womb of the underworld this titanic element, which is always regarded mythologically as the eldest son of the primeval Earth Mother. Hence this patriarchal world takes pride in depicting itself as placing its foot on the head of the conquered dragon of the depths.

The emergence of this Luciferian dragon element with its hostility to Heaven is bound up with the emergence of the Earth archetype; and as the patriarchal means of grace, by whose aid we could identify ourselves with the heavenly side, is no longer at our disposal, we are obliged for better or worse to reach a compromise with this devil side, or rather with this side which up to now has been regarded by us as the Devil. As a result a strange transformation of values gradually becomes clearer and

16. Jung, "Psychology and Religion," CW 11, par. 6.

clearer, according to which the true goal seems to be not the conquest of evil but its redemption, not a patriarchal victory, but a transformation of the lower worlds.

This is made most beautifully clear in a heretical cabbalistic myth of the seventeenth century that has been reported to us by Professor Scholem. It is to be found in the book of Zwi Nathan of Gaza, disciple of Sabbatai, and is characteristically entitled "Treatise on the Dragons." I quote from Scholem's account with some minor omissions:

> At the beginning of the cosmic process En Sof drew back his light into himself, and the primordial space emerged in the centre of En Sof, in which all worlds are born. This primordial space is full of formless hylic powers, the so-called "shells of power." The world process consists of shaping these formless powers by making something out of them. Until that has happened, the primordial space, particularly its lower part, is the bastion of darkness and evil. It is the depth of the great abyss in which the demonic forces have their dwelling. When after the "shattering of the vessels," some sparks of the divine light which radiated out from En Sof fell into the abyss, to create shape and form in the primordial space, the soul of the Messiah also fell which had been embedded in the original divine light. From the beginning of creation, this soul lingered in the depths of the great abyss, in the imprisonment of the shells of power, the kingdom of darkness. Together with this most holy soul at the bottom of the abyss, the serpents have their dwellings; they torment it

and try to seduce it. The "holy serpent," the Messiah, is delivered up to these serpents (does not the Hebraic word for serpent have the same numerical value as the word Messiah?). To the extent that the process of Tikkun, the restoration of all worlds, the separation of good and evil is accomplished in the depths of the primordial space, so the Messiah is freed from its chains. When the process of perfection is completed on which this soul works in its imprisonment, and for which it battles with the serpents or dragons (admittedly, this will not take place till the final completion of the restoration), then the Messiah will leave his prison and reveal himself to the world in an earthly incarnation.

It is a matter of the greatest interest [and I quote still from Scholem] that we encounter the ancient Gnostic myth of the destiny of the soul of the Redeemer in the writings of a young man in the Jerusalem ghetto in the seventeenth century. If we did not actually find the raw material of this doctrine in the Zohar and the writings of Lurjah we might have been tempted to adopt a fundamental, though for us dark, connection between this early Sabbataian myth and the myth of the ancient Gnostic school of the Ophites or Naassenes, who put the mystical symbolism of the serpent at the centre of their Gnosis.[17]

The archetypal image of the redeemer serpent is certainly placed here in opposition to the serpents of evil that battle with it. But why do they both have the same form if

17. Gershom Scholem, *Major Trends in Jewish Mysticism* (New York, 1946), p. 297.

there is only opposition between them? What does it mean that they both dwell in the same place, the depth of the great abyss? Are they not possibly two aspects of the same thing?

We know this image of the redeemer serpent not only from Gnosis and from the Sabbataian myth, but we know of the same serpent rising from below, redeeming and to be redeemed, as the Kundalini serpent in India, and finally from alchemy as the *serpens Mercurii*, the ambiguous serpent whose significance was first made clear to us by Jung's researches.[18]

Since Jung's work on alchemy we know two things. The first is that in its "magnum opus" alchemy dealt with a redemption of matter itself. The second is that *pari passu* with this redemption of matter, a redemption of the individual psyche was not only unconsciously carried out but was also consciously intended. As we know, the serpent is a primeval symbol of the Spirit, as primeval and ambiguous as the Spirit itself. The emergence of the Earth archetype of the Great Mother brings with it the emergence of her companion, the Great Serpent. And, strangely enough, it seems as though modern man is confronted with a curious task, a task which is essentially connected with what mankind, rightly or wrongly, has feared most, namely the Devil.

What has to be redeemed from the hell of Earth and matter, as also from the hell of the human psyche, where redemption is synonymous with transformation, seems to be nothing more or less than "the Spirit of the Earth."

18. Jung, *Psychology and Alchemy*, CW 12, and "The Spirit Mercurius," CW 13.

2

The descent into the darkness of the earth, which stands at the center of every initiation, is enacted in modern man, collectively and individually, as an encounter with the underworld: an encounter that fulfils the human psyche. Certainly there have at all times been invasions and eruptions of the unconscious that in spiritual epidemics such as religions, religious wars, national wars, revolutions, racial, class, and religious persecutions have turned men into monsters. The countless millions of human sacrifices made by the religions, whether directly on their altars as blood offerings or indirectly in wars for the true God, the true faith, the true doctrine—these mountains of corpses are no lower than those sacrificed by races, nations, states, and parties in order to extend a frontier or to secure a position of power or an outlet for their goods.

In this sense the outer situation of modern man does not seem to be much different from what it ever was. The variation provided by a nuclear war threatening a humanity numbered in billions is no more significant, maybe, than the use of iron for killing was for hundreds of thousands, or that of gunpowder for millions. Nevertheless, we maintain that the inner configuration of modern man is different and fundamentally new. But strangely enough this state of affairs, pregnant as it is with the future, results from a loss that may herald a demise as much as a new beginning.

Until now, murderous humanity, given over to its own unconscious, has always had excuses and sacred justifications. It was precisely not its own unconscious to which this humanity was surrendered or to which it surrendered itself whenever it murdered, waged war, burned, tortured, and slaughtered. On the contrary, it was the gods—indeed, Almighty God himself—who demanded these actions. It was a question of the highest values, and the wars that were waged were in every case holy wars.

It is true that we still use the old words, values, and banners as camouflage, but these symbols have become threadbare to us in the sense that it is hard for us not to regard their use as deception and to see through it. Whoever rejects this pious camouflage, considers these deeds to be human deeds, and maybe would even like to prevent such "holy" events: this person is no longer seen as a freethinker, a skeptic, or a heretic. We know about hidden motives, self-deceptive illusions, and aggressive instincts in ourselves. If we consider all this to be evil, we no longer hold the gods responsible for what has happened but understand the shadow and the murderous instinct in ourselves as driving forces.

Even if the individual repeatedly succumbs to infection by the collective sickness, he knows, insofar as he is an individual (and everyone is one at least once), about human guilt and about the earthbound roots of events, roots which penetrate into his own innermost depths. We recognize this driving force in ourselves as something overwhelming, against whose collective power we still know no remedy, but at least we are beginning to experience it as a genuine sickness, a genuine horror, and no longer dignify it with the name "holy sickness" as we have until now.

However, the transformation of the situation and the heroic path of modern man, who is no longer willing to repress and suppress this knowledge of his evil, is now the task of individuals. Since collective insight inevitably lags far and dangerously behind that of the individual, the burden is born by individuals who dare to make the descent into the heart of darkness and who are not spared the initiation into the dark earth of the human psyche.

The Earth and the Underworld seen as a descent but also as a process of transformation not only corresponds to the experience of many individuals in the process of individuation, but it can also be demonstrated to be a collective event in modern culture as a whole. The analysis of this state of affairs falls outside the scope of our present consideration and has already been partially accomplished elsewhere. The task that remains for us is to investigate whether and how a change is arrived at in the meaning of the Earth archetype in the individual's experience of depth, and what the implications of this are.[19]

Submission to and acceptance of the darkness, the shadow, the negative aspects of the anima and animus, the affective and instinctual side of human nature, and assimilation of the unconscious in the sense of an integration of the personality: these, as you know, are some of

19. An attempt to reach a statement that is valid not just for the individual is therefore difficult, because the individual's experience is determined by his personal equation. The significance of the Earth archetype for an introverted intuitive, who by nature is relatively remote from the earth, is completely different from what it is, for example, for an extraverted sensation type who, as the typical representative of our time, is completely governed and grounded in this Earth archetype. However, in spite of all individual variations, the collective determination of the era is so great that it draws all types in the same direction—albeit in different ways. For this reason, the attempt to reach a statement that has a certain comprehensive validity is not in principle impossible.

the most significant phrases that characterize the decisive beginning of the psychic development of modern man. But even these days the alchemical sentence still stands as a motto over this process of transformation: "*visitetis interiora terrae*," "visit the inner parts of the earth." We are all still "descenders" if we venture into the unconscious, which for that very reason is also topographically designated "under"-conscious; we set out from the head, from the outer layer of consciousness, and descend into the "deeper" layers of our psyche and of our symbolic body, and in so doing the symbol of depth, still valid today, is derived from the archetype of Earth, gorge and "depths of the abyss."

As in religious history, the archetypal inhabitant of these female depths is the snake. Just as in Crete and in Greece and with Nathan of Gaza, so even today we are still met there by the snake of the abyss, the Devil, who is at the same time the snake of Mercurius, the spiritual principle that animates the depths, the "Earth Spirit." Seeing this masculine snake-companion of the Great Mother in a phallic sense as a symbol of sexuality corresponds to one of the infinite possibilities and realities of interpretation. On the highest level we are often obliged to interpret it in this way, but never only as such. Even Hermes, the guide of the soul, who is the same god as the alchemists' Mercurius, has a phallic, snake aspect. But whoever mistakes the snake for the penis and the gorge for the female genitals—and without question it is an issue of the earth's womb—offends against the lower as well as against the higher gods by restricting their field of effectiveness and transformation.

Having to descend into the earth really means to fall

into hell, and many dreams, images, and fantasies of modern man show the witch-like character of the earth and the devilish nature of its spirit who dismembers, boils, roasts, tortures, and torments those who become his prey. Leaping into the hell of one's passions and into the emotional side of the underlying nature of humanity is truly a fate that makes plain once and for all to everyone who has experienced it why it is that man's anxiety over consciousness has done everything to denigrate this earth aspect, to warn against it, and to brand it as "the quintessence of danger."

There is only one answer to the question why for God's—or for three devil's—sake modern man nevertheless exposes himself to this horrifying danger, namely that it is no longer possible for contemporary man to avoid it. It is not an arbitrary action, even in the case where it is to a certain extent performed voluntarily, that is to say consciously, but it is in every case recognized, or again, unrecognized destiny. Whoever refuses to accept consciously the problem of the earth that burns in us and of the *deus absconditus* that burns in it, ends up in the same abyss through the collective "earthing" of modern man. It is just that he plunges as a lamb in the flock or as wolf in the pack into the precipitous slide towards collective human catastrophe that characterizes our age. Externally, internally, or both: at all events, no modern man has a happy island of security, a medieval, infantile, or idealistic paradise. The fire that has taken hold of modern man gnaws at him, whether he knows it or not, in atomic explosions, wars, or gas chambers, in crises, neuroses, or psychoses. It grips him in modern art, and in social life it encroaches on him from all directions; there is no way out.

But whoever experiences this terrible character of the psyche as his inner Earth, as the primordial mother of all that is living in him, also experiences change and transformation. Boiling in the retort of one's own captivity in oneself leads to a breakthrough in which the containing mother as well as he who is imprisoned in her is fundamentally altered. With this one arrives at what could be called the initiation into the matriarchal mysterium, in which the earth reveals, beyond her elementary maternal character, her nature as Great Transformer. Now the Earth Mother reveals herself to be the Great Creatrix who, as Nut of Egypt, is also the dark firmament of infinity in which she, as the full moon, lightens her own darkness and in the morning gives birth to the sun and the day. For the Great Transformer is also the source of light and as exalted mother also encompasses the heavens, exactly as Rilke formulates it in an early letter: "But every earth which lives radiates its own heaven and casts starry nights far out into eternity."[20]

At this point I would like to quote a short passage from the active imagination of a patient, in which the phenomenon that I am concerned with here is possibly, clarified. The goddess with the ear of corn, the primordial symbol of the Mother Goddess, appeared to the patient, in his fantasy, by night on a tower, and without his knowing what it meant, she handed over the ear to him. The text then continues:

> the heavens were extinguished as if at a stroke and, looking down from the tower, I suddenly saw the

20. Letter to Lou Andreas-Salomé, 8 Aug. 1903, in *Letters of Rainer Maria Rilke*, tr. Jane Bannard Greene and M. D. Herder Norton, vol. 1 (New York, 1947-1948).

stars in the depths of the earth rising up—an astounding and overwhelming impression. Slowly the earth adorned itself with all the constellations of heaven and the canopy of stars became the earth's robe. But that is not right, since the constellations did not shine on but in the earth at different depths. Just as heaven bore them at different depths, so now did the earth. And she lay radiant before me, not inert mass but enlivened, animated, thoroughly spiritualized essence, pregnant with stars.

As the Great Creatrix, the feminine is no vessel and passage for an alien, masculine Other that condescends towards her, enters into her, and favors her with the seed of living. Life originates in *her* and issues from *her*, and the light that appears projected on the night sky, which she is herself, is rooted in her depths. For she is not only the *protomantis*, the first and great Prophetess, but also she who gives birth to the Spirit-Light, which, like consciousness and the illumination that arises in transformation, is rooted in her creative efficacy. She is the creative Earth, which not only brings forth and swallows life, but as that which transforms also lets the dead thing be resurrected and leads the lower to the higher. All developments and transformations that lead from the simple and insignificant through all gradations of life to the complicated and intricately differentiated fall under her sovereignty. This matriarchal world is geocentric; the stars and signs of the zodiac are the heavenly girdle of the Earth Goddess and are arranged around her as the true center around which everything revolves.

What appears symbolic here and almost mythological

still impresses, we maintain, the being of modern man and our own insight so much that we must at least try to elucidate this phenomenon. It is not difficult for us to comprehend the negative character of the Earth Mother psychologically: it is all too clear that, and how much, the affective and instinctual side of the unconscious is bound up with her image. We have also learned to understand that this Earth archetype of the Great Mother is the birth-place of consciousness: both the history of the origins of consciousness and the daily problems of bringing to consciousness and losing from consciousness have enlightened us on the dependence of consciousness on the unconscious.

But in the image of the constellations in the earth very many more and different things are indicated.

After I had delivered the first part of this lecture in Tel Aviv and before the second part, that is before the motif of the stars in the earth had emerged at all, I was informed by a woman from the audience of the following dream which had been dreamed after the first lecture.

In the depths of the earth. In a domed building, immeasurable, so huge, the orderly layers are set in arches one over the other. On these arches scattered sources of light shine which, although they seem small individually, are so powerful in relation to the vault that they allow the vault to be perceived in the darkness. I myself am enclosed by it all, I am a piece of earth. At the same time watching, but like the interior, dark and light. I say: just as glow-worms have an interior light, so the darkness illuminates itself.

205

This vision is one of many that point in the same direction. It is a question of the same scintillae, sparks in the earth, which, as Jung pointed out,[21] were comparable with the archetypes in the work of the alchemist Khunrath and with the "inner firmament of Paracelsus. That is to say, the contemporary vision relates to the same archetypal phenomenon of "the light in the darkness," of which Jung speaks when he writes about "The Unconscious as a Multiple Consciousness." It is an issue of the recognition of an inner light in the unconscious that becomes distinct in the course of the process of psychic transformation and leads to illumination of the individuality by the *lumen naturæ*. But this *lumen naturæ* must be conceived on a much wider scale than it was, for instance, in Paracelsus, so that we can do justice to all the contents and concepts that appear in modern man along with this transformation in the manifestations of the Earth archetype.

In "On the Nature of the Psyche," Jung has indicated the relationships between inner light, *lumen naturæ,* world-soul, *anima mundi*, and the "Holy Ghost," and he writes: "The world-soul is a natural force which is responsible for all the phenomena of life and the psyche."[22] In the course of time, the emphasis is shifting ever more strongly and decisively onto the autonomy of this natural force. In Paracelsus, the light that appeared in the "inner experience" stands in conflict with the light of the divine

21. Jung, "On the Nature of the Psyche," CW 8, par. 388. [Revised and expanded from "The Spirit of Psychology" = "Der Geist der Psychologie," *EJ 1946*.]
22. Ibid., par. 393.

revelation[23]—a conflict that he himself did not penetrate. In the development of modern man, however, the divine light of revelation has become ever weaker and the earthly light of human experience ever stronger. Modern man's outlook has withdrawn from a heaven that no longer casts light on him and has returned to earth and to himself, and precisely because of this light that shines from below out of darkness and depth is becoming more and more valuable and significant to him. If we now consider the emerging, numinous images with the appropriate religious care, this light is a female light from the earth, a light of Sophia. But this light of Sophia is identical with a newly emerging "Spirit of the Earth."

As C. G. Jung's numerous works on alchemy[24] have demonstrated, the alchemical movement—for a development that has lasted two thousand years must be given this name—represents a subterranean spiritual current in which the Earth archetype began to emerge and to assert itself in a compensatory manner. However, what Jung designates as the "projection of the psychic onto matter," as he himself stressed more than once, is not just the intuition of the transformational contents of the human psyche, but also those of the "world-soul," of the *anima mundi.* That is to say, the process of development (the purport of these experiences) extends beyond the human into the cosmic. Knowledge of the micro/macrocosm equation, of the correspondence of human wholeness with that of the extra-human, leads to a new con-

23. "Paracelsus as a Spiritual Phenomenon," CW 13.
24. *Psychology and Alchemy*, CW 12, and "The Spirit Mercurius," CW 13, et al.

sciousness, in which a new, total man-world continuum becomes visible.

The earth that suffered the Fall together with man is experienced as a world that has remained unconscious along with unconscious humanity, that is to say, unre-deemed. Mankind which was created unconscious is, however, "guiltless-guilty." In an interpretation of the world that is in part similar to Gnosticism, man's devel-opmental path begins with the appearance of the snake, the "cleverest animal," that is, of the instinct for con-sciousness, which leads to and entices one towards knowledge of the principle of contradiction, of good and evil. Through man this is also the developmental path of the world towards a higher, conscious, and no longer merely instinctive knowledge.

According to tradition, the dangerous aspect of this snake-spirit of the earth is still frequently experienced by modern man in the form of the "Devil." As an example, I would like to introduce the dream of a modern woman, though without going into its meaning, that is to say, without discussing at this point the meaning of the epiph-any of the Devil for modern woman or of the "Christian" symbolism for modern Jewish woman:

A symmetrically built, strong, sinewy, tall, and slen-der masculine figure appears before me. He is wear-ing a tightly-fitting, black silk body-stocking from which appear to stand out alternating panels of large black and small white rhomboidal rectangles made of shiny satin. Small rectangles of harsh, dirty red and acid green and yellow are scattered among them and diagonal to their line. I walk quite close up to the lithe figure, which is coming silently towards me. From a distance his costume seemed just like a black and white domino. Not until I am quite close do I see the small colored rectangles that are sprinkled in between. I look solemnly and calmly into the clever, narrow, pale face with thin lips and sharp, narrow nose. Piercing, cold, sparkling, green-black eyes look at me. I meet the gimlet glance. But these contemptuously cold eyes do not allow my glance to enter, they reflect it like gleaming glass. He is much taller than I am, so I have to look up at him. My eye level is at the height of his chest. And suddenly I see that in place of the heart there is a hollow space, which is lined with poisonous green, shiny silk. It is filled with a thick grey mist. From the heartless space, this mist rises in a pillar behind the figure, upwards to infinity. When I look carefully, I notice a continuous changing of the colors. The black rectangles change into white and the white into black and only the lurid, multicolored, small rectangles constantly retain their murky colors; they only gleam with true luster for seconds. The perfectly formed, powerfully lithe legs are relaxed and slightly spread out; between them a long, smooth monkey's tail becomes visible, which moves constantly, gently swinging to and fro. The hard, black tail ends in a thin point on the end of which there is a dully shining, round ball, which seems as if it is made of granite. Now I know that the sad, ambiguous figure, continually changing from black to white, is the Devil. I am not at all afraid, only amazed at the sadness that covers the hybrid figure. Whenever the large rhomboids are white, an all-penetrating sorrow emanates from their glittering luster, like an incomprehensible, unavoidable and increasing torment. I ask myself whether he is really so very much more ambivalent than unambiguously evil. It is a long time before I perceive a tall female figure standing behind him, completely in the shadows: the mourning Mother of Christ (from Eugène Carrière's "Christ on the Cross"). But she is not mourning for her son, who is not there, but for the Devil and I hear her faint, tormented words: "He too is my son"—everything in me resists this image. I do not want to write it down, but it won't let me go to sleep again—until I write it down. Then there is peace. I wanted to resist by force acknowledgment of Christ's substitution by the Devil, but the image was irresistible.

The Mary of this dream is thoroughly earthly—as the dreamer's association of it with a modern painting demonstrates—but the archetypal phenomenon of her two sons, Christ and the Devil, to whose archetypal kinship as brothers Jung has repeatedly referred,[25] indicates the archetypal nature of Mary as well. The dual aspect—Christ the wholesome snake and the Devil, the poisonous snake—corresponds to the dual character of the mercurial snake. This ambivalent character of the snake of the Earth Spirit belongs to the essence of the Earth archetype itself.

I must excuse myself in advance for being able to

25. "A Psychological Approach to the Dogma of the Trinity," CW 11.

indicate only through hints what this new aspect of the Earth archetype might possibly signify. Since we are all caught up in this process of manifestation, we cannot say anything conclusive about it. But on the other hand, a fresh attempt at orientation must always be risked— however premature it may be—for only in this way can that which, among the contents of the unconscious, wishes to make itself intelligible to us be brought into discussion.

I would like to pursue the problem of the "Spirit of the Earth" as a Sophia spirit in two directions and to try to translate into our conceptual language what is initially encountered in mythological images. One indication is related to the "external knowledge," with which we were occupied last year in this same place.[26] It seems that at deeper levels of that which we call the psyche, or even better at a level at which the splitting of psyche and world, earth and heaven, into opposites is no longer or not yet effective, knowledge is to be found of the total reality of the world. This reality has a spiritual and orderly character that goes to the very essence of the archetype, and which on the one hand determines our being and the being of that which appears to us as "World" and, on the other hand, appears as imagery to our psyche. But a spiritual and orderly character means that the world seems to derive its actual organization from this Spirit and does not just seem to us to be organized "in spirit." This spiritual and orderly reality of the archetypal, which at one time we had designated as archetypal field and the

26. I.e., in the author's lecture at the 1952 Eranos conference: "The Psyche and the Transformation of the Reality Planes," in *The Place of Creation* (Essays, vol. 3).

field of the Self that governs this, is nevertheless our real world. This total world, which transcends us at both ends of our being, as psyche and as external world, is neither inside nor outside but everywhere. We are so completely embedded in it that we can only grasp it at all as the determining reality in unusual situations. Generally, however, humanity experiences it on the one hand as archetypal world, that is, as the imaginal world of gods, demons, and archetypes, but also, on the other hand, as "concrete thing," as external, material world.

Here we come to the other indication of what "Earth Spirit" means and this is connected as closely as possible with what has just been said, but is probably easier to understand. Here the issue is that we are only capable of having experience with the help of the psyche. This psyche has its effect and appears in archetypes, that is, in natural symbols, which determine our consciousness and our overall conception of the world.[27]

However, the natural symbol, without our being sufficiently conscious of the fact, is identical with the reality of the world that appears to us, for every object in the natural world is at the same time a symbolic reality to us. The psyche certainly does not use an "object" of nature as a "symbol," but rather the experience of an "object" itself is always already symbolic experience. The star or tree in us is no less real and no less symbolic than it is in outward

27. In his *Philosophy of Symbolic Forms*, E. Cassirer has described the emergence of consciousness from the world of symbols. A depth-psychological treatment of this theme without question would, in a certain sense, have had to go further than his findings—and deeper; it would, nevertheless, have to refer to him in many respects. (See above, essay 2, n. 23.)

experience. For each possibility of experience either presupposes a spiritually forming, that is to say a symbolic
activity, or is identical with this. That is, everything spiritual appears to us first not just in nature but as nature; or
we could formulate this just as well the other way around:
everything natural, whether outward or inward, appears
to us as an image, that is to say as formed spirit. We are
surrounded by images, inwardly and outwardly, but at
the same time formed and determined in all our experiences by the natural symbol as though by a unitary
natural-spiritual reality, for our psychic system only
grasps that which appears to us as the real world through
the world of natural symbolism.

The conceptual world of science is a world of abstraction. In reality, however, it too is only a distillation of
what is primordially given in the natural symbol. What
we encounter in science at the one end, so to speak,
externally as an object, we encounter at the other end,
inwardly in the psyche, as the numinous. Even here, any
statement about the numinous, if it wants to eschew the
natural symbolism in which it is primarily rooted, is a
desperate attempt to abstract, that is, an ultimately vain
effort to escape from myth and symbol. For at the moment when living experience occurs, it is an experience of
the formative psyche.[28]

For this reason, the image as a natural symbol always
refers to an "object" of nature that was worshipped as
numinous, be it mineral, vegetable, or animal, water or
lightning, sun or moon, or something comprehensive

28. Neumann, "The Mythical World and the Individual," tr. R. T.
Jacobson, *Quadrant* 14 (fall 1981). [Orig., *EJ 1949*, and in U. d. M.,
vol. 1.]

such as heaven or earth. The spiritual and symbolic is identical with all this that is given in nature. But this elemental correlation, which as a correspondence between above and below and as the signature of things played a significant role both in antiquity and in medieval thought, becomes a decisive experience only for modern man. Everything that we experience from the image in perception to the inner image, from visible chair to vision of the divine, is forming and formed spirit-psyche. In this sense, if we analyze our experience, there is no matter that stands opposed to spirit and that is free of or alien to the spirit. In their being in and as themselves, just as in their being-for-us, the inorganic and the organic, the ostensibly dead things of physics, just as much as the sensuous, mental unity of the organic and the psychic, are a unity in which the physical spirit is at once visible and invisible.

Humanity is approaching total reality from different directions. Scientifically, it tries to find the laws of the spirit "in" matter—but are the force fields and planes of that which man has called matter spirit or nature? Is the mathematical formula adequate or inadequate? And is not only the unity of what appears as real with what is mathematically conceived the true "spiritual nature" in entirely the sense that Goethe said, "Whoever deals with the Spirit must presuppose nature and whoever speaks of nature must presuppose the Spirit or else silently imply them"?[29] An approach to the unified world of the real is believed not only in science, but just as much in the worship of it as numinosum in religion, in the configura-

---

29. As cited by Paul Schmitt, "Natur und Geist in Goethes Verhältnis zu den Naturwissenschaften," *EJ 1946*.

tions of art, and most of all in the unconscious association of every person with the mundane world itself, with its phenomena and with its things.

If we are enveloped in images, we are also enveloped in forms, in spirit, which is nature, and in nature, which is spirit. Daily and continually we associate with this unified world of nature and spirit without knowing it. But only the person to whom this association has become clear understands what is meant when we talk of Sophia as a heightened and spiritualized earth. But this formulation is already distorted as well. The earth has not changed at all, it is neither heightened and spiritualized: it remains what is always was. Only the person who experiences this Earth Spirit has transformed himself, he alone is changed by it and has, perhaps, been heightened and spiritualized. However, he too remains what he always was and has only become, along with the earth, more transparent to himself in his own total reality.

Here also we must differentiate between the reality of our total existence and the differentiating formulations of our consciousness. Certainly, our consciousness makes the attempt to separate a spiritual from a natural world and to set them in opposition, but this mythical division and opposition of heaven and earth proves more and more impracticable. If, in the process of integration, consciousness allies itself with the contents of the unconscious and the mutual interpenetration of both systems leads to a transformation of the personality, a return to the primordial symbolism of the myth ensues. Above and below, heaven and earth, spirit and nature, are experienced again as *coniunctio*, and the calabash that contains them is the totality of reality itself.

215

Inwardly the psyche, just as outwardly as physis, the reality of the earth, now appears to us as the *coniunctio* of the visible earth with an invisible heaven. Each natural symbol of the psyche, just as each piece of matter, is at the same time both-in-one. Except that the *coniunctio* of the first parents, unified with one another, and of the exalted uroboros will no longer be projected outside as the origin of the world. Thus the earth that is transfigured and becomes transparent is not only experienced inwardly and psychically, but just as much in the actuality of external reality. It seems to me that a significant portion of the new religiosity of modern man consists precisely in this experience of the transparence and transcendence of the earth.

Whether we understand this transparence as the this-worldliness of the beyond or as the otherworldliness of this world or as both, it comes to the same thing; but in no case is separation valid any more. The splitting of heaven from earth, spirit from nature, is resolved by a third position in which their primordial interdependence returns and is comprehended in its primordiality. But this presumes that man himself returns to this primordiality. What is described psychologically as becoming whole in the process of individuation also means this third position, in which this fundamental state of opposition transcends itself.

Man, Thing, Earth. These are the great objects through which modern man, knowingly or unknowingly, confronts himself. And this confrontation is religious precisely because it no longer, or hardly any longer, speaks of the divine. Just as *homo* and *humus*, Adam and *adamah*—that is, Man and Earth—essentially belong together, so a *humilitas*, a humility, is appropriate to this Son of the Earth. This humility belongs to the essence of his new humanity and only just allows him to make statements about the human.

I should like to try to illustrate for you the point which I have reached by two extended examples. One is a passage from Tolstoy's *War and Peace*, the other a passage from one of Rilke's late letters.

The very question that had formerly tormented him, the thing he had continually sought to find— the aim of life—no longer existed for him now. That search for the aim of life had not merely disappeared temporarily—he felt that it no longer existed for him and could not present itself again. And this very absence of an aim gave him the complete, joyous sense of freedom which constituted his happiness at this time.

. . . and suddenly in his captivity he had learned not by words or reasoning but by direct feeling what his nurse had told him long ago: that God is here and everywhere. In his captivity he had learned that in Karatáev God was greater, more infinite and unfathomable than in the Architect of the Universe recognized by the Freemasons. He felt like a man who after straining his eyes to see into the far distance finds what he sought at his very feet. All his life he had looked over the heads of the men around him, when he should have merely looked in front of him without straining his eyes.

In the past he had never been able to find that great inscrutable infinite *something*. He had only felt that it must exist somewhere and had looked for it. In everything near and comprehensible he had seen only what was limited, petty, commonplace, and senseless. He had equipped himself with a mental telescope and looked into remote space, where petty worldliness hiding itself in misty distance had seemed to him great and infinite merely because it was not clearly seen. . . . Now, however, he had learned to see the great, eternal, and infinite in everything, and therefore—to see it and enjoy its contemplation—he naturally threw away the telescope through which he had till now gazed over men's heads, and gladly regarded the ever-changing, eternally great, unfathomable, and infinite life around him. And the closer he looked the more tranquil and happy he became. That dreadful question, "What for?" which had formerly destroyed all his mental edifices, no longer existed for him.[30]

The new, which one should not misunderstand pantheistically, is contained in all parts of this quotation. Neither should one be in any doubt that what Pierre calls "God" has no longer much to do with what was called "God" up to that point and as God of the Revelation and of heaven had given his commandments to fallen man on the accursed earth. And one is perhaps not claiming too much if one suggests that the existential feeling that expresses itself through Pierre could even give up the term "God" too, as for instance in Zen, just as well as lean on this word.

<hr />

30. Tolstoy, *War and Peace*, tr. Louise and Aylmer Maude (New York, 1942), pp. 1226-27 (Book Fifteen, chap. 5).

In Rilke it sounds different, but still with the same sense, when he speaks of the earth and its transformation, in which the correlation Death-Spirit-Invisible is valid for him. Only, Rilke is much more conscious of the new thing which is at issue. In connection with the *Duino Elegies* he writes:

> *Affirmation of life-AND-death appears as one in the "Elegies."* To grant one without the other is, so it is here learned and celebrated, a limitation which in the end shuts out all that is infinite. *Death* is the *side of life* averted from us, unshone upon by us: we must try to achieve the greatest consciousness of our existence which is at home in *both unbounded realms, inexhaustibly nourished from both.* . . . The true figure of life extends through *both* spheres, the blood of the mightiest circulation flows through *both: there is neither a here nor a beyond, but the great unity* in which the beings that surpass us, the "angels," are at home. . . . Transiency everywhere plunges into a deep being. And so all the configurations of the here and now are to be used not in a time-bound way only, but, as far as we are able, to be placed in those superior significances in which we have a share. But *not in the Christian sense* (from which I am more and more passionately moving away), but, in a purely earthly, deeply earthly, blissfully earthly consciousness, we must introduce what is *here* seen and touched into the wider, into the widest orbit. Not into a beyond whose shadow darkens the earth, but into a whole, into *the whole*. Nature, the things of our intercourse and use, are provisional and perishable; but they are, as long as we are here, *our* prop-

erty and our friendship, co-knowers of our distress
and gladness, as they have already been the familiars
of our forbears. So it is important not only not to run
down and degrade all that is here, but just because of
its provisionalness, which it shares with us, these
phenomena and things should be understood and
transformed by us in a most fervent sense. Transformed? Yes, for it is our task to imprint this provi-
sional, perishable earth so deeply, so patiently and
passionately in ourselves that its reality shall arise in
us again "invisibly." *We are the bees of the invisible.*
Nous butinons éperdument le miel du visible, pour
l'accumuler dans la grande ruche d'or de l'Invisible.
. . . The earth has no way out other than to become
invisible: *in* us who with a part of our natures par-
take of the invisible, have (at least) stock in it, and
can increase our holdings in the invisible during our
sojourn here,—*in* us alone can be consummated
this intimate and lasting conversion of the visible
into an invisible no longer dependent upon being
visible and tangible, as our own destiny continually
grows at the same time MORE PRESENT AND
INVISIBLE in us. . . .

and to summarize:

We are, let it be emphasized once more, *in the sense of*
the Elegies, we are these transformers of the earth; our
entire existence, the flights and plunges of our love,
everything qualifies us for this task (beside which there
exists, essentially, no other).[31]

31. Rilke, Letter to Witold van Hulewicz, 13 Nov. 1925, in *Letters*,
vol. 2 (see above, n. 20).

The position of modern man is infinitely different from anything that the numinous of heaven above and earth beneath had ever meant to man. But what is transformation into the invisible other than transformation into spirit, into heaven, though without setting up any kind of opposition to earth. On the contrary, man, who transforms the earth and so transforms himself, becomes the point at which earth and heaven come together again; in the process, however, the transformation from below upwards gains in reality insofar as "more present" also becomes "invisible" at the same time. The weakness of the earth, and with it of man, is here precisely the decisive inception of events, for it is not the perfection of a spiritual and heavenly world, but the limitation and transience of the terrestrial that is the necessary springboard for the leap into a "deeper being."

This essentially religious attitude is free of all conventional and confessional connection. But Rilke's anti-Christian attitude should not be misunderstood as anti-religious any more than our commentary on Pierre's "naming of God." It is only a question of avoiding the conceptual language of theology, not at all of avoiding true numinous experience. Precisely because modern man experiences himself as a Son of the Earth, he instinctively or even consciously avoids the old terminologies that wrench open the opposition between heaven and earth and in so doing rob the earth of spirit. Only when one catches a glimpse of this unconscious tendency towards a new sanctification of real experience, even in the flattest of contemporary empiricism and pragmatism, can one deal with the still partially unconscious value-judgments of modern man.

For him whose unavoidable fate has been to take the passage through the Great Earth Mother and to experience her as terrifying as well as Transforming Mother of the Living, his own being as well as that of the world has become something different. The reality of life has resolved itself out of the opposition of heaven and earth and a third, mediating human element has taken its place. When we try to describe a psychic experience that is still new, we are continually compelled to cling to the old mythological images in which psychic experience takes place. And so our contemplation, which has followed the way of the matriarchal Mysterium through a necessary inner obedience, ends with the symbol that stands at the creative, dawning end of this route: the symbol of the child.

The mythical picture of the matriarchal world knows the Spirit-Progenitor as an invisible, transpersonal masculinity even when the Feminine experiences itself as a creative principle. But the exalted central position which rises above the opposition of the patriarchal and the matriarchal bias is the Divine Child, born of the Feminine.[32] In it, above and below, masculine and feminine, heaven and earth are unified into a "completely Other" and "New."

What is implied, however, by the fact that the appearance of this child in the unconscious of modern man should play such an emphatic role?[33] As you know, the

32. Jung, "The Psychology of the Child Archetype," CW 9,i.

33. The enormous expansion of interest in the psychology of the child and the proof of the fateful significance of childhood for the development of the personality are external symptoms of the appearance of this internal image.

image of the child appears frequently at the center of the mandala, and Jung formulates it as follows:

> Seen as a special instance of "the treasure hard to attain" motif, the child motif is extremely variable and assumes all manner of shapes, such as the jewel, the pearl, the flower, the chalice, the golden egg, the quaternity, the golden ball, and so on. It can be interchanged with these and similar images almost without limit.[34]

In connection with this, one aspect of the mandala must be stressed, to which not enough attention has been paid and which is of particular importance for our study.

The mandala makes use of natural symbols and is an earthly location for the manifestation of that which we designate the Self. This does not mean that the mandala is earth, but it characterizes itself as a position midway between heaven and earth, consciousness and the unconscious. It is the typical "third position" of the transcendent function,[35] in which the opposites are contained and overcome. The dominant human symbol of this earthly manifestation of the third position between masculine and feminine, however, is the child, which is of its very nature hermaphroditic.[36] It is not our task here to add anything to the incomparable presentation of the Child Archetype by Jung; we only want to try to clarify what the appearance of this archetype actually means for modern man and his experience of world and Self.

The child who has not yet had to divide his wholeness

34. "The Psychology of the Child Archetype," par. 270.
35. Jung, *Psychological Types*, CW 6, pars. 825-28.
36. "The Psychology of the Child Archetype," pars. 292-97.

lives in the still undivided world. The earthly is unearthly to him and the unearthly, earthly. He has not yet been compelled to separate and God is father to him and the father is God, the mother is the world, and world and mother are still one and the same thing to him. Here the transparence of the earthly lives in its original wholeness. Everything natural "signifies" and is symbolic, everything symbolic is experienced as nature and as everyday reality. But at the same time this child is unique and alone in his wholeness, and the unrepeatability of the creative life, which reveals the purity of the original world of wholeness in every fully comprehended moment, is precisely contained in the alertness of its being-in-the-present.

The contemporaneity of the child indicates a fulfilled world, just as the focusing only on the future, whether it be a paradise or a messianic time, is the symptom of a spirit oriented towards heaven for which the earth is incomplete and fallen. For the feeling of experiencing the unity of the visible world with the invisible but effective heaven, contemporaneity is at the same time "fullness of time." A time that does not pass in the threefold succession of past, present, and future belongs to the child as well as to the adult who is initiated into the Sophia-Earth mystery. Here a synchrony is experienced in which the past—the ancestors—and the future—the children— are alive in the immediate present, which is the meaning of the symbol. For the lived-through and experienced symbol is just as actual as it is primordial and eternally in the future. This synchrony of the felt symbol—probably best known to you from the symbols of art—is the expression of a creative and at the same time meaningful world. Since the naturally existent is inseparably tied up with the symbolically meaningful for the child, its life is fulfilled and creatively alive. For what we call the "symbolic life" by abstraction is not a complicated and late but an original form of life in this world, consistent with reality.

The world that is originally given and that remains transparent to the child is the same one that modern man reaches momentarily in the process of transformation and permanently on the highest level when, in becoming transparent himself, the transfigured earth becomes transparent as the original otherworldliness of heaven and earth. This symbolic world which belongs to the "child," which lives as symbol in the center of the mandala, is the mandala itself—the mandala as the containing Mother-Spirit, as Sophia. The Sophia-psyche, together with the child, are experiential forms of earthly life, of a life in this world. But this world as an earthly world contains in itself all the gleaming constellations of heaven in its reality. For this heaven full of stars is not a physical but a psychic place, and if it is the "heavenly location" of the archetypes, then these archetypes appear to us as all spiritual impressions of our experience in connection with our earthly givenness. Modern man is in no position to experience his heavenly world and even his infinitude except in most intimate connection with this finitude.

Being devoured by the earth as Terrible Mother and suffering from it belong to the inevitability of our existence. But if we realize this and have plunged outwardly and inwardly into an earthly abyss that seems to be a darkness without light, precisely at that moment the figure of the Earth Mother transforms itself and reveals itself as the transparent and transfigured earth, which is identical with Sophia, the bearer of light, the Spirit-psyche of the real.

The image of the virgin with the golden ear—is the golden ear of corn the heavenly aspect of the stars or the earthly aspect of the Eleusinian mysteries?—is the same image as that of Sophia and child. This Sophia-psyche as the original and as the transfigured earth, as unity of nature and spirit, is, so it seems to us, the last transformation so far of the Earth archetype in modern times. It transcends man, but nevertheless its location is in him. But with the last symbol, that of the child of Sophia, which is actually visible to us only on the edge of our horizon, if we are pursuing the transformation of the Earth archetype in modern times, that is to say in ourselves—with this image something is born, the meaning of which for modern man is not yet in sight at all, namely no more nor less than the "Holy Spirit" of the earth.

V

THE FEAR OF THE FEMININE

"Fear of the Feminine" is a topic that embraces so many phenomena in human existence that we must limit our discussion to circumscribing the range of this fear and to citing its individual manifestations as illustrative hints only. For our task is not merely to elucidate something of the origins of this fear, but, insofar as possible, also to recognize what these phenomena say about the essence of fear.

Our task grows yet more complicated since at many points it is difficult or even impossible to distinguish "fear of the Feminine" from "fear of the Masculine," which complements it. For it also holds true of fear that the conscious constellation is always compensated by an opposed constellation in the unconscious. Hence we often find an overly strong conscious bond, for example to the mother, compensated by an unconscious fear of her as "fear of the Feminine"; but it can also be accompanied by a "fear of the father," i.e., a fear of the Masculine. It seems obvious that we repeatedly come to the point where our present theme intersects the fear of the Masculine when

---

"Die Angst vor dem Weiblichen," in *Die Angst*. Translated by Boris Matthews. (See the editorial note, p. viii.)

we recall that the archetypal figure of the Great Feminine itself is "uroboric"[1] in its undifferentiated form—that is to say, the opposites are still conjoined in it, Masculine and Feminine form a still undissolved unity as the "Great Terrible Mother." Mythologically and symbolically this figure also possesses masculine features, and her attributes can even be the male genitals and the male beard.[2] For this reason those attitudes and effects that one generally ascribes to the Masculine—waging war, killing, hunting, etc.—also belong psychologically to the figure of the Great Terrible Feminine, and "male consorts" later appear beside her as bearers of these functions. Hence the "fear of the Feminine" also includes "fear of the Masculine" wherever it appears as fear of the archaic Feminine, of the "Great Mother." Only in a later, more highly differentiated phase, does the opposition between the Feminine and the Masculine develop, and then the fear of one pole comes into opposition with the fear of the opposite pole.

In another work we presented the extensive mythological and symbolic material belonging to the image of the uroboric Terrible Mother;[3] here we are concerned with the psychic reaction to this image, the fear of the Feminine, and must describe and understand the appearance of this fear in the normal as well as the abnormal development of both males and females.

1. Neumann, *Origins and History*.
2. Neumann, *The Great Mother*.
3. Ibid.

A. FEAR AND THE DEVELOPMENT OF PERSONALITY

I. The Origin of Fear

1. The Significance of the Primal Relationship to the Mother in the Development of Fear

We can grasp the essence of human fear and its genesis only if we have understood the significance and the full range of implications of the initial stage of development specific to humans, the primal relationship to the mother. The compulsion to flee—i.e., the continual readiness to flee and the state of fear underlying it—is an essential feature of the animal world.[4] Although this observation is correct, surely it does not describe the whole of animal existence in the world, an existence to a great extent "guaranteed" by its bondage to instinct. This is just the point at which psychological elucidation must commence by posing and answering a question: Is "fear" associated with the instinct to flee, and if so, to what extent? But in any case, a depiction of the animal's continual "condition of uncertainty" is eminently suited to highlight the difference between the human situation as fundamentally "human" and the existential condition of the animal.

The primal relationship with the mother, and consequently the decisive first phase of childhood and of human development, rests on a phenomenon that Portmann has described and proven as decisive for the human con-

4. H. Hediger, "Die Angst des Tieres," in the symposium *Die Angst* (see the editorial note, above).

dition.[5] The human psychobiological condition preceding all human culture is more decisive than the use of fire, humankind's first significant cultural achievement. The constellation that confronts humankind and separates us from the animal kingdom consists in this: the first year of human life is spent in the primal relationship with the mother in what might be called an "embryonic year"; i.e., only at the end of this "extrauterine embryonic year" does the human infant attain that species-specific degree of maturity that animals—even the closely related anthropoid apes—have already attained at birth. This means that the infant lives psychologically "in" the mother during its first year of life as it did physically prior to birth. It is characteristic of this specifically human constellation that interpersonal relationship—in the form of the primal relationship to the mother and, through her, to the human community and the group of which the mother is a part—is an essential codetermining psychic and cultural factor of the embryonic period in the first year of human development that overrides the biological factor.

The phenomenon of the primal relationship to the mother during the first year of life consists basically in this: even following its birth, the child lives in the mother as "something contained" and is totally dependent on the "positive elementary character" of the mother[6] as the one who provides nourishment, warmth, protection, and tenderness in all areas of its life. Only after completion of the first year does the human infant have the more or less species-specific level of development that grants it the

5. Adolf Portmann, *Zoologie und das neue Bild vom Menschen* (Basel, 1956).
6. *The Great Mother.*

relative ego-stability, freedom of movement, intelligence, etc., that make possible the independence that the animals closest to humans usually have attained at birth.

The infant's initial powerlessness and hence total dependence on the mother in the primal relationship grant her an "archetypal," transpersonal position. No matter how the infant may experience her physically, she is objectively the surrounding world in which and from which it lives. Because she regulates its physical existence, in pleasure or listlessness, pain or hunger, she is simultaneously inside and outside, even if these sorts of distinctions exist only for our consciousness and not for that of the infant. But this unity of a transpersonal structure embracing inside and outside is "archetypal," and in this sense the infant's experience of the mother is an archetypal experience, regardless how unarticulated and unconscious that experience may be. This means that the mother of the primal relationship, as the one who encompasses, contains, and directs life, is at the same time both *world* and *Self* in one.

However, what determines the relationship of the small, dependent creature—the child—to the great life-giver—the mother—is the fundamental situation of security and absence of fear as the foundation of the infant's existence. This means that the infant's security—but also its absence of fear—is part of the actual basis of human existence. Spitz points out that the normal infant who has experienced no birth trauma and who sleeps quietly after birth immediately shows a strong fear reaction if one suddenly removes the support on which it rests.[7]

7. René Spitz, *The First Year of Life* (see above, essay 2, n. 6).

If we are to understand the human condition and its symbols, it is important to see that each life situation is symbolic and that every symbol "represents" a life situation. Whenever we talk about the basis, the foundation, the underpinnings of a situation, we not only employ an "imaginal" symbolic expression but also the unconscious insight into the psychic significance of an actual, existing situation. Just as the actual removal of the mattress triggers fear in the infant, the loss of anything we may designate symbolically as the "basis" also produces fear. The mother of the primal relationship is the basis, the fundament, and the foundation of an infant's existence; it exists bonded with her in security and the absence of fear insofar as its existence is natural. But this means that for the human child and consequently for the human ego, the normal, primal situation of security is one guaranteed by the mother—i.e., by a feminine quality—characterized by the primal relationship to the Feminine.

The fact that the life of the small child in the first phase of development is determined by the mother means that this first phase is typically matriarchal. It is ruled by the mother archetype, and each personal mother fulfills her function as a typical human mother by giving her child security and love, nourishment, warmth and protection, and, as the containing world, makes possible her child's postpartum embryonic development. Each instance of "too much" or "too little" that transgresses the limits of the "species-specific" amount has a negative effect on the child.

The starting point for the child's development is its existence in the psychic unity with the mother who, as world and as Self, continues to carry the newborn child

232

"in herself," as it were, and permits it to develop. This phase of *participation mystique* between mother and child is the breeding ground for the incipient ego development in the child who, as it grows, advances toward experiencing the polar position of reality. Normally the child's fundamental experience is that of protection and security as a small creature in a togetherness with the sheltering Great Mother upon whom it is completely dependent. But as the ego develops, the child begins to sense the opposite, negative position contained in the fundamental experience. Wherever there have been security and togetherness, now insecurity and aloneness are also present, just as satiety and satisfaction alternate with hunger and need, and tenderness and warmth with abandonment and coldness. As with every transition in psychic development, this experience of the opposites is related to the formation of normal anxiety. But so long as the child lives in the primal relationship of the matriarchal phase, its anxiety is always quickly dissipated by the mother's intervention. It is just this maternal regulation of the child's life, a regulation residing in the mother and not in the child itself, that allows us to say that, for this phase, the mother represents the child's Self. As in every exigency, the child alerts the mother whenever anxiety arises, and normally she intervenes immediately in order to dissolve the child's anxiety by regulating the situation to redissolve it in the protectedness of the mother-child unity.

Here we have to make an important reservation about the child's development and the development of its fear. Even when the personal mother plays her role perfectly and with total dedication, she may not be able to give the dependent child all the protection and security it needs.

Although the mother is everything for the small child, its "world," she herself as an individual human being is an integral part of her group, her times, and her destiny. If the mother is filled with fear and anxiety owing to hunger, war, illness, and persecution, or for other reasons, often she may be unable to take away the anxiety and fear of the child that flees to her in its total dependency.

The same thing happens when the child suffers abnormally, i.e., above the typically average level, caused by factors of constitution or fate—for example, illness and pain. In these instances the personal mother "fails" in terms of the child's demands for security in the primal relationship. Although personally she is without fault, the child necessarily experiences her as the negative, "terrible" mother who provides no security.

Because the small child lives in an archetypal rather than a personal world in the pre-ego and early-ego stages of development, it has no possibility of understanding that the personal mother is blameless; rather, it experiences its exposure and vulnerability to the negative world as if to the "negative mother." Since the mother is still archetypally "world," the "negative world" is experienced just like the "negative mother," as well as the other way around when the mother herself is a "negative mother," i.e., when a negative primal relationship has been constellated and the child experiences the positive world as "negative." The child experiences the mother as the surrounding and containing world in whom inside and outside are indistinguishably united. The child "expects" her to allay every dissatisfaction and fear but is unable to distinguish whether the dissatisfaction and fear arise from a slamming door or exploding bombs, from natural hunger preceding the next feeding, or hunger brought on by famine, or hunger because it is ill and cannot assimilate food. In each case, it directs its demand for removal of the fear to the mother, and when the fear is not removed, the mother is perceived as the "terrible" mother who refuses.

The same also holds true for the fear that arises from the child's unconscious, for in this phase it cannot distinguish what is "outside" world and what is "inside" unconscious; both are contained in the *Gestalt* of the mother as Thou and as Not-I that approach the child. But we will not delve deeper into these "atypical" constellations here. They are deviations from the norm, for "on the average" —i.e., normally—the mother is capable of taking away the child's fear. Later we will again speak of fear as one phenomenon of an infantile, "pathological" development in connection with the mother-complex. But our present concern is with normal human development and the role that fear of the Feminine plays in it.

The organic development of the individual is guaranteed by suprapersonal organ systems that are switched on and off independently of the individual's ego and consciousness and ensure and "force" the stages of maturation. Because development is transpersonal and species-specific, we say, for example, that puberty or the climacteric is "premature" or "delayed," or that an individual is "too young" or "too old" for his age. Although the way in which the stages of development are experienced and expressed varies from culture to culture—for example, how a youth or an old man is supposed to act—the basic phenomenon of transformation from one stage of life to another is independent of culture.

Transformation of this sort is always biopsychical, that is, simultaneously physical and psychic; and like physical development and maturation, psychic development is also directed by species-specific transpersonal dominants that we call archetypes. Hence in normal development, the first stage, called matriarchal and governed by the mother archetype, is followed by the patriarchal stage in which the father archetype is dominant. The term "patriarchal stage" signifies that the child has now reached a level in the development of ego and of consciousness in which an increasing importance is given to will, activity, learning, and values, and to integrating the child into the traditional cultural canon of its group, as transmitted by the world of men. By nature each newborn child is "omnipotent," i.e., it is capable of learning any language and adapting to any group in any nation or race. Normally the child can appropriate each cultural canon and that canon's values as its own, i.e., it can become a warrior in a warrior nation, a peasant in an agricultural nation, and a learner in an intellectual nation. While the child is "nature" and develops as nature in the matriarchal phase, its task in the patriarchal phase is to achieve integration into the community of its particular group and their cultural values, and to adapt its individuality to the demands of the particular collective, with or without sacrifice.

This development is already underway in the "matriarchal" phase, since, of course, developmental phases overlap. Just as we summarily refer to that period as puberty when the transition from child to adult is in flux, all other phases of psychological development are also continual, in which, at times slowly and unobtrusively, at other times suddenly, the effects of one constellation—

e.g., the mother archetype—are replaced by the workings of another—e.g., the father archetype.

By the end of the first year of life, if not before, the ego-germ of the child begins to prepare for its subsequent autonomy. Initially this development, too, is sheltered by the mother, who supports and furthers the child's growing independence just as she does its learning to walk and to talk. While the first postnatal, embryonic year still stands under the sign of the unconscious unity of mother and child in the primal relationship in which the mother is simultaneously world and Self, the "migration" (as we have called it elsewhere) of the Self from mother to child gradually begins. With this second birth at the end of the first year of life and "postnatal embryonic period," the ego-development and increasing independence of the child's personality become evident.

The "heroic" character of ego-development, demonstrable in all phases, is perhaps most striking here at the beginning.[8] Because any new development is connected with giving up security, with risking and taking danger and suffering upon oneself, it requires a "heroic" ego. The child's growing independence and its exodus from the matriarchal phase dominated by the mother stands under the sign of the loss of security, of separation from the protection that the mother has promised and given so abundantly and for so long. Behind the outcome of this conflict between the tendency to remain in the security of the primal relationship with the personal mother and the necessity to develop out of this security, we also recognize a transpersonal, archetypal, guiding power. Without the

8. *Origins and History.*

separation that leads away from the mother, the child will not develop into an adult. That is why something in the child itself—the archetype of wholeness, the Self—urges this forward movement and, if necessary, accomplishes it with relentless power.

This central factor—the Self, which determines all human development, not only that of the child—may be clearly seen in a symbolic picture brought by an analysand at the beginning of his development. In this picture the analysand's ego stood at the lowest step of a pyramid. At the apex, however, towered the figure of a crowned elephant standing erect, a sort of Indian Ganesha, who held some flaming object in one hand, a sort of sphere of fire, but he had thrown a similar sphere behind the figure standing below. In order to escape the danger of the fireball exploding behind him, there was only one possibility: ascent.

In the transition from the matriarchal to the patriarchal phase, it seems initially as though the child were caught in a conflict played out between the mother and the father archetypes. But the situation is more complicated, for the workings of the Self, which directs the process and presses for development, are always decisive. It is very helpful when classifying these sorts of phenomena to understand one of the fundamental laws of the psyche: the Self always "disguises" or "clothes" itself in the archetype of the phase toward which progress must advance. At the same time the previously dominant archetype is constellated so that its "negative" side appears. In terms of the developing child with whom we are presently concerned, the Self appears in the archetype of the phase toward which the ego has to evolve, i.e., the father archetype; the archetype of the phase to be overcome, however, appears as the "Terrible Mother."

This constellation, in which the fear of the Feminine *normally* appears as fear of the Terrible Mother, the witch, holds true for children of both sexes, for progress from the matriarchal to the patriarchal phase is a species-specific necessity for the development of the ego and of consciousness, at least so far as we can judge today. The fear-arousing mother appears here as "terrible" because she represents the element that "holds fast" or "arrests," that hinders the development necessary and now "due." This "terribleness" is archetypal, that is, even independent of the personal mother's correct behavior.

It is difficult to step out of security into danger, out of the unconscious unity with a Thou into the loneliness of an independence and autonomy becoming conscious of itself. However, something in the child and in its ego— namely its psychic inertia—corresponds to the safety and security promised by the mother. To be held fast by the mother archetype and to want to remain with her is one and the same thing; only together do they constellate the terrifying aspect of the dragon. And the intent of the ego-hero's struggle is to vanquish the dragon.

2. The Dragon as Symbol of the Feminine

At this point a question arises: Why is the dragon a symbol of the Feminine and not also of the Masculine? The answer is that the dragon can indeed also appear as a symbol of the Masculine because by nature it is often uroboric, i.e., it carries masculine and feminine meaning at the same time. Thus in a certain phase of female development the overwhelming Masculine appears as a male dragon, just as the patriarchal-paternal element appears as father dragon in those instances in which it has to be overcome.[9] This indicates that a symbol can be interpreted correctly only from the perspective of the specific developmental stage of ego-consciousness, as we have discussed elsewhere.[10] Nevertheless we can say that the dragon is usually a symbol of the Feminine.

The primal relationship to the mother is not only the first relationship, it is also the image and prototype of relating in general. It carries this significance especially in the sense of relationship as bond. When the genetic urgency to move "away from mother" arises, the primal relationship comes to symbolize bonding also in the sense of bondage and fixation, which as the Negative Feminine is part of what we designate its "elementary character."[11]

The ego and the consciousness developing with it now come into opposition with that aspect of the Feminine that holds on to or arrests. While the matriarchal-maternal element in the human psyche belongs symbolically to the Feminine and the unconscious, the ego in both sexes—in its heroically active developmental and aggressive character that presses toward becoming conscious—is symbolically masculine. The opposition between the heroic-masculine ego and the Terrible Feminine is intensified since the Feminine of the primal relationship is connected with the symbolism of home, paradise, and the original unitary reality. For the devel-

9. Ibid., pp. 122ff. (the battle with the dragon).

10. Neumann, "The Significance of the Genetic Aspect for Analytical Psychology," tr. R.F.C. Hull, in *Current Trends in Analytical Psychology* (Proceedings of the First International Congress for Analytical Psychology, 1958; pub. 1961), pp. 37ff.

11. *The Great Mother*.

oping ego, however, this matriarchal world is the "forbidden world." Its enticement stands in opposition to the species-specific, innate necessity for ego-development to progress toward the paternal, toward culture and community, to extricate oneself from *participation mystique* and to discover oneself as different and differing from others, that is, to discover one's individuality.

The development of the ego and of individuality has the character of movement and of ascent.[12] In this movement from below to above, from the unconscious toward consciousness, the matriarchal realm takes on the character of what must be overcome: the lower, infantile and archaic, but also abysmal and chaotic. All these symbols are connected with the Terrible Feminine, the devouring feminine "Dragon of the Abyss."[13]

In this sense, the Terrible Feminine becomes the antithesis of the ascending energy of ego-development; it becomes the symbol of stagnation, regression, and death. But this death that the dragon symbol of the terrible Feminine signifies archetypally is not only something passive; rather, as something devouring, it is also an enticing, seductive force sucking one downward. Because the ascending movement of ego-consciousness is heroically connected with suffering and accomplishment, the holding, detaining, captivating power of the dragon may combine with a yearning for peace expressed as tiredness, surrender, and even suicide. The regressive tendency appears as a negative drive, as deadly incest with the Terrible Mother. The danger that issues from the negatively

12. *Origins and History*, pp. 220ff.; *The Great Mother*, pp. 232ff. (the symbol of the ladder).

13. *Origins and History*, index, s.v. Terrible Mother.

constellated unconscious, the Terrible Feminine, corresponds to the regressive drive "backward" of wishing to let go, to fall, and actively to hurl oneself into the abyss. This danger is the basis of what Freud attempted to interpret as the death instinct.

In the heroic battle the dragon of the Terrible Feminine carries a dual aspect. In the one aspect, the dragon appears to the ego frankly as a negative image of the psyche, as the terrifying face of the unconscious that—as drive and affect, as lethargy, cowardice, and the tendency to give up the struggle—attacks the ego from within in all phases and in ever new forms along the path of its development. But this terrible-hostile countenance appears not only undisguised as fear of the unconscious but also indirectly as world and as fear of the world. For in the dragon constellation the world is also an anxiety-arousing aspect of the Terrible Feminine that threatens to devour the ego-hero and drive it back into the arms of the Terrible Mother within, who in her incestuous embrace promises the peace of death through self-surrender.

This "retreat" has many forms; it appears as illness and as fear, but, for example, also as escapism in which a person simply endures the dragon world in comfort and in a "normalcy" that avoids the battle. Individually as well as collectively the consequences of this attitude often are that one is devoured by the dragon without noticing it. Collectively this may be expressed externally in an unavoided war or unavoided dictatorship, etc.; individually, however, it may lead to regression, world renunciation, and illness. Regressions of this sort in which the superior strength of the Terrible Feminine is apparent give rise not only to typical anxiety neuroses and phobias but also, and especially, to addictions and, if the ego is extensively destroyed, to psychoses.

II. Manifestations of Fear of the Feminine

Turning our attention now to the manifestations of fear of the Feminine as it confronts us particularly in therapeutic work, we must distinguish three groups. The one is fear of the Feminine in childhood, a chapter that we can only touch upon briefly since basically it forms part of a psychology of childhood. The other is the adult's fear, which we must treat as two different groups of phenomena since we must consider both the man's fear and the woman's fear of the Feminine. For although the phenomenon of fear of the Feminine plays an essential role in male psychology, extremely important normal as well as pathological reactions in women remain incomprehensible if we fail to make clear the meaning that fear of the Feminine also plays in the life of woman.

1. The Child's Fear of the Feminine

We have emphasized that the "negative" aspect of the archetype of the phase to be overcome is always constellated in the necessary archetypal transition during child development from the matriarchal to the patriarchal world. Regardless how positively and correctly she behaves personally, the mother of the primal relationship must turn into a witch, for the child's early bond to her is, of course, a restrictive and consequently "witchlike" power in the child itself, which the child must overcome in favor of its progressive ego-development; that is, "matricide," which belongs among the hero's tasks, is demanded of the child. But this ego is heroic because it performs the most difficult task: it slays what is most dear to it, the relationship to the mother, under the guise of the dragon that holds it fast.[14] Understandably this deed of the ego is connected with the emergence of guilt feelings, and the guilt feelings that tend to prevent the slaying belong to the dragon's "weapons" with which the ego has to contend.

The attitude of the personal mother toward this archetypally necessary transition is extremely important. What is easier than to increase the child's growing guilt feelings, to demand the child be "good" and thus strengthen its now-regressive bondage to the mother! In contrast to this, a "good" mother in the same situation understands that in the development of the child's ego she necessarily must "become a witch," that she must be overcome and must set her child free. It is precisely her ability not only to protect but also to "deliver up" her child at the developmentally right moment and consciously to expose it to dangers that are necessary for the development of its autonomy that characterize the "good" mother. On the other hand, the true witch will prove to be the witch in "Hansel and Gretel" whose house is made of cake and sugar but who devours the child inside. Her anxiety about the child, like her spoiling it, are fetters, while the good mother, like the animal mother but at a higher, more conscious level, will bite at the child that has achieved autonomy or a certain stage of it in order to send it on its way. Where the clinging, negative-fettering mother intensifies the guilt feelings of the child seeking to free itself

14. *Origins and History.*

from her, the good mother, in accord with the Self pushing toward development, affirms the child's progress, but also its movement away from her.

Here it becomes evident how the intermingling and collaboration of personal and archetypal factors always determine the individual's destiny. The progression from the matriarchal to the patriarchal phase is transpersonal; as an archetypal *Anlage* it is a necessary process of maturation embedded in the species-specific structure of each human child. By contrast, the role of the personal mother who either supports or hampers this progress belongs to the unique and personal constellation of the individual child's destiny.

But guilt feelings arise unavoidably. Precisely because the Self—the highest value—and the extremely intense emotional bonds connected with it have borne the appearance of the archetype that now must be overcome, slaying the dragon always means killing one of the "highest" values and consequently incurring guilt. The heroic combat of the ego always indicates that an old form of the godhead has to be overcome, i.e., "killed," in favor of the new level, the new archetype, the new guise and appearance of the Self, the new god. No ego, however, can take upon itself the slaying of a divinity, even though this may be necessary and demanded, without having guilt feelings arise that must be accepted and made conscious as components of the dragon fight.

However, a normally developed child's ego, reinforced by the security of the primal relationship, will be able to overcome such guilt feelings, especially if they are not strengthened by a clinging mother and if the child can rely on a father figure who supports it in its evolution towards independence and hence relative liberation from the mother.

The child's pathological fear of the Feminine, the "witch" of the actual mother complex, forms a contrast to its normal fear connected with the developmental transition. Schematically we can distinguish three main forms of expression of this complex. The first form is an arrest of the ego by the "Mother," thus preventing the developmentally necessary progression. Second, there is a regressive tendency in the ego, i.e., a disturbance of the child's ego in which the progressive tendency is not strong enough or has been foiled by an instinctive, regressive tendency to seek out the matriarchal phase. Third, however, a constellation can also be present in which an already-achieved, progressive development in the ego is destroyed.

A preponderance of the feminine-matriarchal element that manifests as the "unconscious" can be constitutionally determined; i.e., we must assume that there are individuals in whom the archetypes of the unconscious, for example, are particularly strong so that a priori the activity of the unconscious is more intense than is normally the case. This sort of constellation can prove pathogenic and form the basis for a later neurosis, or especially a psychosis, in which ego-consciousness is not able to attain its normal developmental level of solidity characteristic of and necessary for the healthy person and his adaptation to the world. When we consider that this sort of constitutional overactivation of the unconscious hinders normal ego-development from the start, we more easily understand the possibilities of illness approaching from two sides: from the overly strong unconscious and from underdeveloped ego-strength. Here the fear of the Feminine manifests in the weak ego's anxiety states when faced with an overpowering unconscious that it cannot work through. In our discussion, however, it is of no importance whether the "overactivity" of the unconscious is due to unmanageable drives and affects, to an inundation with archetypal images, or to a mixture of these factors.

On the other hand, as we have already pointed out, an intensification of the negative world factor that exceeds the child's tolerance also leads to an unnatural intensification of the Terrible Feminine in the child. War, hunger, external or internal distress, illness, and every other sort of misfortune affecting the mother, the family, or the child itself that disturbs or destroys the child's necessary and species-specific situation of security and protectedness lets anxiety arise. But in the primal relationship this appears as fear of the Terrible Feminine that even adult consciousness still experiences in the image of "evil nature" or "malicious fate." All these negative conditions lead to a preponderance of the matriarchal, of the "Great Mother" encompassing the unconscious and the world, to which the ego feels "abandoned" in its fear.

If this sort of constitutional or fateful negative predominance of the matriarchal does not assume an extreme form, it can be compensated to a certain extent by the equilibrating intervention of a personal "good" mother. But conversely even if by its nature the child's constitution guarantees a species-specific matriarchal situation as "normal," the negative constellation of fate in the form of family or group conditions can lead to a disruption of ego-development ranging from slight to

catastrophic. Hence in the progression from the matriarchal to the patriarchal phase, an abnormality toward
excessive strength or weakness of the mother or father
can exert a disturbing or pathogenic effect. Of course,
progression toward the patriarchal phase is hampered by
an overly strong mother in the same way as by an unusu-
ally weak father whose normative presence as the representative of the patriarchy in the family is of decisive
significance. It is always a question of the relative balance
of the father and mother figures and of their elasticity,
which conforms to the developmental needs of the child
either by their stepping back or emphasizing their influence. Even though married to a normal father, an excessively strong, binding mother who dominates the family
situation obviously inhibits progress just as much as a
normal mother in the presence of an especially weak
father (through no fault of her own and regardless of the
causes). The absence of a father figure has a disruptive
effect on the child's ego-development regardless whether
the cause of his absence lies in a weakness of character or
an illness, whether he is drawn away by work or by an
extramarital love affair, or whether he is "absent" due to
war or death. The effect on the child is always negative
since the species-specific familial situation is not fulfilled.

But a reversal of this constellation is equally disruptive; i.e., by his frightening predominance an overpowering, "threatening" father impedes the child's progression
toward him, and an excessively weak mother who does
not provide the protection of the matriarchal primal situation in the species-specific manner exerts a negative effect in that she arouses the child's fear of the patriarchal
and strengthens its regressive tendency by her weakness.

Here we clearly see that fear of the Feminine cannot always be separated from fear of the Masculine. For example, the fear of the masculine, paternal element can also activate the image of the "Negative Feminine," the witch, by reinforcing the child's tendency to regression. For even where it is impeded, the progression to the patriarchate is a developmental necessity, and even where it is understandable, remaining with the mother is hostile to development.[15] But in each instance where there is a preponderance of the matriarchal element—for personal rather than constitutional reasons—this maternal element as something that binds, i.e., as the Terrible Feminine, endangers the course of normal development.

Only the analysis of the child's individual situation can reveal the direction in which the emphasis should be shifted, i.e., what is to be done therapeutically. For the progression to the patriarchate can be achieved only when the sense of security in the matriarchal realm has been restored through the intervention of a therapist as a "good" mother; on the other hand, however, a "good" father figure can be helpful and necessary in overcoming the fear of progression toward the patriarchal. But often both paths are natural and viable, and the constellation of

15. In other cultures a different parental constellation can be "natural," and in those instances, too, it can happen that the child's adaptation to the cultural canon that is supposed to be "natural" is disturbed whenever one of the parents does not assume the full function that, according to tradition, the parent must perform for the child's development. Moreover, only as exceptions do we find constellations in which the progression from matriarchal to patriarchal does not have to take place. The patriarchal family situation typical for our culture, however, is by no means the only one that guarantees this sort of progression.

the "good mother" is restricted to a female no more than that of the "good father" is to a male therapist.

But we are confronted with something completely different in the third situation, in which the progression to the patriarchate and separation from the maternal appears successful, but an "attack" by the mother dragon vanquishes and "castrates" the ego that has become "masculine." In regard to age we are usually not concerned here with developmental disturbances of children but rather of adolescents, particularly disturbances at the time of puberty. Corresponding to this, we find in mythology a great number of tragic confrontations between the Terrible Mother and the "youth/lover," confrontations that end with his castration, death, dismemberment, or insanity.[16] In so-called primitive cultures rites of initiation under the protection of the rituals of the collective take place during puberty because this period of time is particularly significant but also dangerous; in such rites the youth is conclusively delivered from the maternal realm and inducted into the patriarchal. By contrast, in our culture, which possesses only remnants of these initiatory rites, this important "transitional phase"—on the way toward a strengthened masculinity and the initial attempts at coming to terms with sexuality, partner, and world—is stigmatized by an abundance of neurotic complaints, even by hebephrenia, an illness typically appearing at this time.

During this developmental epoch the ego faces a multitude of new and difficult tasks, for puberty is characterized not only by the challenge of the world in the form

16. *Origins and History*.

of the collective, now appearing for the first time, but also, and to a greater degree, by a natural activation of the unconscious. The onrush of sexuality and the psychic activation of the archetypes identical with the instinctual activation are typical for this developmental phase—in both its good and its bad aspects; and in both sexes but in different ways the pubescent ego must come to terms with this threat in a new dragon battle.

The fear of the Feminine plays a decisive, but now also conscious, role in the normal spiritual and emotional struggles of this period just as it does in the illnesses associated with it. For the boy the fear of the Feminine appears predominantly as fear of the partner, the girl, while for him the fear of the Masculine is secondary. For the girl, however, the fear of the partner as fear of the Masculine is important, of course, but in addition to it and no less important is her fear of the Feminine, her fear of accepting her own destiny as woman. But first let us turn to the problem of the male and his fear of the Feminine.

2. Men's Fear of the Feminine

We have attempted to elucidate the significance for the child of its primal relationship to the mother. It is a relationship of something dependent and small upon something great and all-embracing, something that contains safety and protection as well as uncertainty and fear, i.e., life and death. Initially the child's relationship—and that of the male child as well—to the elementary character of the Feminine in which the maternal element appears stands under the sign of belonging, of "own-ness," regardless whether it is good or bad. *Participation mys-*

tique with the maternal element initially goes so far that we could say that the mother represents the child's Self, which only gradually migrates to the child as ego-consciousness matures. This sense of belonging to the mother as belonging to one's "own-ness" is so strong that normally the child's differentiation and separation from her also develop under her protection.

But the male's relationship to what we have called the "transformative" character of the Feminine is different.[17] In contrast to stability and what guarantees it, the male experiences the Feminine in its transformative character as something that presses for and brings about change in both a good and a bad sense. Relationship to the female counterpart as to something foreign and other is what manifests clearly in the transformative character of the Feminine and hence legitimately constellates for the man as an "anima figure."[18] This foreign, "other" quality of the transformative character of the Feminine is dangerous, not, as in the instance of the elementary character, because it holds the male fast and fixates him in childish dependency, lack of autonomy, and inertia, but rather precisely because it disquiets the male as the element of inspiration, "animation," and madness.

At first the child also experiences this anima quality in the mother, especially when, as the good mother, she affirms change in the child. But the development of the relationship to the anima (which cannot concern us here) leads away from the mother and toward a relationship with a woman of the same age who can no longer be identified with the mother but initially with the sister.

17. *The Great Mother*.
18. Jung, passim.

252

The essence of the "transformative character" of the Feminine lies in its equal status with the male as a partner. The task of the adult male is to enter into a relationship with this counterpart as a fully developed but essentially different female "thou." Only when a man related to his Self can collaborate and conflict with the foreignness and otherness of another Self, or with a different facet of his Self represented by a woman, can a relationship bear the fruit of the authentic encounter of two individuals.

But frequently in male as well as female development the transformative character of the Feminine is still bound to or fused with the elementary character of the maternal element, and one of the tasks of the hero's battle is that of extricating and liberating the feminine as an autonomous and independent thou from the domination of the mother in the primal relationship. The Feminine intertwined with elementary non-human aspects as water-sprite, snake-woman, centauress, etc., or in human form as the "captive princes" under the power of the dragon which the hero must vanquish are but variations of the same constellation.[19]

In any case, it is part of the normal development of the male ego as hero that he succeed in ransoming the Feminine from maternal domination. It does not matter whether the Feminine itself has remained identical with the mother of the primal relationship and has not become capable of being a partner, or whether the male's image of the Feminine, his anima, is still so thoroughly informed by the image of the mother and his attachment to her that

19. In this context we cannot discuss the constellation in which the dragon refers to a paternal male.

the man himself is still incapable of being a real partner. In both cases liberation of the anima, the Feminine in its transformative character, from the mother with her retentive, elementary character, is necessary for development.[20] This differentiation and liberation is the prerequisite for the *hierosgamos* with the Feminine, the fertile marriage in a relationship of the I to a Thou as Not-I. This relationship is sacred because for both partners it constitutes the prerequisite for the Self-development in which the opposites are contained and wholeness can be achieved. But liberation of the anima presupposes another battle with the dragon, regardless of the content with which this dragon figure is associated, and naturally the ego fears this battle.

Thus this second important fear of the Feminine appearing next to the fear of the mother is the fear of the anima as fear of the transformation to which liberation of the anima from the realm of the dragon and confrontation with the independent otherness of the Feminine will force him.

Wherever the male's ego-development is disturbed and he has not attained independence—e.g., where his ego has remained infantile due to a mother fixation and has not achieved the "combativity" necessary for the heroic ego—each demand for "transformation," every demand to develop toward something unknown and away from whatever provides security, is answered with fear and defensiveness. Since the transformative character always calls for something new and unaccustomed, the anima is that side of the male psyche associated with the

---

20. *Origins and History*, pp. 122ff. (the battle with the dragon).

Feminine that entices the man to adventure, to the conquest of the new. But it is also negatively associated with everything that signifies illusion and delusion, and indeed as madness it signifies a real danger. Just as the hero cannot exist without the conquest of danger, the male cannot develop without stepping into the incalculable danger that transformation demands.

While liberation of the anima and becoming conscious of her are necessary for individuation as the development of individual wholeness, the demands of the cultural canon can be completely opposed to the necessity of individuation. Thus adaptation to the patriarchal culture can also be achieved while avoiding the transformative aspect of the Feminine; that is, stabilization of psychic development after the first part of the species-specific transformative process that ends with puberty is thoroughly desirable for the preservation of the patriarchy. Here authorities in the form of the father archetype, the patriarchal culture canon, and the super-ego are engaged in such a manner as to guarantee a relative stability of the culture by excluding the unsettling, transformative character of the anima and individual development to a great extent. This is why the creative process that is necessarily linked with the fear of the transformative character of the Feminine is shoved off on those who live on the fringes, the creative persons, who comprise the culture's outsiders.

This limitation of development produces a mutilation of the automorphic *Anlage* of the person who by his individual nature is creative and who falls ill when he does not attain real individuation. This is particularly valid for the second half of life because, whenever a person does not fulfill his automorphic potential, the collective adaptation achieved no longer gives a full meaning to the aging person's life. Thanks to this omission, a great number of persons in Western cultures who are "adult" but not "mature" fall ill; but above and beyond this there ensues an undermining of occidental culture itself, which is no longer able to fulfill the inner existential needs of the persons living in it. This constellation holds true even for the "normal" adult in our patriarchal culture for whom the attainment to a genuine automorphic development—i.e., individuation—is possible almost only through severe crises and illnesses.

If we look at the normal goal of development that the male child must attain in our culture, it can be reduced to the following abbreviated formula: development of the ego and of the culture culminates in adaptation to the collective in the sense that the individual becomes fitted to do a job through the development of his specific abilities. Next to be fulfilled after the ability to do a job comes the ability to be a partner. In this, however, we must differentiate several factors that can be fulfilled independently but which only together result in the full ability to be a partner.

One fundamental factor is the capacity for a sexual relationship that moves between the extremes of potent and impotent, but at the human level—and this is characteristic precisely in contrast to the animal world—the capacity for a sexual relationship is inseparable from the capacity to relate to others in general and to a woman in particular. The human capacity for relationship also oscillates between two widely separated poles that perhaps could best be characterized as "being close" and "being distant." Above and beyond the capacity for relationship that encompasses the male-female opposites there is another, supreme form of "partner ability" that we could call integral relationship. No longer are we speaking of the meeting of two partners of different sexes but of the encounter of two human beings whose partnership encompasses the totality of their masculine-feminine individualities of which their gender and gender-related qualities represent only one facet.

The disturbances produced by the fear of the Feminine in the adult male are characterized essentially by the fear fixation to the mother (the mother complex) or the fear fixation to the anima (the anima complex). The mother complex is the earlier and has deeper effects, while a disturbance that is limited to the anima presupposes a certain degree of successful development and hence also a greater possibility for adaptation.

Hence a total mother fixation can lead to complete developmental failure, i.e., to a lack of autonomy that makes not only relationship to a partner but even adequate professional development impossible. Here we find, for example, bachelors and eccentrics who still live with the mother, men who cannot separate from the mother and who, although often nearly fifty themselves, completely collapse following her death. Not only their capacity to relate to a partner is often stunted, but frequently they have not been able to attain the level of professional development possible on the basis of innate capacity and talent either.

Here the conscious bond to the mother corresponds to an exaggerated fear of the Feminine as fear of woman and fear of the world, neither of which can be "conquered." The man does not trust his own masculinity. The unconscious fear of the devouring and castrating Feminine often is accompanied by an equally pronounced fear of the masculine as Oedipal fear of castration by the paternal authority figure.

Here the threatening Masculine turns not only against the personal relationship to the mother; rather, it is often archetypally grounded and represents the transpersonal background of the Oedipus complex. In it the paternal element not only "castrates" and categorically prohibits the Feminine, but demands relinquishment of the mother precisely because the paternal masculine element demands manliness of the son, i.e., his heroism and surrender of the mother and his attachment to her which is the precondition for authentic—and collectively required —individual masculinity. But beneath this layer of fear of the archetypal father there almost always lies a pre-Oedipal fear of the Feminine as the Terrible Mother who does not let go and from whose "claim to ownership" the undeveloped male as son dares not withdraw.

However, this sort of total failure is less common than the many forms of relative failure caused by fear of the Feminine as Terrible Mother. A large group of men damaged in this way can, for example, complete their cultural development through adaptation to job and integration into the collective. Their impairment manifests only in their inability to enter into any relationship with a partner, or to form only a partial one. Here we will point out only some of the constellations that arise in this way.

In this category we find those men fully able to handle a job but who are impotent or fixated on specific perversions, or who are capable only of a homosexual relationship. It is easy to demonstrate the dominant mother complex and the fear of the Feminine for a large number of homosexuals. Here the range extends from a full capacity for physical and spiritual relationship with a male partner, including the emotional, to other instances in which homosexuality may be associated with the capacity for a highly developed but exclusively spiritual relationship to women. Here we are speaking of a partial development of the anima in which the natural sexual aspect remains, to a certain extent, caught in the mother image. Fear of the Feminine is concentrated in fear of the female body, either because the body itself is taboo, or because women, especially the female genitals, are feared as the terrible, castrating "vagina dentata."

Another not uncommon form of failure, a variant first described by Freud, is that of the man who is incapable of experiencing and tolerating woman in her totality.[21] The fear is so overwhelming that it results in splitting woman into a higher and lower femaleness, and the man can have a relationship to only one aspect at a time; that is, on the one hand the man worships the woman and achieves a relationship to her of supremely valuable friendship, but on the other hand a sexual relationship is possible, if at all, only with a prostitute or with a woman of inferior social status. Here, too, it is always a question of "fear of the Feminine," of a "fear of woman" that is experienced as so overwhelming in its totality that the incompletely developed male feels he is no match for it.

Among the relative failures who approach what is

21. Freud, "Contributions to the Psychology of Love" (1910-1917), Standard Ed., vol. 11.

called normalcy, we find the Don Juan type, who is not only potent but has a relatively strong capacity for relationships. His failure lies in his inability to commit himself to a woman, and without exception fear of the Feminine lies behind his inability. Every form of male self-protection—for example even the patriarchal ideology of the "negative Feminine," to which we shall return later—rests on an unsureness of Self, on a feeling of not being a match for the Feminine, that is, on an insufficient development of masculinity, be it that the male fears the binding, arresting, elementary character of the Feminine predominant in the mother, or the opposite, the transformative character embodied in the anima that will not "leave him alone."

We must never forget that, for a man, the Feminine as the "totally other" signifies and must signify something numinous, and that without the fateful confrontation with this numinosum, this other half of the world, no life can attain to its potential for maturity and wholeness (and this, of course, is equally true for woman). It is possible to confront and to come to terms with this numinosum, however, only if one risks one's entire personality without reservations such as may be expressed in a self-protective overestimation or underestimation of the Feminine and of woman.

In another common male type, the "normalcy" of the relationship and commitment to woman and to the Feminine appears at first to be completely attained. We are speaking here of the man who marries a woman "in the image of his mother," a man who acknowledges and loves his wife essentially as mother of the family. This man has separated from his personal mother; his ego and his adaptation to life is fully developed; he is sexually normal and capable of both relationship with and commitment to his wife. To what extent can we still speak of a fear of the Feminine? This brings us to a topic valid for the present-day situation: we could call it "patriarchal normality as a form of fear of the Feminine."

In a certain sense, marriage with a mother or a daughter figure is almost the prescribed formula for a patriarchal marriage, an inference that arises not only from the fact that husband and wife often refer to each other as "father" and "mother." The stability of the family is guaranteed in the patriarchal marriage precisely by the fact that it ensures the unequivocal masculinity of the man and the unequivocal femininity of the woman.[22] For the man this means that he can indeed overcome his initial mother fixation, but in his ego-development he cannot project the anima on his partner in the patriarchal marriage. That is, all "love marriages" are non-patriarchal in this sense. The classical patriarchal marriage was and is un-individual, and is made by families exercising power over their women. It would seem that this classical form of patriarchal marriage has been overcome, but on closer scrutiny we recognize without difficulty that the anima or animus activation leading to the modern "love marriage" usually represents a fleeting stage of premarital relationship that comes to an end when the man identifies with the father figure and the woman with the mother figure in the marriage.

But then the anima and her transformative character is left "outside." It is split off and poses a danger to the

22. See the first essay in this volume.

marriage. More, it threatens all the constants of the patriarchate such as family, security, and position in the
world. Thus the anima turns into a marriage-wrecker
and seductress par excellence, and at a new level we again
find the attempt to overcome the fear of the Feminine by
splitting the Feminine and woman whom the man cannot handle in her wholeness. Countless marital difficulties are based on this fundamental situation, in which
the opposition of patriarchal marriage and extramarital
anima relationship turns into conflict. But this conflict
frequently continues even when the old marriage is dissolved and the man marries the anima figure. A new
patriarchal marriage arises in which the man clings to his
exclusively masculine position and the woman is forced
back into her exclusively feminine stance.

Of course, this fundamental simplification of the patriarchate is also achieved when the man marries a "daughter." In this way the autonomy and the transformation of
the Feminine is made more difficult and the man's patriarchal superiority is guaranteed, which spares him his
own transformation.

An entire ideology of the patriarchy that fundamentally conceives of the Feminine as a "negative Feminine"
is collectively part and parcel of this defensive position in
which the man resists the transformative character of the
Feminine—that is, he defends against the necessity of his
own transformation. In this patriarchal ideology the man
identifies with the "above," with heaven, and the spirit,
i.e., with the father archetype. This identification is understandable; indeed, it seems almost unavoidable when
we recall that the heroic-patriarchal development of the
ego is one of "ascent" and must be oriented to the father
archetype.

This sort of identification is ritualized in puberty and in its initiations, and the symbolic formula "I and the Father are One" is made the foundation of the patriarchally male existence.[23] Consequently the devaluation of the Feminine is to be understood as an attempt at overcoming the fear of the Feminine and its dangerous aspect as the Great Mother and as the anima.

But this means that, in the patriarchate, the unconscious, instinct, sex, and the earth—as "things of this world"—belong to the "negative Feminine" with which the male associates woman and that, in all patriarchal cultures up until the present, woman and the Feminine have suffered under this male defensiveness and contempt. However, this negative valuation applies not only to the elementary character and to the matriarchal aspect but equally to the transformative character, the anima. For the "upper" Masculine she becomes the sorceress, seductress, and witch, and is rejected because of the fear associated with the irrational Feminine. The man is equally ready to denounce the Feminine as enslaving and holding him fast to earthly things and at the same time to accuse "her"—as something confusing and seductive— of endangering the stability of existence. The spirit-man of all shadings who is characteristic of the patriarchate especially rejects the Feminine because it entraps him in marriage, family, and adaptation to reality, and hence confuses him as to his "calling," which, in masculine asceticism, he loves to conceive as "higher" and "spiritual."

However, this same type can negate and split the "earthly" woman in order to be enlivened by *femme inspiratrice* figures. In both cases patriarchal ideology is based

23. *Origins and History.*

on keeping the anima unconscious, and on a conflict in which the Feminine and woman is experienced not as a unity but only as polar opposites. Thus woman and the Feminine appear either as a negative, downward-pulling force, as swamp woman or water sprite, or as a positive, uplifting force, as angel or goddess. But since the patriarchal male is dominated by the upper spiritual element, he withdraws from the reality of earth in ascetic idealism and prefers to ascend toward heaven. It never occurs to him that abduction to heaven might also be a seduction. The result of this one-sided patriarchal stance, demonstrable in all areas of life, is an unintegrated man who is attacked by his repressed side and often enough overwhelmed by it.[24] This transpires not only in the fate of the individual man as seduction by a "lower" anima, but equally through seduction by a compensatory ideology, for example materialism, to which "spirit" men are especially susceptible.

The man wants to remain exclusively masculine and out of fear rejects the transformative contact with a woman of equal status. Negativizing the Feminine in the patriarchate prevents the man from experiencing woman as a thou of equal but different status, and hence from coming to terms with her. The consequence of the patriarchal male's haughtiness toward women leads to the inability to make any genuine contact with the Feminine, i.e., not only in a real woman but also with the Feminine in himself, the unconscious. Whenever an integral relationship to the Feminine remains undeveloped, however,

24. Here we will not address the extent to which the devaluation and negative value assigned to the Feminine increases the male's fear of the Feminine.

this means that, due to his fear, the male is unable to break through to his own wholeness that also embraces the Feminine. Thus the patriarchal culture's separation from the Feminine and from the unconscious becomes one of the essential causes for the crisis of fear in which the patriarchal world now finds itself.

Before we turn to the problem of overcoming fear and of the male's integral relationship to the Feminine, we must outline yet another aspect of the adult's fear of the Feminine: this is the woman's fear of the Feminine.

3. Woman's Fear of the Feminine

In regard to the primal relationship to the mother, i.e., the first phase of childhood, the same conditions hold true for both the boy and the girl. The basic feeling of security is experienced in this phase; and, in a setting of maternal protection, normal fears develop which are integrated when the primal relationship with the mother is positive. The progression from the matriarchal to the patriarchal phase is just as necessary for the female as for the male, at least in modern Western culture. In the typical patriarchal-heroic manner, the girl's developing ego must also break the ties to the Great Mother if she is to become an active member of her patriarchal culture. She must learn; she must develop will and consciousness; and today, almost like a man, she must attain an independence that, in addition to relationship with a partner and founding of a family, leads her also to adaptation to the culture through the fulfillment of a professional role.

But the problems and crises in a woman's development are different from those of a man. And this holds true even if we limit our discussion to our theme and do not consider woman's central problem, her fear of the Masculine.

Fear of the Masculine is a significant impediment in the girl child's progression to the patriarchate and in her acceptance of love for the father, an acceptance connected with the archetypal constellation of the Oedipus complex. Here we cannot discuss her way of coming to terms with the Father Dragon, typical for women but differing from the male pattern.[25] But progression to the patriarchate, the girl child's necessary love relationship with the father, forms the backdrop to the role that the mother of the primal relationship plays for the girl in this context.

We have drawn attention elsewhere to the decisive significance of the fact that by separating from the mother and joining the father's world, the boy "comes into his own" because the Self represented by the father archetype has the same gender as he does.[26] The reverse holds true for the girl. Even after the Self has "migrated" from the mother to the daughter, this childlike, daughterly Self remains identical to the gender of the mother archetype. This symbolic fact means that the mother-daughter relationship with its more intimate connection of ego and Self as well as consciousness and the unconscious is fundamentally closer to nature than is the mother-son relationship. The greater tension between male ego-consciousness and the "contrasexual" mother archetype—i.e., the matriarchal unconscious, also a naturally determined tension—accounts for fundamental

25. See the first three essays in this volume, and Neumann, *Amor and Psyche*.

26. Neumann, "Narcissism, Normal Self-Formation, and the Primary Relation to the Mother," tr. Hildegard Nagel, *Spring 1966* (orig. 1955).

differences between female and male development, especially in regard to the manner of male creativity.

The girl's closer tie to the mother archetype and to the matriarchal phase make her separation especially difficult. Persistence in the primal relationship and hence persistence in an essentially unconscious, matriarchal existence is a distinct possibility and temptation for the woman, especially because that sort of fixation is not really pathogenic, although it strengthens the opposition to the patriarchal world and her fear of it. Indeed, we may even assume that this basic matriarchal stance remains primary for the primitive woman in a patriarchal culture.

The matriarchal world is essentially "man-hating" because it is a world in its own right with values and attitudes differing from those of the patriarchate.[27] The juxtaposition of matriarchy and patriarchy as opposites also includes a mutual devaluation; as we have attempted to demonstrate, this very juxtaposition is what makes the transition from the one phase to the other so very difficult for the child's ego. The attachment to the mother, the tie to the matriarchal world, and the fear-laden negation of the Masculine, however, also lead, in the instance of the woman, to an unavoidable conflict between the mother archetype of the phase to be overcome and the Self's emphasis on the father archetype toward which the ego must advance. But this constellates the Great Mother in her negative, terrifying—i.e., fear-inspiring—aspect; that is to say, she becomes the witch who wants to impede progress.

For the girl the situation is complicated in that the

27. See the second essay in this volume.

phase of unity with the mother as the phase of Self-conservation is not only peacefully undisturbed but also carries a feminine accent; however, progression to the patriarchate is identical with the conquest of fear of the Masculine, a conquest that forces the girl into danger, indeed into the death of Self-surrender, which we have described as the "death-marriage."[28] In this sense, the matriarchal witch not only binds the girl fast, she induces in her a sense of guilt at having "betrayed the mother," a guilt that runs deeper than in the boy because the girl child's "betrayal of the mother" can easily be interpreted as a betrayal of her essence, and her movement into the father world as surrender of her own nature.

It turns out in this situation that the binding and man-hating mother archetype does not correspond to the female Self but rather, to illustrate this constellation with the myth of Persephone, the Self, affirming the progress of individuation, is represented not by Demeter, who refuses to release her daughter, but by Gaia, who knows of Hades' abduction of Persephone.

The defeat of the matriarchal witch and the transition to the patriarchate and its values leads to the girl child's partial identification with her masculine, "animus" side, which must be developed. This identification inevitably brings with it the danger that the girl child will get lost in the Masculine in a way that has nothing to do with feminine giving in Self-surrender, in the sense of that sort of surrender and devotion through which alone she comes to the experience of her feminine nature.

This mode of losing oneself to the male realm repre-

28. See the first three essays in this volume, and *Amor and Psyche*.

sents the danger of masculinization in the form of developing a pseudo-masculinity in which the woman runs the danger of losing her essential femininity. Without a doubt, the task confronting the woman in our culture is to develop the masculine and patriarchal aspects of the psyche without thereby giving up her feminine being, and this task is especially difficult thanks to its equivocal and ambiguous nature.

In this constellation the woman can be even further endangered when the personal mother and the world of the Feminine belonging to her lose their original security that comes from being rooted in the matriarchal ground. This maternal element is often damaged by the negative value placed on the Feminine in the patriarchate and hence made unsure of its femininity. In this case the mother already fears the Feminine as her denied and rejected "authentic Self." Then the negative mother appears to the daughter as the patriarchal witch who overrates the Masculine and the son but underrates the Feminine and the daughter, and who thus endangers the daughter's development. Such a mother robs her daughter of the primal security that is necessary during the phase of Self-preservation and then delivers her without any protection to the superior masculinity of the patriarchy.

The threat posed by the Masculine and the fear associated with it is ultimately the fear of Self-devaluation and Self-estrangement that women experience. In this situation the woman often sees no choice left her but to rid herself of her femininity and to transform herself into a quasi-masculine being. This danger is especially great when, as in Western patriarchal culture, the figure of the archetypal Feminine as a deity and as the incarnation of the female Self is absent.

But in a certain sense Nature has limited the danger that the woman can betray herself to the Masculine and lose her connection to the fundamental archetypal *Gestalt* of the Feminine. For no matter how far the daughter as a woman may have distanced herself from the matriarchal world of the maternal ground and how much she succumbs to the patriarchal male's negative disparagement of her, she typically enters a developmental phase of her female existence in which the great totality of feminine nature almost always rights and corrects all deviations from her feminine essence.

This rectification happens independently of the woman's knowledge and consciousness of everything that "really" happens during that phase decisive for woman signified by the advent not of marriage but of pregnancy and childbirth. When the woman bears a child, she experiences a Self-discovery that is so deeply anchored in her biopsychic existence that it is missed only in the most unusual cases. The unity of mother and daughter celebrated in the Eleusinian mysteries is established in the female rites of initiation in which the old women introduce the young women to the fundamental situations of female existence. However, this unity is present wherever the daughter, as the birth-giver, becomes a mother, and it exists for every woman, even for the "uninitiated," regardless what occurs in the consciousness of the woman giving birth. Even where the relationship to the personal mother is disturbed or destroyed and the latter as patriarchal witch endangers the woman's Self-worth, this existential situation produces a connection with the archetypal Feminine as Great Mother and as Self. Beyond all patriarchal judgments and misunderstandings and the female consciousness proceeding from them, the woman can experience herself as creatrix and as the source of life, irrefutably and to a depth that makes all the aberrations and wrong attitudes of her consciousness superficial.[29] But even this profound Self-experience of woman as birth-giver can remain hidden in darkness; here the modern woman's ego can even experience a deep fear of the Feminine as a fear of herself, as fear of the incomprehensible numinosity of feminine nature.

A similar fear of the Feminine and of its essence can also arise in the second half of life during the process of individuation, for woman's individuation as Self-discovery demands of her something extraordinarily difficult: redemption from domination by the archetypal Masculine and the patriarchal mentality and its values. For this reason a woman's discovery of herself is frequently connected with a marital crisis, especially when the marriage has been a patriarchal one in which the dependency and one-sidedness of each partner was the prerequisite for the symbiosis of togetherness in the marriage.

Because relating is one of life's crucial contents for woman—if not the primary and decisive one—any "dissolution of ties" in the sense of becoming independent represents a particularly difficult crisis and problem. Even when she dissolves the ties to the mother of the primal relationship, this factor of "faithfulness" to a relationship plays an essential—and inhibiting—role. How-

29. Carol Baumann, "Psychological Experiences Connected with Childbirth," *Studien zur analytischen Psychologie C. G. Jungs* (Festschrift for Jung's eightieth birthday, 1955), vol. 1.

ever, in each progression the Self forces the ego to move forward and to overcome imprisonment. In the instance of separation from the mother, the Self assumes the form of the father archetype; in the present context it is the female Self that pushes the ego forward. But in this situation one must experience and decide whether it is a question of a woman's authentic Self-discovery—i.e., Self-discovery necessary if she is to fulfill her destiny—or of a neurotic confusion in which the ego is only fleeing from its duties to the earth and to reality. For although woman can and must come into opposition to the archetypal Masculine and to the patriarchy as she comes to herself, by her very nature she nevertheless experiences a greater and more comprehensive kind of relatedness, that is, her capacity for love grows. By contrast a neurotic pseudo-development that, for example, gives up one's relationship with husband and family under the slogan of "doing your own thing" reveals an egotistical impoverishment of the capacity to love that stands in direct opposition to authentic female Self-discovery.

Woman's fear of the female Self, of the experience of the numinous archetypal Feminine, becomes comprehensible when we get a glimpse—or even only a hint— of the profound otherness of female selfhood as contrasted to male selfhood. Precisely that element which, in his fear of the Feminine, the male experiences as the hole, abyss, void, and nothingness turns into something positive for the woman without, however, losing these same characteristics. Here the archetypal Feminine is experienced not as illusion and as maya but rather as unfathomable reality and as life in which above and below, spiritual and physical, are not pitted against each other; reality as eternity is creative and, at the same time, is grounded in primeval nothingness. Hence as daughter the woman experiences herself as belonging to the female spiritual figure Sophia, the highest wisdom, while at the same time she is actualizing her connection with the musty, sultry, bloody depths of swamp-mother Earth. However, in this sort of Self-discovery woman necessarily comes to see herself as different from what presents itself to men—as, for example, spirit and father, but often also as the patriarchal godhead and his ethics. The basic phenomenon— that the human being is born of woman and reared by her during the crucial developmental phases—is expressed in woman as a sense of connectedness with all living things, a sense not yet sufficiently realized, and one that men, and especially the patriarchal male, absolutely lack to the extent women have it.[30]

To experience herself as so fundamentally different from the dominant patriarchal values understandably fills the woman with fear until she arrives at that point in her own development where, through experience and love that binds the opposites, she can clearly see the totality of humanity as a unity of masculine and feminine aspects of the Self.

B. THE ESSENCE, THE ORIGIN, AND THE CONQUEST OF FEAR

The paradoxical role the ego plays in the psychic life of the individual is expressed also in the fact that it may be

30. *The Great Mother*, pp. 325ff. (Sophia).

considered with equal justification as the place where fear originates and where it is overcome. Vis-à-vis the great existential powers—whether they are called the world, the Self, or the archetype of the unconscious— the ego remains something small and perpetually endangered. Psychic development takes three directions: extraversion (orientation towards the world), introversion (orientation toward the unconscious), and centroversion (the orientation to the Self). Movement toward one of these existential directions always means movement away from another. While looking at and moving toward the "world" the danger is always constellated that the "other" neglected and hostile realm at our back will generate fear. Even the "Big Third," the world of the Self, which as totality constellates the to-and-fro movement between the opposing worlds and their unity, is by no means only and always a support and source of safety for the ego; rather, it is often equally something incomprehensible, a source of fear, until a relatively late degree of development has been attained.

In human development the ego is employed as representative of the totality, and balancing the individual in his or her intermediate position between the outer and the inner worlds has fallen to the lot of this ego and the consciousness associated with it.[31]

With this "filialization,"[32] in which to some extent the ego represents the Self, the ego also assumes the duty of monitoring, of protecting consciousness against each and every superior force. This is why the ego must entrench

31. *Origins and History.*
32. Ibid.

itself in the mandala of consciousness and carefully guard the entrance and exit gates so as to preserve the unity of consciousness and to avoid disintegration through flooding by unconscious or worldly contents. This relative stability of the conscious system that forms the basis for a person's reliability is demanded by the collective, and rightly so. This is why stability of the ego counts among the goals of all patriarchal initiations: the demand is placed on the male that he prove himself steadfast and heroic against the powers that threaten to dissolve the unity of the personality, be they hunger or pain, drives or demons.

The centrally positioned constellation of the ego signifies that what is familiar and has already been experienced supports stability as something belonging to consciousness; whatever is unknown and unfamiliar, since it is threatening, is held at the greatest possible distance from what exists, or it is admitted only to the extent that it can be assimilated and does not disturb the established unity. This is to say that an attitude that defends consciousness and the established and familiar order is demanded of the adult ego and of the personality adapted to the cultural canon; this contrasts to the heroic, progressive attitude of the ego (outlined earlier) that must forfeit the old security in order to attain a new, archetypally prescribed phase. In the adult world this heroic attitude of active conquest of the new continues to be handed over to the peripheral personalities in the culture, the creative persons, while the collective composed of grown-ups assumes the essentially conservative task of defending and transmitting the cultural values. The collective rewards creative persons with high prizes for all those accomplishments that further and expand, decorate and equip the existing culture. Typical examples of this attitude are the church and the court cultures of monarchs, as well as the support for these sorts of creative persons in Russia and America. A revolutionary creative accomplishment, on the other hand, is punished by death, in the present as in the past.

But this sort of "division of labor" within a culture can be carried through only to a certain extent if the individuals are to remain healthy. Since each individual is creative according to his or her own nature, a conflict arises between the collectively demanded, conservative nature of defense of the existing cultural values (by the ego) and the pressing unconscious forces that intend the individual's further development and that strive to force the surrender of the old position by exerting ever greater pressure. Because this constellation is especially evident today, we live in a time when an ever greater number of individuals experience their exposure to the threat posed by unknown and ego-alien qualities of existence.

These fear-laden experiences that often appear in the second half of life after the individual has attained and consolidated his position in the collective and the collective has confirmed his contribution to it frequently manifest, during this phase of life, in the symbol of death. The fear induced by the unfamiliar, which is associated with the central symbol of death, assumes many faces. The depression and fears of living, the neuroses and crises of the adult and even of successful people often stand under the sign of meaninglessness and of the fear that one may be missing, or may have missed, one's entire life; we encounter these depressions and fears equally often in the fear of illness, diminishing vitality, and actual death.

Behind these fears, hiding under the sign of death and attacking and reaching the individual in the center of his or her fortress of consciousness, however, we find the movement of the Self forcing transformation in the person who wants to hang on. It is almost always fear of transformation that arouses anxiety in the person constricted by the old; but while he believes it is the new that is frightening him, the anxiety derives in fact from the limitedness of the old life paralyzed in the prison of habit.

At this mid-life point or later at the climacteric with the reduction of the biological-collective tasks, what is life and what is death become almost inscrutable and indistinguishable for the ego. For as the ego, afraid of transformation, clings rigidly to the "old life," this very same, hotly defended "old life" turns out to be death, and the death of the ego brought about through transformation proves to be life. In the unwillingness to let go of the old, fear rises, depression arises, for new forces rise up that want access to life and that press against the entrenched ego. But if the ego surrenders its defensive position and throws itself heroically into the jaws of the dragon of death—into the night sea journey of the sun hero—death proves itself to be life, and surrender of what one had held fast becomes a new way of living and of overcoming fear.

The development of human consciousness through archetypal phases is species-specific; i.e., every member of the human species passes through them, and in their development both the ego and consciousness follow transpersonal directives that are inherent in the psyche and that come to maturity. But the Self, the imaginary center of wholeness, directs not only the species-specific but also the individual development of the human being. That is to say, in the human individual the Self exerts its effects as the tendency not only to play the typical role in one's adaptation to life but also to discover one's own authentic beingness and to achieve Self-realization through life and the collective; i.e., to actualize one-Self in one's own unique suchness. But for Self-realization all the phases of transformation are necessary.

The great, and to some extent ultimate, task posed here is that of understanding fear in all its forms as an instrument of the Self. Fear of the unknown and of all that is ego-alien turns out to be fear of the unknown aspects of "one-Self" and of "one-Self" as the unknown. In this sense the transformation process of becoming one-Self again and again embraces new unknowns, indeed, ever-new worlds of fear-inspiring unknowns.

In development through the archetypal stages, the individual must overcome fear with each transition from one phase to another, which, of course, always means the new phase of an existence unknown until that time. In this context we cannot take up the various ways in which men and women overcome fear, nor can we address the striking and as yet not well understood fact that the manner in which the ego overcomes fear is symbolically "genital," i.e., is coordinated with the specific form of the genitals. Thus the male form of overcoming fear is active, intrusive, and pugnaciously heroic just as the typical form of fear appears as "castration" fear. Conversely, the woman's fear is the fear of rape, and her way of overcoming fear is not actively heroic but passively heroic, accepting and incorporating it in her surrender to fear.

But always and independently of any of its forms, overcoming fear represents a specific form of integration in which something alien to the ego, some piece of Not-I, is recognized and realized as one's own. Thus the man experiences the Terrible Feminine in its character of anima and transformation as belonging to his own psyche, just as he experiences the maternal and elementary character as "his own," and only after assimilating all these aspects of the Feminine will a man attain to his own authenticity as a human Self that is male and female simultaneously. Only when the "pure masculinity" of the patriarchy has been overcome through this process of transformation does a man overcome the fear in which his "pure masculinity" screened itself from the otherness that appeared symbolically as feminine. The same holds true for woman and her fear of the Masculine, which she has only concealed by her identification with the animus world demanded by the patriarchy.

In this experience of transformation the human individual becomes conscious of the relentless power of the Self, which recasts all phases of development as well as all ego-conquests of the outer and inner worlds into aspects of Self-realization that manifest from the very beginning as automorphism, as a tendency at work in the psyche. When the personal Self that manifests as a fear-inducing world assaulting the ego from within and from without is integrated, not only the one who fears and the one who overcomes fear but that which arouses fear can be seen as belonging together. Just as the good and the evil gods in the *Bardo Thödol*[33] are one and turn out to be only projections of an underlying third thing, here we are led to experience the unity of Self and world. Destiny in its unity of inside and outside that arouses fear from without and from within turns out to belong to humankind and to be the living experience of the personal Self. World events appearing from outside just as much as inner, fear-inducing phenomena of the psyche prove to be disguises of the Self. Inner and outer realities that at first appear strange and hence frightening are later experienced and "unmasked" as belonging to one's very own authentic being, and thereby lose their foreign as well as their fearsome character. In this transformation the ego experiences that it belongs fundamentally to the Self, and that, in the form of the ego-Self axis, this "belongingness" has determined the entire development of personality on a new level. When the ego grasps the degree to which the Self directs fear and uses it as a "tool for transformation," it also experiences itself as embraced by the Self's demand for transformation. In this way, however, the ego unmasks its own annihilation through fear and recognizes it as a process of negation brought about by something unfamiliar that proves itself to be one's most essential nature, and one gains a paradoxical security in the Self that creatively forces the ego into continual transformation. As the ego becomes the transparent exponent of the Self, this agent of transformation, the Self, becomes one's most treasured essence that remains fearlessly cre-

33. W. Y. Evans-Wentz, *The Tibetan Book of the Dead* (3rd ed., with psychological commentary by C. G. Jung, 1957).

ative throughout all transformations. Only in this way does fearlessness arise for the ego that no longer clings to itself but rather in transformation surrenders and devotes itself to the Self as to its "own." Thus the ego-Self axis becomes humankind's guarantee of a creative existence, i.e., of an existence of transformation. Despite this ego-Self unity, however, the opposition persists in which the ego, as a smaller part, is subjected to a Self that is existentially superior to and more than a match for the ego. This means that the ego must necessarily continue to experience fear. Fear disappears only when the ego has come to that stage of the conquest of fear in which the human being's sense of security lies in existing not only as an ego but, in a mysterious and numinous way, also as a Self that guides the personality through all ego-phases and turns all of the ego's fear-constellations into stages of transformation in which existence reveals itself as an unending metamorphosis of aspects of the creative.

INDEX

INDEX